# CASEBOOK SERIES

JANE AUSTEN: *Emma* (Revised) David Lodge
JANE AUSTEN: *'Northanger Abbey'* & *'Persuasion'* B. C. Southam
JANE AUSTEN: *'Sense and Sensibility'*, *'Pride and Prejudice'* & *'Mansfield Park'*
  B. C. Southam
BECKETT: *Waiting for Godot* Ruby Cohn
WILLIAM BLAKE: *Songs of Innocence and Experience* Margaret Bottrall
CHARLOTTE BRONTE: *'Jane Eyre'* & *'Villette'* Miriam Allott
EMILY BRONTE: *Wuthering Heights* (Revised) Miriam Allott
BROWNING: *'Men and Women'* & *Other Poems* J. R. Watson
CHAUCER: *The Canterbury Tales* J. J. Anderson
COLERIDGE: *'The Ancient Mariner'* & *Other Poems* Alun R. Jones & W. Tydeman
CONRAD: *'Heart of Darkness'*, *'Nostromo'* & *'Under Western Eyes'* C. B. Cox
CONRAD: *The Secret Agent* Ian Watt
DICKENS: *Bleak House* A. E. Dyson
DICKENS: *'Hard Times'*, *'Great Expectations'* & *'Our Mutual Friend'* Norman Page
DICKENS: *'Dombey and Son'* & *'Little Dorrit'* Alan Shelston
DONNE: *Songs and Sonets* Julian Lovelock
GEORGE ELIOT: *Middlemarch* Patrick Swinden
GEORGE ELIOT: *'The Mill on the Floss'* & *'Silas Marner'* R. P. Draper
T. S. ELIOT: *Four Quartets* Bernard Bergonzi
T. S. ELIOT: *'Prufrock'*, *'Gerontion'* & *'Ash Wednesday'* B. C. Southam
T. S. ELIOT: *The Waste Land* C. B. Cox & Arnold P. Hinchliffe
T. S. ELIOT: *Plays* Arnold P. Hinchliffe
HENRY FIELDING: *Tom Jones* Neil Compton
E.M. FORSTER: *A Passage to India* Malcolm Bradbury
WILLIAM GOLDING: *Novels 1954–64* Norman Page
HARDY: *The Tragic Novels* (Revised) R. P. Draper
HARDY: *Poems* James Gibson & Trevor Johnson
HARDY: *Three Pastoral Novels* R. P. Draper
GERARD MANLEY HOPKINS: *Poems* Margaret Bottrall
HENRY JAMES: *'Washington Square'* & *'The Portrait of a Lady'* Alan Shelton
JONSON: *Volpone* Jonas A. Barish
JONSON: *'Every Man in his Humour'* & *'The Alchemist'* R. V. Holdsworth
JAMES JOYCE: *'Dubliners'* & *'A Portrait of the Artist as a Young Man'* Morris Beja
KEATS: *Odes* G.S. Fraser
KEATS: *Narrative Poems* John Spencer Hill
D.H. LAWRENCE: *Sons and Lovers* Gamini Salgado
D.H. LAWRENCE: *'The Rainbow'* & *'Women in Love'* Colin Clarke
LOWRY: *Under the Volcano* Gordon Bowker
MARLOWE: *Doctor Faustus* John Jump
MARLOWE: *'Tamburlaine the Great'*, *'Edward II'* & *'The Jew of Malta'* J. R. Brown
MARLOWE: *Poems* Arthur Pollard
MAUPASSANT: *In the Hall of Mirrors* T. Harris
MILTON: *Paradise Lost* A. E. Dyson & Julian Lovelock
O'CASEY: *'Juno and the Paycock'*, *'The Plough and the Stars'* & *'The Shadow of a*
  *Gunman'* Ronald Ayling
EUGENE O'NEILL: *Three Plays* Normand Berlin
JOHN OSBORNE: *Look Back in Anger* John Russell Taylor
PINTER: *'The Birthday Party'* & *Other Plays* Michael Scott
POPE: *The Rape of the Lock* John Dixon Hunt
SHAKESPEARE: *A Midsummer Night's Dream* Antony Price
SHAKESPEARE: *Antony and Cleopatra* (Revised) John Russell Brown
SHAKESPEARE: *Coriolanus* B. A. Brockman

SHAKESPEARE: *Early Tragedies* Neil Taylor & Bryan Loughrey
SHAKESPEARE: *Hamlet* John Jump
SHAKESPEARE: *Henry IV Parts I and II* G.K. Hunter
SHAKESPEARE: *Henry V* Michael Quinn
SHAKESPEARE: *Julius Caesar* Peter Ure
SHAKESPEARE: *King Lear* (Revised) Frank Kermode
SHAKESPEARE: *Macbeth* (Revised) John Wain
SHAKESPEARE: *Measure for Measure* C. K. Stead
SHAKESPEARE: *The Merchant of Venice* John Wilders
SHAKESPEARE: *'Much Ado About Nothing' & 'As You Like It'* John Russell Brown
SHAKESPEARE: *Othello* (Revised) John Wain
SHAKESPEARE: *Richard II* Nicholas Brooke
SHAKESPEARE: *The Sonnets* Peter Jones
SHAKESPEARE: *The Tempest* (Revised) D. J. Palmer
SHAKESPEARE: *Troilus and Cressida* Priscilla Martin
SHAKESPEARE: *Twelfth Night* D. J. Palmer
SHAKESPEARE: *The Winter's Tale* Kenneth Muir
SPENSER: *The Faerie Queene* Peter Bayley
SHERIDAN: *Comedies* Peter Davison
STOPPARD: *'Rosencrantz and Guildenstern are Dead', 'Jumpers' & 'Travesties'*
    T. Bareham
SWIFT: *Gulliver's Travels* Richard Gravil
SYNGE: *Four Plays* Ronald Ayling
TENNYSON: *In Memoriam* John Dixon Hunt
THACKERAY: *Vanity Fair* Arthur Pollard
TROLLOPE: *The Barsetshire Novels* T. Bareham
WEBSTER: *'The White Devil' & 'The Duchess of Malfi'* R. V. Holdsworth
WILDE: *Comedies* William Tydeman
VIRGINIA WOOLF: *To the Lighthouse* Morris Beja
WORDSWORTH: *Lyrical Ballads* Alun R. Jones & William Tydeman
WORDSWORTH: *The 1807 Poems* Alun R. Jones
WORDSWORTH: *The Prelude* W. J. Harvey & Richard Gravil
YEATS: *Poems 1919–35* Elizabeth Cullingford
YEATS: *Last Poems* Jon Stallworthy

*Issues in Contemporary Critical Theory* Peter Barry
*Thirties Poets: 'The Auden Group'* Ronald Carter
*Tragedy: Developments in Criticism* R.P. Draper
*The Epic* Ronald Draper
*Poetry Criticism and Practice: Developments since the Symbolists* A.E. Dyson
*Three Contemporary Poets: Gunn, Hughes, Thomas* A.E. Dyson
*Elizabethan Poetry: Lyrical & Narrative* Gerald Hammond
*The Metaphysical Poets* Gerald Hammond
*Medieval English Drama* Peter Happé
*The English Novel: Developments in Criticism since Henry James* Stephen Hazell
*Poetry of the First World War* Dominic Hibberd
*The Romantic Imagination* John Spencer Hill
*Drama Criticism: Developments since Ibsen* Arnold P. Hinchliffe
*Three Jacobean Revenge Tragedies* R.V. Holdsworth
*The Pastoral Mode* Bryan Loughrey
*The Language of Literature* Norman Page
*Comedy: Developments in Criticism* D.J. Palmer
*Studying Shakespeare* John Russell Brown
*The Gothic Novel* Victor Sage
*Pre-Romantic Poetry* J.R. Watson

# CONTENTS

*System of Titling*: in the Contents listing and in the Selection, exterior quotemarks are used for editorially devised captions. In other cases, the caption employs the original title of the writer's book, chapter or section of a book, article or essay (in some instances abbreviated from that), and it is displayed without exterior quotemarks.

# GENERAL EDITOR'S PREFACE

The Casebook series, launched in 1968, has become a well-regarded library of critical studies. The central concern of the series remains the 'single-author' volume, but suggestions from the academic community have led to an extension of the original plan, to include occasional volumes on such general themes as literary 'schools' and genres.

Each volume in the central category deals either with one well-known and influential work by an individual author, or with closely related works by one writer. The main section consists of critical readings, mostly modern, collected from books and journals. A selection of reviews and comments by the author's contemporaries is also included, and sometimes comment from the author himself. The Editor's Introduction charts the reputation of the work or works from the first appearance to the present time.

Volumes in the 'general themes' category are variable in structure but follow the basic purpose of the series in presenting an integrated selection of readings, with an Introduction which explores the theme and discusses the literary and critical issues involved.

A single volume can represent no more than a small selection of critical opinions. Some critics are excluded for reasons of space, and it is hoped that readers will pursue the suggestions for further reading in the Select Bibliography. Other contributions are severed from their original context, to which some readers may wish to turn. Indeed, if they take a hint from the critics represented here, they certainly will.

A. E. Dyson

# INTRODUCTION

Literary history has tended to marginalise the eighteenth-century Gothick. There is a strong tradition, deriving from the late Victorian and early twentieth century period, which represents the Gothick novel or romance as one of the minor products of a great movement in the history of taste – a forerunner, or a by-blow, of Romanticism proper. Such an attitude pigeon-holed the Gothick as part of an excessive reaction against the dominance of Augustan rationalism, a fashionable rush into nostalgia for a more vigorous, primitive life by an age that had grown weary of Enlightenment values. These early novels of terror, so the account ran, with their stereotypical trappings – their old castles, sensibility-ridden maidens, evil villains, monks, abbeys, Shakespearean ghosts, inflated and melodramatic diction – are nothing more than the bric-à-brac of pre-Romanticism, possessing, at most, a mere curiosity-value for a modern reader.

But the actual history of critical opinion is much more diverse and interesting than such a literary–historical judgement would give us the right to expect.[1] The impact of these novels on their contemporary and subsequent readership reveals a surprising range of responses. The *genre* is not a dusty corner but an arena open, from the first, to the social and political interests of the day. Both the literary form and the commentary on it are permeated by controversy, and this fact alone explains something about the value of a species of writing which remained part of the pulse of literary expectation for three generations of readers, during a period of rapid social change and political transition.

More than this, there has been a marked revival of interest in the Gothick novel during recent years, supported by the currency of the mode in the modern cinema and the growth of a more broadly cultural approach to the literary *genre*.

What follows is a mosaic, pieced together from a number of different sources, which tries to give the reader some sense of the contours of critical opinion. Some of this material I have been able to represent directly in the Casebook selection of criticism. Other important sources of information and comment I have been obliged to exclude for reasons of space from the main body of the selection. Some of this latter material I have attempted to bring to the reader's attention in the course of the following brief, contextual survey.

## Overt Critics and Covert Readers

Horace Walpole, antiquarian, collector, designer of the famous 'Gothick' villa Strawberry Hill and member of parliament, is usually regarded as the father of the Gothick Novel. But his paternity was curiously shy: the first edition of *The Castle of Otranto* (1764) was introduced to the public as a translation of a medieval manuscript by one 'Onuphrio Muralto'. Purportedly, the translator was 'William Marshall, Gent.' The contemporary reviewer in the *Critical* is slightly uneasy – anxious not to be taken in by a possible hoax, yet concerned at the same time to assert correct standards of judgement:

Such is the character of the work given us by its judicious translator; but whether he speaks seriously or ironically, we neither know nor care. The publication of any work at this time in England, composed of such rotten materials, is a phænomenon we cannot account for. . . .[2]

But if the critic, beneath his apparent indifference to irony, is doubtful and hostile, the public had no such difficulties with the book. They were so enthusiastic that the first edition sold out in three months. Walpole, encouraged by his success to relinquish the shelter of his twin personae, wrote the preface to the second edition in his own person. It took the form of a conscious manifesto for what he called the 'Gothick story': a deliberate hybrid of the ancient and the modern, of history and fiction.

Looking back over the whole of the period which followed, this rather devious beginning seems thoroughly appropriate to the *genre*. During the next sixty years, the Gothic novel survived and flourished, despite – or perhaps because of – a barrage of official discredit. It was repeatedly denounced as a dangerous form of the romance: a term which is commonly used to mean, after Cervantes, an improbable, absurdly hyperbolic kind of writing either in, or deriving from, the Romance languages. And meanwhile, during that same sixty years, readers went on devouring these books in greater and greater numbers, and booksellers and circulating library-owners began to die rich men.

Some idea of the climate of 'official' opinion against which Walpole and his fellow-Gothicists of the later eighteenth century had to contend can be gained from the magisterial strictures of Samuel Johnson's *Rambler* paper of 1750[*] Here, the Great Cham of

[*] Here, and elsewhere in the Introduction, an asterisk within square brackets indicates reference to material in the Casebook selection. Numbered references to material or writers cited relate to the Notes for the Introduction, below.

Literature provides the standard, mid-century Augustan opposition to all forms of romance:

Why this wild strain of imagination found reception so long, in polite and learned ages, it is not easy to conceive; but we cannot wonder that, while readers could be procured, the authors were willing to continue it: for when a man had by practice gained some fluency of language, he had no further care than to retire to his closet, let loose his invention, and heat his mind with incredibilities; a book was thus produced without fear of criticism, without the toil of study, without knowledge of nature or acquaintance with life.

The actual occasion of these remarks seems to have been a defence of Richardson against Fielding's 'comic romance' parody, and Johnson is thinking essentially about Ariosto and Spenser and their prose derivatives. But the mixture of moral and aesthetic objections to fantasy and 'incredibilities' in this paper are precisely those which will recur later – in Jane Austen [*] and, to an extent, in Scott [*] – with regard to the Gothick romance. Such doughty opposition explains, at least in part, Walpole's reluctance to own his fiction.

Readers may differ profoundly from critics, but critics always have to begin by being readers; there is generally an air of covertness about the readership of romance which complicates the politics of its reception. Those who pronounce most solemnly on the defects of the romance are sometimes found, secretly, in the ranks of its most avid consumers. Samuel Johnson is a case in point. Boswell records that he was wont to attribute his early inability to rise in public life to a compulsive reading of the romances of chivalry, the forerunners of the heinous Gothick romances.[3] On a visit to a Scottish bishop, Johnson disappeared into the library for a whole weekend, rudely ignoring his host. Later, he admitted he had been reading romances. And on his trip to the Western Isles, at his first sight of the castles and landscape of the Hebrides, he is reported as remarking: 'The fictions of the Gothic romance were not so remote from credulity as they are now thought.'[4]

Perhaps less surprisingly, Edmund Burke [*] admitted to having whiled away many important hours – when he should have been devoting his attention to more weighty matters – reading romances. And Macaulay, whose essay on Horace Walpole was not published until 1838 [*], was a lifelong addict of romances and novels: a compulsion which is at first hard to detect from the balanced, carefully-considered tone of the essay.[5] But Macaulay ends up conceding, in a kind of backhanded compliment, Walpole's sheer narrative power over him in *Otranto*.

Many an eminent Victorian must have acquired the habit, like

Macaulay, by subscribing to that great source of the Gothick, the Minerva Press Library, founded by William Lane as early as 1773. Leigh Hunt, for example, was a subscriber to Lane's library in the 1790s, while still at school; and he continued to be ever after, on his own admission, 'a glutton of novels'. Later, of course, he was to become Mary Shelley's influential editor and friend. Shelley himself, it seems, obtained his Gothic *sub rosa* at the more discreet circulating library of P. Norbury in Brentford.[6]

Subterfuge, for both reader and supplier of the Gothick, often had to be resorted to, as is confirmed by the testimony of a circulating-library manager, given in *Pratt's Family Secrets* (1797). He used to dispose of his 'good things': 'Sometimes tricked between muslins, cambrics, silks, sattins, and the like, or rolled in a bundle, then thrown into a coach by some of my fair smugglers; the old ones, meanwhile, Mams and Dads, never the wiser.'

There is a tinge of partisanship about circulating libraries in Jane Austen's letter of 1798 to her sister Cassandra, in which she comments that the family are 'all great Novel-readers & not ashamed of being so'. Both she and Peacock would no doubt have agreed that by far the majority of volumes that rolled in an unceasing tide during the 1790s from the presses of Lane's establishment in Leadenhall Street were, as he put it, 'completely expurgated of any of the higher qualities of mind'. Yet there is a fascination and an intimacy in both their parodies of the Gothick, which testifies to their close readerly awareness of the mode.[7]

And even if, like Hester Thrale, the robust and perspicacious friend of Samuel Johnson, you belonged to an older generation, the influence of the Gothick was still strong. Mrs Thrale's debunking of Mrs Radcliffe reveals, at the same time, what excitement there was about the newest sensation of 1794:

We have all been reading the Mysteries of Udolpho; 'tis very horrible indeed, says one; very like Macbeth, says another: Yes truly, replied H.L.P.: as like Pepper-Mint water is to good Brandy . . . .[8]

But despite her disapproval of Beckford's character, Mrs Thrale had already admitted the sublimity of parts of *Vathek*, and by 1820 we find her yielding with a regretful sigh to the dominance of the Gothick:

How changed is the taste of verse, prose, and painting from le bon vieux temps! Nothing attracts us but what terrifies and is within a hair's breadth of positive disgust; some of the strange things they write remind me of Squire Richard's visit to the Tower Menagerie when he says, 'They are pure grim devils' – particularly a wild and hideous tale called Frankenstein. . . .[9]

It sounds as if Mrs Thrale does not know who the author is, and Scott in his review of *Frankenstein* [*] assumes that it was written by Percy Bysshe, not Mary Shelley. Female authors, female readers: the Gothick gained its hold through the expansion of the readership, and in particular through the increase in 'fair smugglers'.

The basic metaphor of the period for reading is that of appetite; and, by the latter half of the 1790s, when the cult of the Gothick was at its height, the potential dangers for women of excessive reading, on the analogy of gin or laudanum, are a subject of widespread comment in the magazines. Two short articles out of many usefully represent this new concern. That in the *Scots Magazine* for 1797 [*] discourses in patriarchal style on the corrupting effect of romance on the female reader. The other, a witty, reflexive piece from a woman's magazine, the *Lady's Monthly Museum* for 1798 [*] argues, in the manner of earlier eighteenth-century satire, that bad novels (and we infer, from the imagery of the piece, Gothick novels) are good, because they induce enough literacy in the female reader to lead to their own eventual rejection. The piece is an educative spoof: it contains the usual jibe at the gullibility of the female reader, but plays this off against the pomposity and dullness of the *Scots Magazine*'s pronouncements, showing a refreshing awareness of male vanity. If the Gothick romance is a means to the enlightenment of women, then let it be written and read unreservedly, bad as it undoubtedly is.

I would include in this context of female readership Henry Tilney's famous rebuke to Catherine Morland from Jane Austen's *Northanger Abbey* [*]. This novel was probably written between 1799 and 1801, but not published until 1818, after the author was dead. The book is quite justly treated by modern readers as a timeless Olympian satire on the Gothick, and I have also included a passage of sparkling parody of Mrs Radcliffe [*]. But it was composed with one eye on this contemporary debate in the magazines about the female reader. It is easy to forget, moreover, that Henry himself is being guyed by the author, even as he shatters Catherine's dreams – for who would want to live in a 'neighbourhood of voluntary spies'? Reader and critic of romance meet here in the open, and neither escapes unscathed.

## RELIGION AND POLITICS

Proscribed by the canons of good taste and morality, manufactured and consumed in large doses by women and sometimes by critics, the Gothick novel expanded like an open secret in the last decades of the eighteenth century. Locked into our distant modern view, the *genre* looks all too unified, but the fiction market of the 1790s was polarised by a range of contradictory social and political factors – by methodism, by female emancipation, by political radicalism, by anti-Catholicism and by anti-Jacobinism, to name a few of the strongest lobbies. A romance launched on this stormy sea was likely to be attacked or supported from all sorts of unexpected quarters. For T. J. Mathias, the topical satirist of the poem, *The Pursuits of Literature*, female novelists like Charlotte Smith, Mrs Inchbald or Mary Robinson, were all 'tainted with democracy'. Only Mrs Radcliffe escaped political censure.[10] But for writers like Clara Reeve, the Gothick motifs, drawn from the age of chivalry, could be used to redress the levelling tendencies that followed in the wake of the French Revolution – she consciously wrote a kind of counter-Gothick. In 1800 the Marquis de Sade revealed an equally political interest in the Gothick novel, reading Ann Radcliffe and Lewis as a partly unconscious response to the revolutionary upheavals that had recently shaken Europe [*]. Thus, tug and counter-tug from the beginning weave a tradition of cultural appropriation in the history of critical opinions about the Gothick romances.

Nothing illustrates this process more aptly than the reception in 1796 of one of the central texts of the Gothick, Lewis's *The Monk*. The rhetoric of this novel, like that of both Radcliffe's *Udolpho* (1794) and Maturin's *Melmoth the Wanderer* (1820), uses the anti-Catholic prejudice of the audience as a tactic to gain acceptance. Coleridge, in his famous review of 1797 [*], might have been expected to respond sympathetically, since he shared the prejudice with many of Lewis's readers; but he attacks the novel in the *Critical Review* because he thinks it blasphemous. At the time, blasphemy was actionable in common law. It was classified as a political crime, technically a 'crime against the King's peace' and almost undistinguishable from sedition. It was punishable by flogging, fine or imprisonment. Lewis, who had recently become member of parliament for Hindon, Wiltshire, ironically inheriting William Beckford's seat, withdrew the first edition of the novel, taking occasion to excise and alter numerous passages of sexual explicitness as well. He may have got wind of a rumour that legal papers were being drawn up against him.[11]

But besides this furore, caused perhaps unwittingly by Coleridge's review, Lewis had also fallen foul of various other lobbies. The puritans, marginally more interested in obscenity that anti-Catholicism, assailed him. At the same time he was attacked from another direction by the pro-Catholic *European Magazine* for aligning himself, in his libel on the convents of Rome, with 'democratical atheists and atheistical devotees'. To make matters worse, *The Monk* was reviewed sympathetically (probably by the painter Fuseli) in the pages of the *Analytical Review*: a paper regarded in Government circles as a dangerous nest of Jacobins, feminists and radicals, whose editor was eventually arrested in 1799.[12] Interest in Lewis's novel was registered at Cabinet level. In 1796, William Wilberforce noted in his diary:

Dined Lord Chancellor's – Loughborough, William Pitt, Lord Chatham, Westmoreland &c – talk rather loose. I fear I [sic] not guarded and grave enough. Much talk about 'The Monk', a novel by Lewis's son.

Already in 1784, Loughborough, the Lord Chancellor, had directed a savage campaign against another Gothick writer, Beckford, which had resulted in his enforced exile in Italy and France. Beckford, who had just become a member of parliament, formed an amazingly indiscreet homosexual attachment to young William Courtenay, Loughborough's nephew.[13] Mrs Thrale, alongside qualified approval of *Vathek*, notes the scandal in her diary.[14]

Is there any truth in this contemporary suspicion that the Gothick novelists were subversives? Walpole, Beckford, Burke – whose powerful treatise *On the Sublime and the Beautiful* (1757) provided a vital source for much of the imagery and the rhetoric of the Gothick novel [*] – and Lewis were all Whig members of parliament. With the exception of Burke, whose character is somewhat different, the others may be said to form a tradition of Whig dilettantism which one might broadly speak of as a form of cultural dissent.

The dissent is more theatrical, more *épatant* perhaps, than strictly political, and yet it is difficult to draw this line in the atmosphere of the 1790s. All three were concerned with Europe. Walpole had connections with the French Encyclopaedists, who were thought of in England as a dangerous company of atheists. In the 1790s, he returned to the Gothick with a sensational play about incest, *The Mysterious Mother*, said to have been a strong influence on Shelley's *The Cenci*. Beckford and Lewis were connected with French and German culture respectively. The latter two were open homosexuals, in whom 'camp' sexual mores coexisted with the demands of public reputation and practical politics.

Beckford was actually present in Paris at the time of the French Revolution and was well-received by the revolutionary government. He is well-known as an eccentric collector of art and *bon viveur*, but it seems that he made some attempts from Europe to bring about a treaty between the English and the French. His satire *Modern Novel*

*Writing or the Elegant Enthusiast* (1796) addresses the literary supporters of Pitt the Younger, whose magazine the *British Critic* had been launched with secret service money. The satire was written in the guise of a woman, 'Lady Harriet Marlow'. His *Azemia* (1797) was published under the name of 'Jacquetta Maria Jenks'. These pieces reveal Beckford's distaste for a political regime which had suspended the Habeas Corpus Act. The mask of female authorship was so successful that his works here were often attributed to Charlotte Smith, well-known for her 'democratic' views. The eagle-eyed Mrs Thrale, however, detected his hand. Beckford is attempting to parody the Gothick in these works (presumably because of its growing *anti*-democratic associations), but even the reviewers noticed the way the satire breaks down into something nearer sincerity. It could not be 'meant as a jeer on Mrs Radcliffe' wrote one critic, because 'it has all the marks of intentional seriousness . . .'[15] Much of Beckford's behaviour, including his ambiguous attitudes towards religion, for example, lurked behind a mask.[16]

A similar difficulty of tone is present in *The Monk*. When Lewis censored his own novel, he was not always censoring heterosexual outrage – as, for example, in the famous seduction of Antonia by Ambrosio – but a series of coterie homosexual jokes too, which already involved, for some readers, the transposition of boy for girl. Thus Rosario in the plot of that novel is a girl pretending to be a boy: but the jest – from an author with whom Byron said he refused to dine because he filled up his table with young ensigns and had looking-glass panels in his bookcases – is about the androgyne. It is with some of Lewis's characters as it is with Shakespeare's actors – boy plays girl plays boy.

But such is the difficulty of Lewis's tone that there is room for Robert Kiely to argue in his 1973 analysis of the novel [*] that such ambiguity of characterisation in *The Monk* should be taken, not so much as camp transvestism, but as the emblem of a true subversion of identity. Ambrosio, insists Kiely, in discovering his true self, presses beyond any given role, ending up as a combination of all, as 'lecher-virgin-saint-murderer-man-woman-rapist-victim. . .' .

Camp or not, Lewis's pro-German enthusiasms were carefully monitored throughout the latter years of the 1790s by that venerable governmental organ, the *Anti-Jacobin; or Weekly Examiner*. This paper, in a parody of Schiller's *The Robbers* called *The Rovers*, associated the *Sturm und Drang* with the desire to 'unhinge the present notions of men with regard to the obligations of Civil Society'.

The development of the Gothick Villain, that gigantic sinister figure, needs to be seen in this context of political suspicion, because the archetype partly derives from English translations during the period 1794–96 of Schiller's *The Ghost-Seer*, Schink's self-styled 'magico-political tale' *Victim of Magical Delusions* and, most famous of all, the Marquis Grosse's *Horrid Mysteries*. Secret conspiratorial societies were generally associated with the Germans – societies such as the Illuminati, the Rosicrucians and the Jesuits. A vestige of these associations is to be found in Peacock's parody of Shelley in *Nightmare Abbey* [*], in the conjunction between Scythrop's 'passion for reforming the world' and his habit of sleeping with a copy of *Horrid Mysteries* under his pillow.

The horror and fascination of the Villain and of secret societies like the Illuminati spread across the Atlantic at this time in the work of the American Gothick novelist, Charles Brockden Brown – often described in literary histories as the first American novelist. Brown was a writer of great vigour and power who looked eagerly towards Europe and the new radicalism of Godwin – himself the author of two very interesting novels in the Gothick mode, *Caleb Williams* (1794) and *St Leon* (1799). And Brown's novels fed back immediately into the main stream of the Gothick in England because, during the early years of the nineteenth century, the Minerva Press happily pirated all his major works and published them under the Leadenhall Street imprint.[17] Leslie Fiedler's lively piece from *Love and Death in the American Novel* [*] attempts to reclaim Brown's importance for American literature. Fiedler argues, in an entertaining pastiche of Freud and the Marquis de Sade, that the Gothick comes to Brown through Richardson and the sentimental novel. The American novel began with Brown, and Fiedler contends that this Gothick strain took visible root in the major authors of the nineteenth century: Poe, Hawthorne and Melville.

The 1790s, as Professor Tompkins shows in her survey of the Gothic Romance [*], were a whirlpool of influences and pressures. What looks, from the narrow, literary-historical point of view, like a *genre* in the making, was more like a struggle to possess and appropriate the available language of cultural division. So radical-democratic and conservative strains of Gothick shared the same motifs. Mrs Radcliffe's politics, for example, like Clara Reeve's, were quite different from those of Beckford, Walpole and Lewis. Her ancestors were Dutch Protestants, impeccably orthodox, and her cousin was surgeon to George III. Externally, she was a zealous reformation patriot, repelled by southern Catholic Europe,[18] which she obviously regarded as backward and superstitious. Yet all her novels are set in France and Italy, and she is fascinated, like many Gothick novelists, by the secret workings of the Inquisition. The evil, totally unscrupulous Villain stalks her pages just as surely as he does those of Beckford and Lewis. Her preoccupation with this figure originates in her native Shakespeare and Milton, in *Hamlet* and *Macbeth*, in *Comus* and the Satan of *Paradise Lost*; but her Montoni and Schedoni, unforgettable characters, who move with such breathtaking ease outside law and conventional ethics, share the fascination of figures who threaten the current fabric of social organisation with Schiller's Armenian and Lewis's Ambrosio. As Marilyn Butler has pointed out, the anti-Jacobin movement, which wanted above all to assert common sense and conformity, 'paid unwilling tribute to the power and fascination of the superhuman individual'.[19] Such 'unwilling tribute' opens out into dramatic conflict in *The Mysteries of Udolpho* and *The Italian*.

## THE TERM 'GOTHICK'

The Gothick novel, then, is a specialised form of the historical romance, a form of fantasy about past history and alien cultures which has a meaning for its present audience through a variety of cultural and political reflexes. Its hallmark is a deliberate archaism. But what did 'Gothick' mean? The label itself was heavily nuanced in the eighteenth century, more so than modern readers tend to imagine. 'Gothick' could connote any of a wide range of overlapping senses: horrid, barbarous, superstitious, Tudor, Druid, English, German, and even Oriental.[20] Its most obvious reading for a modern reader is perhaps 'anti-Classical' or 'medieval', and this is how Bishop Hurd is using it in his *Letters on Chivalry and Romance* of 1762 [*], in which he defends the taste for the labyrinthine form of 'Gothick' (i.e. Tudor) organisation in everything from landscape gardening to the wandering narrative of the Spenserian romance.

But it is doubtful if all eighteenth-century readers saw the relation between the present and the past in such a schematic way as the opposition between 'classical' and 'anti-classical' implies. 'Anti-classical' covers a whole host of things. One familiar meaning of 'Gothick', for example, assumes that it is barbarous, Catholic, feudal and Norman in origin – everything opposed to the civilised 'Augustan' classicism of contemporary England. But, as Samuel Kliger shows in his fascinating historiographical survey, 'The Goths in England', [*] there is a well-established Whig tradition which sees 'Gothick' as native, Protestant and 'democratic' and the very foundation of contemporary English culture. The pointed arch was thought by some to derive from the groves of the Druids, and it was elided, as a symbol, with the social system of the Germanic tribes of Northern Europe from which the English derive their social organisation. Blake's paintings often embody this interpretation of 'Gothick'. Burke's response to Westminster Abbey, for example, is a thrill of awe at a *national* institution, which the 'Gothick' nature of the architecture induces, without any sense of contradiction:

... the moment I entered I felt a kind of awe pervade my mind which I cannot describe: the very silence seemed sacred: Henry vii's chapel is a very fine piece of Gothic architecture, particularly the roof . . .[21]

In religio-political terms, Luther's second rejection of the Empire of Roman Catholicism is assimilated to the first sack of Rome by the Goths. 'Gothick', in this tradition, suggests not darkness but a rude form of 'democratic' enlightenment.

Beckford is equally enthusiastic about the architecture of the Catholic abbey church of Batalha in Portugal, calling it 'the best style of Gothic at its best period', and an uncharacteristic wave of patriotism steals over him as he contemplates the tombs in the crypt:

I withdrew from the contemplation of these tombs with reluctance; every object in the chapel which contains them being so pure in taste, so harmonious in colour; every armorial device; every mottoed lambel, so tersely and correctly sculptured, associated so closely with historical and English recollections – the garter, the leopards, the fleur-de-lys 'from haughty Gallia torn'; the Plantaganet cast of the whole chamber conveyed home to my bosom a feeling so interesting, so congenial, that I could hardly persuade myself to move away.  . . .[22]

For Beckford, more psychologically appreciative of Catholic ritual than Burke, say, or Mrs Radcliffe, and scornful of the vulgarity of Protestant iconography, 'Gothick' could mean 'English' too, but via a different cluster of associations. For him, it was Catholic, feudal and Anglo–Norman, and no doubt it was these associations that lay uppermost in his mind as he was building Fonthill Abbey.

Thus the term 'Gothick' itself is an ambiguous one, incorporating many shades and combinations of association. For the eighteenth-century reader, it was an almost unpredictable intersection of religious belief, of aesthetic taste and political inclination.

## THE WATERSHED: SCOTT AND THE END OF A CULT

Literary history marks a conventional ending for the cult of the Gothick at about 1820. The posthumous publication of *Northanger Abbey* in 1818, despite the fact that *Frankenstein* was published in the same year, contributes strongly to the sense of an historical watershed, the wit of Jane Austen's novel perhaps matching the feeling of the times that the literary cult of terror and the sublime has a touch of the *grand guignol* about it. The rough date of 1820, too, marks the decline of Lane's circulating library as a source of Gothick. As if blushing at the maturity of the new century, the Minerva Press went over into publishing childrens' books, which it continued to do well into the Victorian era.

Maturin's *Melmoth the Wanderer*, when it came out in 1820, fared badly at the hands of the reviewers, despite the support and encouragement of Scott and Coleridge, with whom he had corresponded. The reviewer in the *Scots Magazine* gives one the sense that he feels the whole scale of this kind of writing belongs to the experience of an earlier generation. Writers, he argues, who have witnessed the upheavals and violence of revolution early in life, and then have lived through the recent Apocalypse of the Napoleonic period, 'Those, we say, to whom such marvels have been familiar from their infancy, cannot easily now reduce their imaginations within the vulgar "visible diurnal sphere" of common existence.' . . .[23]

There is a new sense of the 'modern', and the 'rational' which absorbs the anarchic play of the old Gothick with history, converting it wherever possible, by a kind of retrospective evolution, into the harbinger of the 'modern' historical romance. This view is most subtly articulated in Walter Scott's scrupulous discussions of the Gothick novelists in his reviews and prefaces, and in his important essay on the supernatural in the *Foreign Quarterly Review* of 1827 [*], in which he describes some of the changes in religious belief during the recent past. In these and other pieces, Scott naturalises superstition. He tends to represent the older authors – in a financial metaphor that seems the symptom of a new realism about belief – as 'drawing too much on the credit of their readers'. Scott requires 'dignity of explanation' for this new age of universal incredulity. The wild excesses of these earlier romances are justified for Scott only when they are obviously symptomatic of an earlier stage of culture. The question of probability runs like a thread through his discussions of the Gothick, and where he sees value in the writing (and to be fair to him, he often does), he tends to associate it with historical or psychological probability. Conversely, *dis*value associates for him with the 'overheated imagination'. Thus it is Scott who is fascinated by Mrs Radcliffe's rationalism and it is he who really begins the tradition of talking about her in terms of the 'explained supernatural' [*].

James Hogg, in our extract from the *Noctes Ambrosianae* dialogue of 1826 [*], echoes this feeling of Scott's about the Gothick. Hogg had helped Scott collect oral legends in Scotland, and he was suspicious of the 'literary' quality of the Gothick. Although his character feels respect for 'the enchantress', as Mrs Radcliffe was called, he also criticises her on the grounds of probability and belief – the ghost loses his effect, either because he is not a 'real' ghost or because you see too much of him and he loses his supernatural quality altogether. Hogg went on to solve this problem in a radical psychological presentation of schizophrenic hallucination in his novel, *The Private Memoirs and Confessions of a Justified Sinner*.

But, by 1845, the conservative appropriation of Scott himself was complete, as an anonymous Tory writer in *Blackwoods Magazine* on 'The Historical Romance' was able to prove to his own satisfaction:

> It is not going too far to say, that the romances of Sir Walter Scott have gone far to neutralise the dangers of the Reform Bill. Certain it is that they have materially assisted in extinguishing, at least, in the educated classes of society, that prejudice against the feudal manners, and those devout aspirations [sic] on the blessings of democratic institutions, which were learned over Europe in the close of the eighteenth century. Like all other great and original minds, so far from being swept away by the errors of his age, he rose up in direct opposition to them. Singly he set himself to breast the flood which was overflowing the world. Thence the reaction in favour of the institutions of the olden time in church and state, which became general in the next generation, and is now so strongly manifesting itself, as well in the religious contexts as in the lighter literature of the present day.[24]

Scott's project to produce a watershed and modernise the historical romance is politically appropriated by this writer as a defence of feudalism and 'the olden time in Church and State'. Such an interpretation does no justice to the ambiguity of Scott's presentation of history, but it indicates how the wheel of appropriation can come full circle. Scott's newly-created historical romance was recycled by Victorian readers into their prejudices about their own recent past.

## VICTORIAN SURVIVAL

If Scott's commentaries absorbed, contained and historicised the literary cult of the Gothick for the benefit of the Victorians, the popular cult went on disseminating itself through the Romantics into the penny dreadful in the work of Reynolds and Ainsworth. The years 1820–50 are testimony to the fact that the popular love of the supernatural and the macabre was still very strong. *Blackwoods Magazine* flourished during this era, specialising in ghost stories and the bizarre tale. And other presses took over from Lane. Henry Colburn, for example, edited the *New Monthly Magazine*, which published several articles about Mrs Radcliffe, including a posthumous fragment. Colburn also had a circulating library which reprinted many of the old Gothick titles during this period. Maturin may have failed with the reviewers in England and sunk into oblivion, but he was an instant success in France, influencing Baudelaire and inspiring Balzac to write *Melmoth Reconcilié*. Beckford's *Vathek* was not reprinted by the early Victorians, and had to wait until Stephane Mallarmé rescued it in the 1870s. But *Frankenstein* was a resounding success. On her return to England in 1823, Mary Shelley was 'much amused', as she wrote to a friend, to see her novel on the stage at the English Opera House, adapted into a melodrama called *Presumption*, which appeared, she noted, 'to excite a breathless eagerness in the audience'. This piece was still playing in 1887, having been performed almost annually until 1850. In the twentieth century there have been dozens of Frankensteins, the film industry often using ideas that were first developed in stage productions of the novel.[25]

But Mary Shelley did not leave *Frankenstein* to the tender mercies of literary history or popular tradition. The most important of the new studies of the novel by Mary Poovey (1980) [*] reveals that there are significant differences between the texts of the 1818 first edition and the second edition which she saw through the press in 1831. Poovey shows how, as time went on, Mary Shelley responded more critically to the Romantic myth of the artist-creator which had been the corner stone of Shelley's work and that of the other male Romantic poets of their acquaintance. For Mary Shelley, the act of imagination, symbolised in Frankenstein's action in creating the monster, was free if uncaptured in a text, a public statement. But she had become a public figure by 1831, an editor and literary widow, and art had become for her part of a process of personal suffering. The critique of Romantic self-indulgence and personal destructiveness, implicit in the original novel, sharpens in hindsight; and the notion that Victor Frankenstein, instead of being the autonomous Promethean, is actually a victim of external forces is intensified in the pattern of the later textual changes. In the 1831 *Frankenstein*, which is often taken as the standard text of the novel and reprinted without comment, Mary Shelley gave expression, argues Poovey, to a growing guilt about her own former audacity. She embraced powerlessness while criticising a male Romantic myth, and thus this act of 'feminisation' is, like her own complex personality, equivocal, a form of self-appropriation.

Thus the 'watershed' of c. 1820 forms a convenient guideline, but it is really the sign, not so much of the death of the Gothick as of the scattering and transmutation of the tangible literary form into a mode of sensibility. In 1842, for example, the young Wilkie Collins [*], himself to become one of the most prolific popular authors of the middle and late Victorian periods, writing to his father about a visit to some country cousins, shows a strong sense of the continuous tradition of popular Gothick. Instinctively, when wanting to frighten his gullible audience, he invokes all the old names, together with Macbeth, forming a complete mini-spectrum of pantomine oral tradition, a tiny glimpse into the survival of the mode as a reference point.

As George Saintsbury points out in his *The Peace of the Augustans* [*] Wilkie Collins in his own novels is, along with several other writers in this tradition, using a form of Mrs Radcliffe's 'explained supernatural'. This passage reveals a paradox about the Victorian attitudes to the Gothick. Saintsbury is no longer sure whether the Gothick novels referred to by Isabella Thorpe in *Northanger Abbey* existed or not, and it took until the 1920s for them to be unearthed again by Mackillop and Sadleir. The contemporary point of Austen's satire has been completely lost, and yet, almost in the same breath, Saintsbury makes a telling point about the survival of Mrs Radcliffe's rhetoric of natural explanation in the nineteenth-century ghost story. A similar technique of equivocal explanation of irrational phenomena was developed to an elaborate degree by a whole range of eminent and familiar Victorian writers: Poe, Hogg, Stevenson and Sheridan Le Fanu[26] and later, M. R. James and Conan Doyle. Even Henry James's *Turn of the Screw* pays lip-service to the earlier romances; and the debt of the Brontë's to them has been commented on by other critics.

But it is Dickens who provides one with the most striking emblem of the survival of the Gothick in his last novel, *Edwin Drood* (1870). In the gardens and alleys of the ancient, respectable, claustrophobic medieval town of Cloisterham, the children are making mud pies out of the remains of abbots and friars – a macabre image of recycled Gothick.

### Modern Approaches: Freud and the Surrealists

Freud's essay of 1919, 'The Uncanny' [*], heralds a new and essentially modern line of thought, which has had an enormous influence of critical approaches to the Gothick novel. Freud analyses Hoffman's famous story 'The Sandman', rejecting the idea that horror is connected to what he calls 'intellectual uncertainty'. Instead, he introduces the notion that the whole structure and mood of horror fiction is a projection, in heavily codified form, of deeply instinctual drives in the unconscious mind. He accounts for the recurrent motifs of this kind of fiction by seeing them, not as literary devices, but as projections of what he calls 'repetition-compulsion' – the primary activity of the pleasure principle which drives us compulsively to repeat experiences which we find pleasurable – acting here in repressed, inverted form. Thus the traditional idea of the 'explained supernatural', in Freud's argument, becomes part of the mechanism of evasion or repression, by the conscious mind, of the instinctual drives of the unconscious. The whole shape of this kind of fiction for author and reader alike becomes, in Freud's view, a distorted projection of desire for the womb, the ultimate target of the unconscious.

Freud uses some very interesting philological materials as evidence for his argument, but he does not really develop the cultural implications of his thought. He is attempting to expand a unitary explanation of the literary *genre* and the experience of the 'uncanny' in life, based on the instinctual drives of the individual.

André Breton [*], on the other hand, while clearly developing a Freudian analysis in his comments on the eighteenth-century English Gothick has a cultural perspective too. Breton appropriates the Gothick as the ancestor of modern surrealism, and in doing so takes up the Marquis de Sade's comment – that it is a collective myth – and reapplies it. Breton was in part attempting to sell surrealism to the English and his comments should be seen in the context of the Surrealist exhibition which he was taking to London. But his piece of 1936 seems to be an attempt to marry the Marxism of the 1930s with the Freudian mechanism of individual repression. Thus the English Gothick of the eighteenth century is seen as a collective symptom of the political pressures felt all over Europe at the time. Breton interprets Walpole's account of the genesis of *Otranto* as indicating that it was a species of automatic or unconscious writing. He argues that when a writer, particularly one of Walpole's conscious political awareness, yields himself to the deeper layers of the mind, it is precisely such *random* images from the unconscious which reveal the great determining patterns of social repression. He calls it, in an obvious glance at Freud, the revenge of the pleasure principle on the reality principle.

Breton's comments also have been extremely influential in stimulating the 'modern' view of the Gothick. How serious either his Marxism or his Freudianism is, it is difficult to say, but Montague Summers, the English bibliographer of the Gothick, obviously regards Breton's appropriation of the *genre* as a form of political threat. 'If surrealism', he comments in his book, *The Gothic Quest*, 'is knit to Communism it can have nothing to do with the Gothic novel, nor indeed with romanticism at all.'[27]

## CULTURAL AND HISTORICAL APPROACHES

The 1930s also saw a challenge to the Marquis de Sade's version of the Gothick. Eleanor Sickels in *The Gloomy Egoist* [*] explores the relation between the Gothick novel and the cult of religious melancholy in the earlier eighteenth century. This study goes right outside questions of literary *genre* or arguments about the romance. The importance of this contribution is that it does not rest with individual psychology, but attempts, convincingly I think, a cultural analysis of the literary form. Modestly presented, this work is not to be taken as a dull piece of empirical literary history; it is based on the more interesting assumption that theological doctrine plays a conditioning or determining role in the obsessively-repeated motifs of the Gothick romance. The background to this assumption is the argument – first made in the 1920s by Sickels's mentor, Professor Draper, in his book *The Funeral Elegy and the Rise of Romanticism* – that there is a cultural connection between the centrifugal tendency of eighteenth-century Protestantism and Romantic solitariness in aesthetics. Emergent socio-economic groups have a different psychological response to the demands of theological doctrine (melancholy tends to be Puritan for example, rather than Cavalier); and earlier, severer versions of Calvinism are bourgeoisified and sentimentalised in the eighteenth century. Hence the overlap between literary genres which Sickels surveys in her chapter 'King Death' – the 'graveyard school' in poetry meets the Gothick romance.

## LITERARY ARCHETYPES

The more purely literary approach in the modern period yields insights too. Mrs Radcliffe and Lewis were plundering Shakespeare for effects in their novels, and there is a strong cross-fertilisation between Shakespearean tragedy and Milton and the Gothick. Exponents of the Longinian tradition in eighteenth-century thought always quoted certain parts of Shakespeare and Milton as authorities for the sublime. Burke's excitement, for example, over certain passages of *Paradise Lost* is a case of this [*]. Coral Ann Howell [*], in her sensitive analysis of the relations between rhetoric and feeling in *The Mysteries of Udolpho* shows how this tradition of induced sublimity actually works in readerly practice.

In broader terms, however, the whole *genre* has been viewed as a mode of live pastiche, an endless rewriting of major scenes and effects from literary tradition. The Villain/Hero of the Gothick begins to be seen in the modern period as an Elizabethan or Jacobean stage hero, playing out a later career between the covers of an eighteenth-century novel. The most comprehensive and fascinating study of literary transmission is Mario Praz's *The Romantic Agony*, in which the author traces the transcultural development of romantic archetypes, many of them central to the Gothick – the pale, vampiric maiden, for example, and the Satanic Hero. Praz's chapter [*] on the metamorphosis of Satan generates all kinds of insights into this part of the tradition. The assumption behind his survey is much more Jungian than Freudian as far as one can see: that the project of the Gothick is the transformation and the representation of archetypes. Hence the concentration is on the minute comparison and contrast of structural features over an enormous range of texts. Praz's book was reprinted many times after the war, and it became an indispensable text in the study of the Gothick. His tact as a critic and his research over large areas of empirical materials prevent his typology from ever becoming reductive. His argument had the virtue of reactivating interest in the fact that the materials of literature are held in suspension between different historical periods, often in process of re-emergence and re-shaping. Byron's heroes, for example, have their ancestry in the Gothick novel, whose Satanic figures, in turn, can be seen as transformations of the heroic contradictions of Milton's character in *Paradise Lost*. And Praz went on to show how the image of the artist in Romantic thought is also drawn into this process of transformation, so that the Lucifer Prometheus figure is common to literature and biography in the period.

## FEMINIST APPROACHES

The most interesting and important recent work on the Gothick has been feminist. The pioneer essay in the 1970s by Ellen Moers, 'Female Gothic' sparked off a new approach to the *genre*,[28] and this is directly taken up in Sandra Gilbert and Susan Gubar's piece, 'Horror's Twin' on Mary Shelley's *Frankenstein* [*]. Here the literariness of the Gothick is given a new twist and development. The Freudian allegory of the 'family romance', the primal, Oedipal reaction of the children against the Father, is imported into the perception of literary tradition. The authors argue, after Harold Bloom in his book *The Anxiety of Influence*, that *Frankenstein* is an allegorical exorcism of Mary Shelley's literary patriarch, Milton. It is a fictionalised rendition of the meaning to women of the myth of *Paradise Lost*. The authors' theme is bibliogenesis – the book, they argue, is a displaced 'birth myth' in which the Monster, by inversion, is Eve. They point to a reduplication in the language of the text of all the roles from the biblical story of Genesis, which Milton himself had rewritten. *Frankenstein*, suggest Gilbert and Gubar, rescues female experience. The analysis tackles a problem felt by generations of readers that the female characters in the novel are all strangely passive. The men are actually women. Frankenstein himself is an Eve-figure, too; and his Monster, who reads *Paradise Lost* as a 'true story', is another comment on Eve's narcissism, a reperception by Mary Shelley of the female self as monstrous and the identity as extra-familial. The book is frankly and challengingly allegorised as a Miltonic nightmare, delivered from the imaginative womb of one of the Patriarch's nineteenth-century daughters.

Mary Poovey [*], on the other hand, takes issue with this 'optimistic' interpretation of *Frankenstein*. She faces us, as I have already pointed out, with some fascinating scholarly facts about the text, and her complex conclusions are regretfully 'revisionist'.

This debate, amongst others I have no space to represent, carries interest in the Gothick, alive and kicking, into the present day.

NOTES

1. Anyone consulting the enormous amount of material collected in D. J. McNutt (ed.), *The XVIIIth Century Gothic Novel: An Annotated Bibliography of Criticism* (London, 1975) – Introduction by D. P. Varma and M. Levy – will see immediately what I mean. I suppose I am thinking of the kind of attitude George Saintsbury shows in *The Peace of the Augustans* (excerpted in our selection, below). The most intelligent version of the literary-historical picture is to be found in E. Legouis and L. Cazamian, *A History of English Literature* (London, 1947), pp. 923ff. There is an interesting survey of historical theories in M. Levy, *Le Roman 'Gotique' anglais, 1764–1824* (Paris, 1960), pp. 600–20.

2. *Critical Review*, xx (1765), p. 51.

3. Boswell, *Life of Samuel Johnson* (London, 1934): I pp. 48–9; IV, pp. 1–17.

4. This remark of Johnson's is quoted in C. Baker, 'The Cham on Horseback', *Virginia Quarterly Review*, 26 (1950), p. 82.

5. Macaulay confessed to his sister Hannah as late as 1832: 'My tastes are, I fear, incurably vulgar, as you perceive by my fondness for Mrs Meeke's novels'; quoted in D. Blakey, *The Minerva Press, 1790–1820* (London, 1939), p. 60. Mrs Meeke was a Minerva Press authoress.

6. Blakey, ibid., pp. 111–12.

7. I am indebted to Blakey, op, cit., for all these details. Jane Austen's letter quoted above actually reveals her contempt for the snobbery of those subscription-library readers whose appetite for 'literature' was well developed but who looked down on readers of novels. A new library was about to be opened on 14 January 1798 by one Mrs Martin. Jane Austen commented to her sister on 18 December 1798:

'As an inducement to subscribe Mrs Martin tells us that her collection is not to consist only of Novels, but of every kind of Literature &.& – She might have spared this pretension to *our* family who are great Novel-readers & not ashamed of being so; – but it was necessary I suppose to the Self-Consequence of half her Subscribers.'

*Jane Austen's Letters To Her Sister Cassandra And Others*, collected and edited by R. W. Chapman, 2nd ed. London, 1952, pp. 38–9.

8. *Thraliana: The Diary of Mrs Hester Lynch Thrale, 1776–1809*, 2 vols (Oxford, 1951): ii, p. 886.

9. Quoted in E. F. Carritt (ed.), *A Calendar of British Taste, 1600–1800* (London, 1949), p. *xii*.

10. See A. Parreaux, *The Publication of 'The Monk': A Literary Event, 1796–1798* (Paris, 1960). For comment on Clara Reeve, see A. L. Cooke, 'Some Sidelights on the theory of the Gothic Romance', *Modern Language Quarterly*, xii (1951), pp. 429–36.

11. See Parreaux, op. cit., pp. 88–90.

12. For the attribution of this and other reviews and for an account of the political orientation of the magazines, see D. Roper, *Reviewing before The Edinburgh, 1788–1802* (London, 1978), p. 142.

13. For a full account of this scandal, see A. Parreaux, *William Beckford* (Paris, 1960), pp. 69–78.

14. *Thraliana*, op. cit.; ii, p. 799.

15. See A. Parreaux, 'The Caliph and the Swinish Multitude', in Fatma Moussa Mahmoud (ed.), *William Beckford and Fonthill, 1760–1844: Bicentenary Essays* (Port Washington, Kennika, 1960; reprint of 1972), pp. 1–15. For an account of Lewis's talent for self-parody, see *The Reminiscences of Henry Angelo* (1828–30: reprinted with Introduction by Lord Howard de Walden, and Notes and Memoir by H. Lavers Smith, London, 1904), 2 vols: ii, pp. 151–2.

16. For the complexities of Beckford's attitudes towards Catholicism, see William Beckford, *Excursion à Alcobaça et Batalha*, edited with Introduction (in French) by André Parreaux (Lisbon, 1956), p. *xxiv*.

17. Blakey, op. cit., p. 43.

18. See the biographical account of Mrs Radcliffe by T. M. Talfourd, Serjeant-at-Law, 'Memoir of the Life and Writings of Mrs Radcliffe', prefixed to her novel *Gaston de Blondeville* (London, 1826; reprinted New York, 1972).

19. Marilyn Butler, *Jane Austen and the War of Ideas* (Oxford, 1975), pp. 114–19. For further comment on the connections between Jacobinism

and the Gothick romance, see Gay Kelly, *The English Jacobin Novel, 1780–1805* (Oxford, 1976).

20. For a survey of some of the meanings of the term 'Gothick', in particular the Oriental connection, see A. O. Lovejoy's pioneering study, 'The First Gothic Revival and the Return to Nature', *Modern Language Notes*, XLVII, 7 (1932), pp. 419–46.

21. Quoted in Carritt, op. cit. n. 9 above, p. 252.

22. Beckford, *Excursion*. . ., op. cit., pp. 96–8.

23. *Scots Magazine*, n.s. LXXXVII (1821), p. 413.

24. 'The Historical Romance', *Blackwood's Magazine*, 58 (July–Dec. 1845), p. 347.

25. There is an excellent account of the penny dreadful in Louis James, *Fiction for the Working Man* (London, 1963), pp. 72–96. For a full account of the stage history of Frankenstein, see E. Nitchie, *Mary Shelley* (New Brunswick, N.J., 1953), App. IV, pp. 218–31.

26. Le Fanu wrote to his publisher, George Bentley, that in *The Haunted Baronet* he was deliberately striving for an effect of 'equilibrium between the natural and the *super*natural, the supernatural phenomena being explained on natural theories – and people left to choose which explanation they please'; quoted in Julia Briggs, *The Rise and Fall of the English Ghost Story* (London, 1978), p. 49.

27. M. Summers, *The Gothic Quest* (London, 1938), p. 412.

28. Ellen Moers, *Literary Women* (London, 1975).

PART ONE

# Critical Comment & Opinion c. 1750–c. 1840

# *Samuel Johnson*   (1750)

'This wild strain of imagination'[1]

... The works of fiction, with which the present generation seems more particularly delighted, are such as exhibit life in its true state, diversified only by accidents that daily happen in the world, and influenced by passions and qualities which are really to be found in conversing with mankind.

This kind of writing may be termed not improperly the comedy of romance, and is to be conducted nearly by the rules of comic poetry. Its province is to bring about natural events by easy means, and to keep up curiosity without the help of wonder: it is therefore precluded from the machines and expedients of the heroic romance, and can neither employ giants to snatch away a lady from the nuptial rites, nor knights to bring her back from captivity; it can neither bewilder its personages in desarts, nor lodge them in imaginary castles.[2]

I remember a remark made by Scaliger upon Pontanus, that all his writings are filled with the same images; and that if you take from him his lillies and his roses, his satyrs and his dryads, he will have nothing left that can be called poetry. In like manner, almost all the fictions of the last age will vanish, if you deprive them of a hermit and a wood, a battle and a shipwreck.

Why this wild strain of imagination found reception so long, in polite and learned ages, it is not easy to conceive; but we cannot wonder that, while readers could be procured, the authors were willing to continue it: for when a man had by practice gained some fluency of language, he had no further care than to retire to his closet, let loose his invention, and heat his mind with incredibilities; a book was thus produced without fear of criticism, without the toil of study, without knowledge of nature, or acquaintance with life.

The task of our present writers is very different; it requires, together with that learning which is to be gained from books, that experience which can never be attained by solitary diligence, but must arise from general converse, and accurate observation of the living world. Their performances have, as Horace expresses it, *plus oneris quantum veniae minus* [*Epistles*, II i 170], little indulgence, and therefore more difficulty. They are engaged in portraits of which every one knows the original, and can detect any deviation from exactness of resemblance. Other writings are safe, except from the malice of learning, but these are in danger from every common reader; as the slipper ill executed was censured by a shoemaker who happened to stop in his way at the Venus of Apelles.

But the fear of not being approved as just copyers of human manners, is not the most important concern that an author of this sort ought to have before him. These books are written chiefly to the young, the ignorant, and the idle, to whom they serve as lectures of conduct, and introductions into life. They are the entertainment of minds unfurnished with ideas, and therefore easily susceptible of impressions; not fixed by principles, and therefore easily following the current of fancy; not informed by experience, and consequently open to every false suggestion and partial account.

That the highest degree of reverence should be paid to youth, and that nothing indecent should be suffered to approach their eyes or ears; are precepts extorted by sense and virtue from an ancient writer, by no means eminent for chastity of thought. The same kind, tho' not the same degree of caution, is required in every thing which is laid before them, to secure them from unjust prejudices, perverse opinions, and incongruous combinations of images.

In the romances formerly written, every transaction and sentiment was so remote from all that passes among men, that the reader was in very little danger of making any applications to himself; the virtues and crimes were equally beyond his sphere of activity; and he amused himself with heroes and with traitors, deliverers and persecutors, as with beings of another species, whose actions were regulated upon motives of their own, and who had neither faults nor excellencies in common with himself.  . . .

SOURCE: extract from *The Rambler*, no. 4 (Saturday, 31 March 1750).

NOTES

1. [Ed.] The caption is devised from a phrase in Johnson's text. It was Arthur Murphy's opinion that Johnson wrote this essay in distaste at the success of Smollett's *Roderick Random* and Fielding's *Tom Jones*, which he compared unfavourably with the works of Richardson.

2. [Ed.] Nevertheless, for evidence of Johnson's own addiction to romances, see our Introduction, page 11 above.

## *Edmund Burke* (1757)

### Of the Sublime

Whatever is fitted in any sort to excite the ideas of pain, and danger, that is to say, whatever is in any sort terrible, or is conversant about terrible objects, or operates in a manner analogous to terror, is a source of the *sublime*; that is, it is productive of the strongest emotion which the mind is capable of feeling. I say the strongest emotion, because I am satisfied the ideas of pain are much more powerful than those which enter on the part of pleasure. Without all doubt, the torments which we may be made to suffer, are much greater in their effect on the body and mind, than any pleasures which the most learned voluptuary could suggest, or than the liveliest imagination, and the most sound and exquisitely sensible body could enjoy. Nay I am in great doubt, whether any man could be found who would earn a life of the most perfect satisfaction, at the price of ending it in the torments, which justice inflicted in a few hours on the late unfortunate regicide in France.[1] But as pain is stronger in its operation than pleasure, so death is in general a much more affecting idea than pain; because there are very few pains, however exquisite, which are not preferred to death; nay, what generally makes pain itself, if I may say so, more painful, is, that it is considered as an emissary of this king of terrors. When danger or pain press too nearly, they are incapable of giving any delight, and are simply terrible; but at certain distances, and with certain modifications, they may be, and they are delightful, as we every day experience. The cause of this I shall endeavour to investigate hereafter. . . .

### Of the passion caused by the sublime

The passion caused by the great and sublime in *nature*, when those causes operate most powerfully, is Astonishment; and astonishment is that state of the soul, in which all its motions are suspended, with some degree of horror. In this case the mind is so entirely filled with its object, that it cannot entertain any other, nor by consequence reason on that object which employs it. Hence arises the great power of the sublime, that far from being produced by them, it anticipates our reasonings, and hurries us on by an irresistible force. Astonishment, as I have said, is the effect of the sublime in its highest degree; the inferior effects are admiration, reverence and respect.

## Terror

No passion so effectually robs the mind of all its powers of acting and reasoning as fear. For fear being an apprehension of pain or death, it operates in a manner that resembles actual pain. Whatever therefore is terrible, with regard to sight, is sublime too, whether this cause of terror, be endued with greatness of dimensions or not; for it is impossible to look on any thing as trifling, or contemptible, that may be dangerous. There are many animals, who though far from being large, are yet capable of raising ideas of the sublime, because they are considered as objects of terror. As serpents and poisonous animals of almost all kinds. And to things of great dimensions, if we annex an adventitious idea of terror, they become without comparison greater. A level plain of a vast extent on land, is certainly no mean idea; the prospect of such a plain may be as extensive as a prospect of the ocean; but can it ever fill the mind with any thing so great as the ocean itself? This is owing to several causes, but it is owing to none more than this, that the ocean is an object of no small terror. Indeed terror is in all cases whatsoever, either more openly or latently the ruling principle of the sublime. Several languages bear a strong testimony to the affinity of these ideas. They frequently use the same word, to signify indifferently the modes of astonishment or admiration and those of terror. Θάμβος is in greek, either fear or wonder; δεινός is terrible or respectable; αἰδέω, to reverence or to fear. *Vereor* in latin, is what αἰδέω is in greek. The Romans used the verb *stupeo*, a term which strongly marks the state of an astonished mind, to express the effect either of simple fear, or of astonishment; the word *attonitus*, (thunderstruck) is equally expressive of the alliance of these ideas; and do not the french *etonnement*, and the english *astonishment* and *amazement*, point out as clearly the kindred emotions which attend fear and wonder? They who have a more general knowledge of languages, could produce, I make no doubt, many other and equally striking examples.

## Obscurity

To make any thing very terrible, obscurity seems in general to be necessary. When we know the full extent of any danger, when we can accustom our eyes to it, a great deal of the apprehension vanishes. Every one will be sensible of this, who considers how greatly night adds to our dread, in all cases of danger, and how much the notions of ghosts and goblins, of which none can form clear ideas, affect minds, which give credit to the popular tales concerning such sorts of beings. Those despotic governments, which are founded on the passions of men, and principally upon the passion of fear, keep their chief as much as may be from the public eye. The policy has been the same in many cases of religion. Almost all the heathen temples were dark.[2] Even in the barbarous temples of the Americans at this day, they keep their idol in a dark part of the hut, which is consecrated to his worship. For this purpose too the druids performed all their ceremonies in the bosom of the darkest woods, and in the shade of the oldest and most spreading oaks. No person seems better to have understood the secret of heightening, or of setting terrible things, if I may use the expression, in their strongest light by the force of a judicious obscurity, than Milton. His description of Death in the second book is admirably studied; it is astonishing with what a gloomy pomp, with what a significant and expressive uncertainty of strokes and colouring he has finished the portrait of the king of terrors.

> *The other shape,*
> *If shape it might be called that shape had none*
> *Distinguishable, in member, joint, or limb;*
> *Or substance might be called that shadow seemed,*
> *For each seemed either; black he stood as night;*
> *Fierce as ten furies; terrible as hell:*
> *And shook a deadly dart. What seemed his head*
> *The likeness of a kingly crown had on.*
> [*P. Lost*, II 666–73, but misquoted]

In this description all is dark, uncertain, confused, terrible, and sublime to the last degree. . . .
. . . The ideas of eternity, and infinity, are among the most affecting we have, and yet perhaps there is nothing of which we really understand so little, as of infinity and eternity. We do not any where meet a more sublime description than this justly celebrated one of Milton, wherein he gives the portrait of Satan with a dignity so suitable to the subject.

> *He above the rest*
> *In shape and gesture proudly eminent*
> *Stood like a tower; his form had yet not lost*
> *All her original brightness, nor appeared*
> *Less than archangel ruin'd, and th' excess*

*Of glory obscured: as when the sun new ris'n*
*Looks through the horizontal misty air*
*Shorn of his beams; or from behind the moon*
*In dim eclipse disastrous twilight sheds*
*On half the nations; and with fear of change*
*Perplexes monarchs.*

[*P. Lost,* 1 589–99]

Here is a very noble picture; and in what does this poetical picture consist? in images of a tower, an archangel, the sun rising through mists, or in an eclipse, the ruin of monarchs, and the revolutions of kingdoms. The mind is hurried out of itself, by a croud of great and confused images; which affect because they are crouded and confused. For separate them, and you lose much of the greatness, and join them, and you infallibly lose the clearness. The images raised by poetry are always of this obscure kind; though in general the effects of poetry, are by no means to be attributed to the images it raises; which point we shall examine more at large hereafter. But painting, when we have allowed for the pleasure of imitation, can only affect simply by the images it presents; and even in painting a judicious obscurity in some things contributes to the effect of the picture; because the images in painting are exactly similar to those in nature; and in nature dark, confused, uncertain images have a greater power on the fancy to form the grander passions than those have which are more clear and determinate. But where and when this observation may be applied to practice, and how far it shall be extended, will be better deduced from the nature of the subject, and from the occasion, than from any rules that can be given.

I am sensible that this idea has met with opposition, and is likely still to be rejected by several.[3] But let it be considered that hardly any thing can strike the mind with its greatness, which does not make some sort of approach towards infinity; which nothing can do whilst we are able to perceive its bounds; but to see an object distinctly, and to perceive its bounds, is one and the same thing. A clear idea is therefore another name for a little idea. There is a passage in the book of Job amazingly sublime, and this sublimity is principally due to the terrible uncertainty of the thing described. *In thoughts from the visions of the night, when deep sleep falleth upon men, fear came upon me and trembling, which made all my bones to shake. Then a spirit passed before my face. The hair of my flesh stood up. It stood still,* but I could not discern the form thereof; *an image was before mine eyes; there was silence; and I heard a voice,—Shall mortal man be more than just God?* [*Job,* IV 13–17]. We are first prepared with the utmost solemnity for the vision; we are first terrified, before we are let even into the obscure cause of our emotion; but when this grand cause of terror makes its appearance, what is it? is it not, wrapt up in the shades of its own incomprehensible darkness, more aweful, more striking, more terrible, than the liveliest description, than the clearest painting could possibly represent it? When painters have attempted to give us clear representations of these very fanciful and terrible ideas, they have I think almost always failed; insomuch that I have been at a loss, in all the pictures I have seen of hell, whether the painter did not intend something ludicrous. Several painters have handled a subject of this kind, with a view of assembling as many horrid phantoms as their imagination could suggest; but all the designs I have chanced to meet of the temptations of St. Anthony, were rather a sort of odd wild grotesques, than any thing capable of producing a serious passion. In all these subjects poetry is very happy. Its apparitions, its chimeras, its harpies, its allegorical figures, are grand and affecting; and though Virgil's Fame, [*Aeneid*, IV 173 ff.], and Homer's Discord [*Iliad*, IV 440–5] are obscure, they are magnificent figures. These figures in painting would be clear enough, but I fear they might become ridiculous.

## Power

Besides these things which *directly* suggest the idea of danger, and those which produce a similar effect from a mechanical cause, I know of nothing sublime which is not some modification of power. And this branch rises as naturally as the other two branches, from terror, the common stock of every thing that is sublime. The idea of power at first view, seems of the class of these indifferent ones, which may equally belong to pain or to pleasure. But in reality, the affection arising from the idea of vast power, is extremely remote from that neutral character. For first, we must remember, that the idea of pain, in its highest degree, is much stronger than the highest degree of pleasure; and that it preserves the same superiority through all the subordinate graduations. From hence it is, that where the chances for equal degrees of suffering or enjoyment are in any sort equal, the idea of the suffering must always be prevalent. And indeed the ideas of pain, and above all of death, are so very affecting, that whilst we remain in the presence of whatever is supposed to have the power of inflicting either, it is impossible to be perfectly free from terror. Again, we know by experience, that for the enjoyment of pleasure, no great efforts of power are at all necessary; nay we know, that such efforts would go a great way towards destroying our satisfaction: for pleasure must be stolen, and not forced upon us; pleasure follows the will; and therefore we are generally affected with it by many things of a force greatly inferior to our own. But pain is always inflicted by a power in some way superior, because we never submit to pain willingly. So that strength, violence, pain and terror, are ideas that rush in upon the mind together.   . . .

SOURCE: extracts from *A Philosophical Enquiry into the Origins of Our Ideas of the Sublime and the Beautiful* (1757); modern edition, edited by J. T. Boulton (London, 1958), pp. 39–40, 57–9, 61–5.

NOTES

1. [Ed.] A reference to the protracted execution of Robert–François Damien, who attempted to assassinate Louis xv on 5 January 1757.
2. [Ed.] Burke may be recalling here F. Hutcheson's observation in his *An Enquiry into the Original of our Ideas of Beauty and Virtue* (1725), p. 76: 'The cunning of the Heathen Priests might make such obscure Places the Scene of the fictitious Appearances of their Deitys.'
3. [Ed.] Burke's expectation was realised. Cf. *Literary Magazine*, ii, p. 183: 'Obscurity, our author observes, increases the sublime, which is certainly very just; but from thence erroneously infers, that clearness of imagery is unnecessary to affect the passions; but surely nothing can move but what gives ideas to the mind.' Similarly the writer in the *Monthly Review*, xvi , p. 477n. observes: 'Distinctness of imagery has ever been held productive of the sublime . . . .

*Richard Hurd*   (1762)

'Gothic method of design'

[Hurd has been arguing that such poets as Spenser have their own special kind of rule of Unity – Ed.] . . . This, it is true, is not the classic Unity, which consists in the representation of an entire action: but it is an Unity of another sort, an entity resulting from the respect which a number of related actions have to one common purpose. In other words, it is an unity of *design*, and not of action.

This Gothic method of design in poetry may be, in some sort, illustrated by what is called the Gothic method of design in gardening. A wood or grove cut out into many separate avenues or glades was amongst the most favourite of the works of art, which our fathers attempted in their species of cultivation. These walks were distinct from each other; had, each, their several destination, and terminated on their own proper objects. Yet the whole was brought together and considered under one view by the relation which these various openings had, not to each other, but to their common and concurrent center. . . .

SOURCE: extract from *Letters on Chivalry and Romance* (1762), pp. 66–7. A modern reprint, edited by Hoyt Trowbridge, was issued by the Augustan Reprint Society (Los Angeles, 1963).

# *S. T. Coleridge* (1797)

## 'The blasphemy of *The Monk*'

The horrible and the preternatural have usually seized on the popular taste, at the rise and decline of literature. Most powerful stimulants, they can never be required except by the torpor of an unawakened, or the languor of an exhausted, appetite. The same phænomenon, therefore, which we hail as a favourable omen in the belles lettres of Germany, impresses a degree of gloom in the compositions of our countrymen. We trust, however, that satiety will banish what good sense should have prevented; and that, wearied with fiends, incomprehensible characters, with shrieks, murders, and subterraneous dungeons, the public will learn, by the multitude of the manufacturers, with how little expense of thought or imagination this species of composition is manufactured. But, cheaply as we estimate romances in general, we acknowledge, in the work before us, the offspring of no common genius. The tale is similar to that of Santon Barsista in the Guardian. Ambrosio, a monk, surnamed the Man of Holiness, proud of his own undeviating rectitude, and severe to the faults of others, is successfully assailed by the temper of mankind, and seduced to the perpetration of rape and murder, and finally precipitated into a contract in which he consigns his soul to everlasting perdition.

The larger part of the three volumes is occupied by the underplot, which, however, is skilfully and closely connected with the main story, and is subservient to its development. The tale of the bleeding nun is truly terrific; and we could not easily recollect a bolder or more happy conception than that of the burning cross on the forehead of the wandering Jew (a mysterious character, which, though copied as to its more prominent features from Schiller's incomprehensible Armenian, does, nevertheless, display great vigour of fancy). But the character of Matilda, the chief agent in the seduction of Ambrosio, appears to us to be the author's master-piece. It is, indeed, exquisitely imagined, and as exquisitely supported. The whole work is distinguished by the variety and impressiveness of its incidents; and the author everywhere discovers an imagination rich, powerful, and fervid. Such are the excellences; – the errors and defects are more numerous, and (we are sorry to add) of greater importance.

All events are levelled into one common mass, and become almost equally probable, where the order of nature may be changed wherever the author's purposes demand it. No address is requisite to the accomplishment of any design; and no pleasure therefore can be received from the perception of *difficulty surmounted*. The writer may make us wonder, but he cannot surprise us. For the same reasons a romance is incapable of exemplifying a moral truth. No proud man, for instance, will be made less proud by being told that Lucifer once seduced a presumptuous monk. *Incredulus odit*. Or even if, believing the story, he should deem his virtue less secure, he would yet acquire no lessons of prudence, no feelings of humility. Human prudence can oppose no sufficient shield to the power and cunning of supernatural beings; and the privilege of being proud might be fairly conceded to him who could rise superior to all earthly temptations, and whom the strength of the spiritual world alone would be adequate to overwhelm. So falling, he would fall with glory, and might reasonably welcome his defeat with the haughty emotions of a conqueror. As far, therefore, as the story is concerned, the praise which a romance can claim, is simply that of having given pleasure during its perusal; and so many are the calamities of life, that he who has done this, has not written uselessly. The children of sickness and of solitude shall thank him. – To this praise, however, our author has not entitled himself. The sufferings which he describes are so frightful and intolerable, that we break with abruptness from the delusion, and indignantly suspect the man of a species of brutality, who could find a pleasure in wantonly imagining them; and the abominations which he pourtrays with no hurrying pencil, are such as the observation of character by no means demanded, such as 'no observation of character can justify, because no good man would willingly suffer them to pass, however transiently, through his own mind'. The merit of a novelist is in proportion (not simply to the effect, but) to the *pleasurable* effect which he produces. Situations of torment, and images of naked horror, are easily conceived; and a writer in whose works they abound, deserves our gratitude almost equally with him who should drag us by way of sport through a military hospital, or force us to sit at the dissecting table of a natural philosopher. To trace the nice boundaries, beyond which terror and sympathy are deserted by the pleasurable emotions, – to reach those limits, yet never to pass them, – *hic labor, hic opus est*. Figures that shock the imagination, and narratives that mangle the feelings, rarely discover *genius*, and always betray a low and vulgar *taste*. Nor has our author indicated less ignorance of the human heart in the management of the principal character. The wisdom and goodness of providence have ordered that the tendency of vicious actions to deprave the heart of the perpetrator, should diminish in proportion to the greatness of his temptations. Now, in addition to constitutional warmth and irresistible opportunity, the monk is impelled to incontinence by friendship, by compassion, by gratitude; by all that is amiable, and all that is estimable; yet in a few weeks after his first frailty, the man who had been described as possessing much general humanity, a keen and vigorous understanding, with habits of the most exalted piety, degenerates into an uglier fiend than the gloomy imagination of Dante would have ventured to picture. Again, the monk is described as feeling and acting under the influence of an appetite which could not co-exist with his other emotions. The romance-writer possesses an unlimited power over situations; but he must scrupulously make his characters act in congruity with them. Let him work *physical* wonders only, and we will be content to *dream* with him for a while; but the first *moral* miracle which he attempts, he disgusts and awakens us. Thus our judgment remains unoffended, when, announced by thunders and earthquakes, the spirit appears to Ambrosio involved in blue fires that increase the cold of the cavern; and we acquiesce in the power of the silver myrtle which made gates and doors fly open at its touch, and charmed every eye into sleep. But when a mortal, fresh from the impression of that terrible appearance, and in the act of evincing for the first time the witching force of this myrtle, is represented as being at the same moment agitated by so fleeting an appetite as that of lust, our own feelings convinced us that this is not improbable, but impossible; not preternatural, but contrary to nature. The extent of the powers that may exist, we can never ascertain; and therefore we feel no great difficulty in yielding a temporary belief to any, the strangest, situation of *things*. But that situation once conceived, how beings like ourselves would feel and act in it, our own feelings sufficiently instruct us; and we instantly reject the clumsy fiction that does not harmonise with them. These are the two *principal* mistakes in *judgment*, which the author has fallen into; but we cannot wholly pass over the frequent incongruity of his style with his subjects. It is gaudy where it should have been severely simple; and too often the mind is offended by phrases the most trite and colloquial, where it demands and had expected a sternness and solemnity of diction.

A more grievous fault remains, – a fault for which no literary excellence can atone, – a fault which all other excellence does but aggravate, as adding subtlety to a poison by the elegance of its preparation. Mildness of censure would here be criminally misplaced, and silence would make us accomplices. Not without reluctance then, but in full conviction that we are performing a duty, we declare it to be our opinion, that the Monk is a romance, which if a parent saw in the hands of a son or daughter, he might reasonably turn pale. The temptations of Ambrosio are described with a libidinous minuteness, which, we sincerely hope, will receive its best and only adequate censure from the offended conscience of the author himself. The shameless harlotry of Matilda, and the trembling innocence of Antonia, are seized with equal avidity, as vehicles of the most voluptuous images; and though the tale is indeed a tale of horror, yet the most painful impression which the work left on our minds was that of great acquirements and splendid genius employed to furnish a *mormo* for children, a poison for youth, and a provocative for the debauchee. Tales of enchantments and witchcraft can never be *useful*: our author has contrived to make them *pernicious*, by blending, with an irreverent negligence, all that is most awfully true in religion with all that is most ridiculously absurd in superstition. He takes frequent occasion, indeed, to manifest his sovereign contempt for the latter, both in his own person, and (most incongruously) in that of his principal characters; and that his respect for the *former* is not excessive, we are forced to conclude from the treatment which its inspired writings receive from him. Ambrosio discovers Antonia reading –

He examined the book which she had been reading, and had now placed upon the table. It was the Bible.

'How!' said the friar to himself, 'Antonia reads the Bible, and is still so ignorant?'

But, upon a further inspection, he found that Elvira had made exactly the same remark. That prudent mother, while she admired the beauties of the sacred writings, was convinced that, unrestricted, no reading more improper could be permitted a young woman. Many of the narratives can only tend to excite ideas the worst calculated for a female breast: every thing is called plainly and roundly by its name; and the *annals of a brothel would scarcely furnish a greater choice of indecent expressions.* Yet this is the book which young women are recommended to study, which is put into the hands of children, able to comprehend little more than those passages of which they had better remain ignorant, and which but too *frequently inculcates the first rudiments of vice,* and gives the first alarm to the still sleeping passions. Of this was Elvira so fully convinced, that she would have preferred putting into her daughter's hands 'Amadis de Gaul,' or 'The Valiant Champion, Tirante the White'; and *would sooner have authorised her studying the lewd exploits of Don Galaor, or the lascivious jokes of the Damsel Plazer di mi vida.* [II p. 247 – Coleridge's italics]

The impiety of this falsehood can be equalled only by its impudence. This is indeed as if a Corinthian harlot, clad from head to foot in the transparent thinness of the Cöan vest, should affect to view with prudish horror the naked knee of a Spartan matron! If it be possible that the author of these blasphemies is a Christian, should he not have reflected that the only passage in the scriptures,* which could give a *shadow* of plausibility to the *weakest* of these expressions, is represented as being spoken by the Almighty himself? But if he be an infidel, he has acted consistently enough with that character, in his endeavours first to influence the fleshly appetites, and then to pour contempt on the only book which would be adequate to the task of recalming them. We believe it not absolutely impossible that a mind may be so deeply depraved by the habit of reading lewd and voluptuous tales, as to use even the Bible in conjuring up the spirit of uncleanness. The most innocent expressions might become the first link in the chain of association, when a man's soul had been so poisoned; and we believe it not absolutely impossible that he might extract pollution from the word of purity, and, in a literal sense, *turn the grace of God into wantonness.*

We have been induced to pay particular attention to this work, from the unusual success which it has experienced. It certainly possesses much real merit, in addition to its meretricious attractions. Nor must it be forgotten that the author is a man of rank and fortune. – Yes! the author of the Monk signs himself a legislator! We stare and tremble.

Source: review of *The Monk. A Romance*, by M. G. Lewis, Esq. M.P., 3 vols (Bell, London, 1796), in the *Critical Review* (February 1797), pp. 194–200.

* *Ezekiel*, xxiii [Coleridge's note].

## Anonymous    (1797)

### 'On the corruption of the female reader'

. . . To indulge in a practice of reading romances, is, in several other particulars, liable to produce mischevous effects. Such compositions are, to most persons, extremely engaging. That story must be uncommonly barren, or wretchedly told, of which, after having heard the beginning, we do not desire to hear the end. To the pleasure of learning the ultimate futures of the heroes and heroines of the tale, the novel commonly adds, in a greater or a less degree, that which arises from animated description, from lively dialogue, or from interesting sentiment. Hence the perusal of one romance leads, with much more frequency than is the case with works of other kinds, to the speedy perusal of another. Thus, a habit is formed, a habit at first, perhaps, of limited indulgence, but a habit that is continually found more formidable and more encroaching. The appetite becomes too keen to be denied; and, in proportion as it is more urgent, grows less nice and select in its fare. What would formerly have given offence, now gives none. The palate is vitiated or made dull. The produce of the book-club, and the contents of the circulating library are devoured with indiscriminate and insatiable avidity. Hence the mind is secretly corrupted. Let it be observed, too, that in exact correspondence with the increase of a passion for reading novels, an aversion to reading of a more improving nature will gather strength. There is yet another consequence too important to be overlooked. The catastrophe and the incidents of romances commonly turn on the vicissitudes and effects of a passion the most powerful of all those which agitate the human heart. Hence some of them frequently create a susceptibility of impression and a premature warmth of tender emotions, which, not to speak of other possible effects, have been known to betray young women into a sudden attachment to persons unworthy of their affection, and thus to hurry them into marriages terminating in their unhappiness. . . .

SOURCE: unsigned article in the *Scots Magazine*, LXIX (June 1797), p. 375.

# '*E.A.*'   (1798)

'Bad novels are . . . most excellent things'

. . . If we look at the female part of mankind, and speak of it as one individual, we shall perceive that it is just emerging from infancy. If, however, we separate the particles of this Composition, we shall find that the appearance of refinement, which had induced us to suppose this *emerging*, is not produced by an equal improvement in the whole; but rather, many enlightened, some splendid, individuals among them serve to illumine the features of the rest; while the greater part are, in themselves, buried in the profoundest night. Now, I contend that, if this period of female mental infancy be compared with that of the male, the ladies will suffer nothing in the comparison: so that we may reasonably hope, and, indeed, particular examples assure us, that their maturity may hereafter vie with our own.

Have we forgotten that, when *we* first began to cultivate our understanding, *we* had our Monkish legends, our crusades, and our hobgoblins; and witchings;, and our conundrums? Have we forgotten these things, that we look so haughtily upon the fair who now admire them?

Let us observe the utility of these compositions which the greater part of our novels imitate so well.

They induce persons to read, who, but for these, would never read at all.  . . .

Let me see a girl take up an absurd novel; if she is pleased with it, I will pronounce that it is perfectly fitted for her capacity: as methodism is the most proper religion for those whose minds are weak and depraved enough to applaud it. In ninety-nine instances these predilections will produce the misery of the admirer; but in the hundredth a strong understanding will learn, from the very lessons, to despise the instructor. A good taste will spring from the detestation of the bad; and thus, spreading itself to myriads of mankind, in luxuriant branches from the well-nourished root, will have ample vengeance for the ninety-nine who have been destroyed.  . . .

Bad novels, then, are most excellent things: and the worse they are written, so much the better for society: they will gain the greatest number of those who have, hitherto, never read – for such cannot understand any part of a book that is tolerably put together – and what is best of all, they will at the same time, have the fewest admirers: because the more glaring the absurdity is, the greater will be the number of those who discover it! Moreover, I do really, and not jocularly, wish to see stupid stories written (and, thanks to *circulating libraries*, I shall not wish in vain); because they attract readers. These, having tasted books, commonly seek for others and it is hard, indeed, if some of the latter are not moderately good; and the reader is by this time prepared to comprehend them. . . .

Go on, therefore, you who write vile novels! Croud absurdity upon absurdity; patch deformity with deformity; caricature the works of Providence; mar the outlines of his wisdom, till its form is rendered doubtful, and its beauty denied; twist the paths of virtue till their end and object are lost; strew those of vice so thick with flowers, that their characteristics may become equivocal, and their way-marks uncertain; draw fantastick characters; paint their countenances woful; and then tell your readers, that *you are almost inclined to doubt the goodness of God in making them so** – If, indeed, you mean *their maker, their Creator*, I doubt with you! Go on: – do these things; and my earnest wishes attend you! – And you, fair Ladies, read on; gather together all the novels that you can find; read them till – till you have acquired enough sense to see their worthlessness!

SOURCE: article in the *Lady's Monthly Museum*, I (1798), excerpted from pp. 258–9.

# *Jane Austen*    (c. 1800)

### I 'A cold sweat stood on her forehead'

. . . The dimness of the light her candle emitted made her turn to it with alarm; but there was no danger of its sudden extinction, it had yet some hours to burn; and that she might not have any greater difficulty in distinguishing the writing than what its ancient date might occasion, she hastily snuffed it. Alas! it was snuffed and extinguished in one. A lamp could not have expired with more awful

---

* Expression in an admired Novel [anonymous author's footnote].

effect. Catherine, for a few moments, was motionless with horror. It was done completely; not a remnant of light in the wick could give hope to the rekindling breath. Darkness impenetrable and immoveable filled the room. A violent gust of wind, rising with sudden fury, added fresh horror to the movement. Catherine trembled from head to foot. In the pause which succeeded, a sound like receding footsteps and the closing of a distant door struck on her affrighted ear. Human nature could support no more. A cold sweat stood on her forehead, the manuscript fell from her hand, and groping her way to the bed, she jumped hastily in, and sought some suspension of agony by creeping far underneath the clothes. To close her eyes in sleep that night, she felt must be entirely out of the question. With a curiosity so justly awakened, and feelings in every way so agitated, repose must be absolutely impossible. The storm too abroad so dreadful! – She had not been used to feel alarm from wind, but now every blast seemed fraught with awful intelligence. The manuscript so wonderfully found, so wonderfully accomplishing the morning's prediction, how was it to be accounted for? – What could it contain? – to whom could it relate? – by what means could it have been so long concealed? – and how singularly strange that it should fall to her lot to discover it! Till she had made herself mistress of its contents, however, she could have neither repose nor comfort; and with the sun's first rays she was determined to peruse it. But many were the tedious hours which must yet intervene. She shuddered, tossed about in her bed, and envied every quiet sleeper. The storm still raged, and various were the noises, more terrific even than the wind, which struck at intervals on her startled ear. The very curtains of her bed seemed at one moment in motion, and at another the lock of her door was agitated, as if by the attempt of somebody to enter. Hollow murmurs seemed to creep along the gallery, and more than once her blood was chilled by the sound of distant moans. Hour after hour passed away, and the wearied Catherine had heard three proclaimed by all the clocks in the house, before the tempest subsided, or she unknowingly fell fast asleep.  . . .

II 'What ideas have you been admitting?'

. . . 'If I understand you rightly, you had formed a surmise of such horror as I have hardly words to – Dear Miss Morland, consider the dreadful nature of the suspicions you have entertained. What have you been judging from? Remember the country and the age in which we live. Remember that we are English, that we are Christians. Consult your own understanding, your own sense of the probable,

your own observation of what is passing around you – Does our education prepare us for such atrocities? Do our laws connive at them? Could they be perpetrated without being known, in a country like this, where social and literary intercourse is on such a footing; where every man is surrounded by a neighbourhood of voluntary spies, and where roads and newspapers lay every thing open? Dearest Miss Morland, what ideas have you been admitting?'

They had reached the end of the gallery; and with tears of shame she ran off to her own room. . . .

SOURCE: extracts from *Northanger Abbey*, probably written between 1799 and 1801, posthumously published in 1818; new edition, edited by John Davie (Oxford, 1971; 1980), pp. 135–6, 159.

## Marquis de Sade    (1800)

### 'The fruit of revolutionary tremors'

. . . Man is subject to two weaknesses which cling to his existence, and give it its character. Universally he must pray, universally he must love; and in this lies the essence of all novels – they are either produced in order to depict those beings whom he has worshipped, or to celebrate those whom he has loved. The former, motivated by terror or hope, ought to be sombre, gigantic, full of lies and fictions, such as were composed by Esdras[1] at the time of Babylon's thrall: the latter filled with delicacy and sentiment, such as those of Theagenes and Chariclea by Heliodorus. But since man has prayed and since he has loved, everywhere, at any given point on this habitable globe, it follows that there will be novels, that is works of fiction, which as often as they portray the mythical objects of his worship, celebrate those more real ones of his love. . . .

Hence it is unnecessary to set oneself the task of finding the origin of this *genre*, favouring such and such a culture above such and such as a home for it. It should be abundantly clear from what has just been said that all of them have more or less employed, according to which bias they have manifested, either love or superstitition. . . .

Perhaps at this point we should analyse these recent novels the magic and fantasmagoria of which constitute nine-tenths of their worth, giving pride of place to *The Monk*, superior on all counts to the bizarre flashes of the brilliant imagination of Radcliffe. But such a dissertation would be too long: let us agree that this species of writing, whatever one might say about it, is assuredly not without merit. It became the necessary fruit of the revolutionary tremors felt by the whole of Europe. For anyone who was familiar with the extent of the miseries which evil men were able to heap upon mankind, the novel became as difficult to write as it was monotonous to read. In four or five years, there was not an individual left who had not experienced misfortunes and who, in a century famous for its writing, was not able to depict them. In order therefore to confer some interest on their productions, it was necessary to appeal to hell for aid and to find chimeras in the landscape: a thing which one perceived at the time by a mere glance through the history of mankind in this age of iron. But how many infelicities presented themselves in this mode of writing; nor has the author of *The Monk* avoided them any more than Radcliffe. Here one must choose one of two things: either one must bring forth the magic spell, after which interest is lost, or one must never raise the curtain at all, and then one enters the realms of the most frightful truthlessness. Let there appear in this *genre* a work of sufficient quality to attain its goal without foundering on one or other of these reefs, and, far from criticising its methods, we will offer it up as a model. . . .

SOURCE: extracts from 'Idée sur les romans', in *Les Crimes de l'Amour* (Paris, 1800), pp. 102–3, 120–1 – translated for this Casebook by Victor Sage.

NOTE

1. [Ed.] The allusion is to the second book of Esdras, in the *Apocrypha* – a record of revelations and visions predictive of destruction for the wicked and salvation for the righteous.

## Henry Crabb Robinson   (1816)

### 'Read *Vathek* till past one'

*March 3rd* . . . Read till near one the beginning of *Vathek*.[1]   . . .
*March 4th* . . . Continued till near one *Caliph Vathek*, a book which is quite original in its style. It is marvellous without surfeiting and, without falling into the ridiculous, is humorous. I know not when I have been so amused.

*March 5th* . . . Read *Vathek* till past one – the tale increases in horror, perhaps it becomes disgusting as it advances. It is a powerful production. . . .

*March 10th* . . . Finished *Vathek*. As I advanced in this book it pleased me less. There is a strange want of keeping in the style, Johnsonian parade being blended with colloquial familiarities, and an unsuccessful attempt to unite the description of horrid situations and incidents with strokes of humour. The finest part is the description of hell at the close. The immense and gorgeous hall surrounded by objects of magnificence and wealth, full of wretches each tormented by an incessantly burning heart and each bearing his torment in mournful seclusion from others, all crowded together and each bearing his own suffering and further tormented by his hatred of his former friends – this is a very fine picture certainly. But the philosophy of the tale is not better than the philosophy of other like tales. If all the sufferers like Vathek have been wrought on by the agency of the necromancer and Giaour who wrought the Caliph's downfall, the same objection will apply to all. Either such an agent was not wanted to effect the perdition of the individual, and then he is an impertinent intruder; or he was, and then why was he permitted to ruin those who otherwise would have remained innocent?

How glad I should be if such an objection never occurred to me but on the perusal of a fairy tale! . . .

SOURCE: extracts from Robinson's *Diaries*, first published posthumously in 1869, edited by T. Sadleir.

NOTE

1. [Ed.] Variously known as *An Arabian Tale*, as *Vathek, An Arabian Tale* and as *The History of the Caliph Vathek*, the tale was originally written by Beckford in French and translated from MS by the Rev. S. Henley for publication in English in 1786. The French version was published in 1787.

# *Thomas Love Peacock* (1818)

## 'Distempered ideas of metaphysical romance'

Shortly after the disastrous termination of Scythrop's passion for

Miss Emily Girouette, Mr Glowry found himself, much against his
will, involved in a lawsuit, which compelled him to dance attendance
on the High Court of Chancery. Scythrop[1] was left alone at
Nightmare Abbey. He was a burnt child, and dreaded the fire of
female eyes. He wandered about the ample pile, or along the garden-
terrace, with 'his cogitative faculties immersed in cogibundity of
cogitation'. The terrace terminated at the south-western tower,
which as we have said, was ruinous and full of owls. Here would
Scythrop take his evening seat, on a fallen fragment of mossy stone,
with his back resting against the ruined wall, – a thick canopy of
ivy, with an owl in it, over his head, – and the Sorrows of Werter in
his hand. He had some taste for romance reading before he went to
the university, where, we must confess, in justice to his college, he
was cured of the love of reading in all its shapes; and the cure would
have been radical, if disappointment in love, and total solitude, had
not conspired to bring on a relapse. He began to devour romances
and German tragedies, and, by the recommendation of Mr Flosky[2],
to pore over ponderous tomes of transcendental philosophy, which
reconciled him to the labour of studying them by their mystical
jargon and necromantic imagery. In the congenial solitude of
Nightmare Abbey, the distempered ideas of metaphysical romance
and romance metaphysics had ample time and space to germinate
into a fertile crop of chimeras, which rapidly shot up into vigorous
and abundant vegetation.

He now became troubled with the *passion for reforming the world.**
He built many castles in the air, and peopled them with secret
tribunals, and bands of illuminati, who were always the imaginary
instruments of his projected regeneration of the human species. As
he intended to institute a perfect republic, he invested himself with
absolute sovereignty over these mystical dispensers of liberty. He
slept with Horrid Mysteries under his pillow, and dreamed of
venerable eleutherarchs and ghastly confederates holding midnight
conventions in subterranean caves. He passed whole mornings in
his study, immersed in gloomy reverie, stalking about the room in
his nightcap, which he pulled over his eyes like a cowl, and folding
his striped calico dressing-gown about him like the mantle of a
conspirator.

'Action', thus he soliloquised, 'is the result of opinion, and to
new-model opinion would be to new-model society. Knowledge is
power; it is in the hands of a few, who employ it to mislead

* See *Forsyth's Principle of Moral Science* [Peacock's footnote – Ed.].

the many, for their own selfish purposes of aggrandisement and appropriation. What if it were in the hands of a few who should employ it to lead the many? What if it were universal, and the multitude were enlightened? No. The many must be always in leading-strings; but let them have wise and honest conductors. A few to think, and many to act; that is the only basis of perfect society. So thought the ancient philosophers: they had their esoterical and exoterical doctrines. So thinks the sublime Kant, who delivers his oracles in language which none but the initiated can comprehend. Such were the views of those secret associations of illuminati, which were the terror of superstition and tyranny, and which, carefully selecting wisdom and genius from the great wilderness of society, as the bee selects honey from the flowers of the thorn and the nettle, bound all human excellence in a chain, which, if it had not been prematurely broken, would have commanded opinion, and regenerated the world.'

Scythrop proceeded to meditate on the practicability of reviving a confederation of regenerators. To get a clear view of his own ideas, and to feel the pulse of the wisdom and genius of the age, he wrote and published a treatise, in which his meanings were carefully wrapt up in the monk's hood of transcendental technology, but filled with hints of matter deep and dangerous, which he thought would set the whole nation in a ferment; and he awaited the result in awful expectation, as a miner who has fired a train awaits the explosion of a rock. However, he listened and heard nothing; for the explosion, if any ensued, was not sufficiently loud to shake a single leaf of the ivy on the towers of Nightmare Abbey; and some months afterwards he received a letter from his bookseller, informing him that only seven copies had been sold, and concluding with a polite request for the balance.

Scythrop did not despair. 'Seven copies', he thought, 'have been sold. Seven is a mystical number, and the omen is good. Let me find the seven purchasers of my seven copies, and they shall be the seven golden candle-sticks with which I will illuminate the world.'

Scythrop had a certain portion of mechanical genius, which his romantic projects tended to develope. He constructed models of cells and recesses, sliding panels and secret passages, that would have baffled the skill of the Parisian police. He took the opportunity of his father's absence to smuggle a dumb carpenter into the Abbey, and between them they gave reality to one of these models in Scythrop's tower. Scythrop foresaw that a great leader of human regeneration would be involved in fearful dilemmas, and determined, for the benefit of mankind in general, to adopt all possible precautions for the preservation of himself.

The servants, even the women, had been tutored into silence. Profound stillness reigned throughout and around the Abbey, except when the occasional shutting of a door would peal in long reverberations through the galleries, or the heavy tread of the pensive butler would wake the hollow echoes of the hall. Scythrop stalked about like the grand inquisitor, and the servants flitted past him like familiars. In his evening meditations on the terrace, under the ivy of the ruined tower, the only sounds that came to his ear were the rustling of the wind in the ivy, the plaintive voices of the feathered choristers, the owls, the occasional striking of the Abbey clock, and the monotonous dash of the sea on its low and level shore. In the mean time, he drank Madeira, and laid deep schemes for a thorough repair of the crazy fabric of human nature.

SOURCE: chapter II of *Nightmare Abbey*, first published in 1818. [For critical discussion of it, in context with his other novels, see the Casebook on Peacock's *Satirical Novels* – Ed.]

NOTES

1. [Ed.] Scythrop Glowry is a parody of many characteristics of Shelley, a close acquaintance of Peacock's.
2. [Ed.] Mr Flosky is a caricature of Coleridge.

## *Sir Walter Scott*   (1818)

### On types of romantic fiction

[*Frankenstein*] is a novel, or more properly a romantic fiction, of a nature so peculiar that we ought to describe the species before attempting any account of the individual production.

The first general division of works of fiction, into such as bound the events they narrate by the actual laws of nature, and such as, passing these limits, are managed by marvellous and supernatural machinery, is sufficiently obvious and decided. But the class of marvellous romances admits of several subdivisions. In the earlier productions of imagination, the poet, or tale-teller does not, in his own opinion, transgress the laws of credibility, when he introduces into his narration the witches, goblins, and magicians, in the existence of which he himself, as well as his hearers, is a firm believer. This good faith, however, passes away, and works turning upon the marvellous are written and read merely on account of the exercise which they afford to the imagination of those who, like the poet Collins, love to riot in the luxuriance of Oriental fiction, to rove through the meanders of enchantment, to gaze on the magnificence of golden palaces, and to repose by the water-falls of Elysian gardens. In this species of composition, the marvellous is itself the principal and most important object both to the author and reader. To describe its effect upon the mind of the human personages engaged in its wonders, and dragged along by its machinery, is comparatively an inferior object. The hero and heroine, partakers of the supernatural character which belongs to their adventures, walk the maze of enchantment with a firm and undaunted step, and appears as much at their ease, amid the wonders around them, as the young fellow described by the *Spectator*, who was discovered taking a snuff with great composure in the midst of a stormy ocean, represented on the stage of the opera.

A more philosophical and refined use of the supernatural in works of fiction, is proper to that class in which the laws of nature are represented as altered, not for the purpose of pampering the imagination with wonders, but in order to show the probable effect which the supposed miracles would produce on those who witnessed them. In this case, the pleasure ordinarily derived from the marvellous incidents is secondary to that which we extract from observing how mortals like ourselves would be affected,

> By scenes like these which, daring to depart
> From sober truth, are still to nature true.

Even in the description of his marvels, however, the author who manages this stile of composition with address, gives them an indirect importance with the reader, when he is able to describe with nature and with truth, the effects which they are calculated to produce upon his dramatis personæ. It will be remembered, that the sapient Partridge was too wise to be terrified at the mere appearance of the ghost of Hamlet, whom he knew to be a man dressed up in pasteboard armour for the nonce – it was when he saw the 'little man', as he called Garrick, so frightened, that a sympathetic horror took hold of him. . . . But success in this point is still subordinate to the author's principal object, which is less to produce an effect by means of the marvels of the narrations, than to open new trains and channels of thought, by placing men in supposed situations of an extraordinary and preternatural character, and then describing the mode of feeling and conduct which they are most likely to adopt.

To make more clear the distinction we have endeavoured to draw between the marvellous and the effects of the marvellous, considered as separate objects, we may briefly invite our readers to compare the common tale of *Tom Thumb* with *Gulliver's Voyage to Brobdingnag*; one of the most childish fictions, with one which is pregnant with wit and satire, yet both turning upon the same assumed possibility of the existence of a pigmy among a race of giants. In the former case, when the imagination of the story-teller has exhausted itself in every species of hyperbole, in order to describe the diminutive size of his hero, the interest of the tale is at an end; but in the romance of the Dean of St Patrick's, the exquisite humour with which the natural consequences of so strange and unusual a situation is detailed, has a canvass on which to expand itself, as broad as the luxuriance even of the author's talents could desire. Gulliver stuck into a marrow bone, and Master Thomas Thumb's disastrous fall into the bowl of hasty-pudding, are, in the general outline, kindred incidents; but the jest is exhausted in the latter case, when the accident is told; whereas in the former, it lies not so much in the comparatively pigmy size which subjected Gulliver to such a ludicruous misfortune, as in the tone of grave and dignified feeling with which he resents the disgrace of the incident.

In the class of fictitious narrations to which we allude, the author opens a sort of account-current with the reader; drawing upon him, in the first place, for credit to that degree of the marvellous which he proposes to employ; and becoming virtually bound, in consequence of this indulgence, that his personages shall conduct themselves, in the extraordinary circumstances in which they are placed, according to the rules of probability, and the nature of the human heart. In this view, the *probable* is far from being laid out of sight even amid the wildest freaks of imagination; on the contrary, we grant the extraordinary postulates which the author demands as the foundation of his narrative, only on condition of his deducing the consequences with logical precision.

We have only to add, that this class of fiction has been sometimes applied to the purposes of political satire, and sometimes to the general illustration of the powers and workings of the human mind. Swift, Bergerac, and others, have employed it for the former purpose, and a good illustration of the latter is the well known *Saint Leon* of William Godwin. In this latter work, assuming the possibility of the transmutation of metals and of the *elixir vitæ*, the author has deduced, in the course of his narrative, the probable consequences of the possession of such secrets upon the fortunes and mind of him who might enjoy them. *Frankenstein* is a novel upon the same plan with *Saint Leon*; it is said to be written by Mr Percy Bysshe Shelley,[1] who, if we are rightly informed, is son-in-law to Mr. Godwin; and it is inscribed to that ingenious author. . . .

SOURCE: extract from review of *Frankenstein: or, The Modern Prometheus*, first published 1818, in *Blackwood's Magazine*, II (1818).

NOTE

1. [Ed.] A shrewd but erroneous assumption by Scott; on the anonymity of the first edition of *Frankenstein*, see Introduction, page 12, above.

## Sir Walter Scott  (1824)

### 'An age of universal credulity'

. . . Mrs Radcliffe, as an author, has the most decided claim to take her place among the favoured few, who have been distinguished as the founders of a class, or school. She led the way in a peculiar style of composition, affecting powerfully the mind of the reader, which has since been attempted by many, but in which no one has attained or approached the excellences of the original inventor, unless perhaps the author of *The Family of Montorio*.

The species of romance which Mrs Radcliffe introduced, bears nearly the same relation to the novel that the modern anomaly entitled a melo-dramo does to the proper drama. It does not appeal to the judgment by deep delineations of human feeling, or stir the passions by scenes of deep pathos, or awaken the fancy by tracing out, with spirit and vivacity, the lighter marks of life and manners, or excite mirth by strong representations of the ludicrous or humorous. In other words, it attains its interest neither by the path of comedy nor of tragedy; and yet it has, notwithstanding, a deep, decided, and powerful effect, gained by means independent of both – by an appeal, in one word, to the passion of fear, whether excited by natural dangers, or by the suggestions of superstition. The force, therefore, of the production, lies in the delineation of external incident, while the characters of the agents, like the figures in many landscapes, are entirely subordinate to the scenes in which they are placed; and are only distinguished by such outlines as make them seem appropriate to the rocks and trees, which have been the artist's principal objects. The persons introduced – and here also the correspondence holds betwixt the melo-dramo and the romantic novel – bear the features, not of individuals, but of the class to which they belong. A dark and tyrannical count; an aged crone of a housekeeper, the depositary of many a family legend; a garrulous waiting-maid; a gay and light-hearted valet; a villain or two of all work; and a heroine, fulfilled with all perfections, and subjected to all manner of hazards, form the stock-in-trade of a romancer of a melo-dramatist; and if these personages be dressed in the proper costume, and converse in language sufficiently appropriate to their stations and qualities, it is not expected that the audience shall shake their sides at the humour of the dialogue, or weep over its pathos.

When applied to Mrs Radcliffe herself, the tone of criticism which we allude to will, when justly examined, be found to rest chiefly on that depreciating spirit, which would undermine the fair fame of an accomplished writer, by showing that she does not possess the excellences proper to a style of composition totally different from that which she has attempted. The question is neither, whether the romances of Mrs Radcliffe possess merits which her plan did not require, nay, almost excluded; nor whether hers is to be considered as a department of fictitious composition, equal in dignity and importance to those where the great ancient masters have long pre-occupied the ground. The real and only point is, whether, considered as a separate and distinct species of writing, that introduced by Mrs Radcliffe possesses merit, and affords pleasure; for, these premises being admitted, it is as unreasonable to complain of the absence of advantages foreign to her style and plan, and proper to those of another mode of composition, as to regret that the peach-tree does not produce grapes, or the vine peaches. A glance upon the face of nature is, perhaps, the best cure for this unjust and unworthy system of criticism. We there behold, that not only each star differs from another in glory, but that there is spread over the face of Nature a boundless variety; and that as a thousand different kinds of shrubs and flowers, not only have beauties independent of each other, but are more delightful from that very circumstance than if they were uniform, so the fields of literature admit the same variety; and it may be said of the Muse of Fiction, as well as of her sisters,

Mille habet ornatus, mille decenter habet.

It may be stated to the additional confusion of such hypercritics as we allude to, that not only does the infinite variety of human tastes require different styles of composition for their gratification; but if there were to be selected one particular structure of fiction, which possesses charms for the learned and unlearned, the grave and gay, the gentleman and the clown, it would be perhaps that of those very romances which the severity of their criticism seeks to depreciate. There are many men too mercurial to be delighted by Richardson's beautiful, but protracted display of the passions; and there are some too dull to comprehend the wit of Le Sage, or too saturnine to relish the nature and spirit of Fielding: And yet these very individuals will with difficulty be divorced from *The Romance of the Forest*, or *The Mysteries of Udolpho*; for curiosity and a lurking love of mystery, together with a germ of superstition, are more general ingredients in the human mind, and more widely diffused through the mass of humanity, than either genuine taste for the comic, or true feeling of the pathetic. The unknown author of *The Pursuits of Literature*, who, in respect to common tales of terror,

> boasts an English heart,
> Unused at ghosts or rattling bones to start,

acknowledges, nevertheless, the legitimate character of Mrs Radcliffe's art, and pays no mean tribute to her skill. Of some sister novelist he talks with slight regard.

> Though all of them are ingenious ladies, yet they are too frequently whining and frisking in novels, till our girls' heads turn wild with impossible adventures; and now and then are tainted with democracy. Not so the mighty magician of *The Mysteries of Udolpho*, bred and nourished by the Florentine muses in their secret solitary caverns, amid the paler shrines of Gothic superstition, and in all the dreariness of enchantment; a poetess whom Ariosto would with rapture have acknowledged as,
> > La nudrita
> Damigella Trivulzia AL SACRO SPECO.        [*Orlando Furioso*, XLVI][1]

Mrs Radcliffe was not made acquainted with this high compliment till long after the satire was published; and its value was enhanced by the author's general severity of judgment, and by his perfect acquaintance with the manners and language of Italy, in which she had laid her scene.

It is farther to be observed, that the same class of critics who ridiculed these romances as unnatural and improbable, was disposed to detract from the genius of the author, on account of the supposed facility of her task. Art or talent, they said, was not required to produce that sort of interest and emotion, which is perhaps, after all, more strongly excited by a vulgar legend of a village ghost, than by the high painting and laboured descriptions of Mrs Radcliffe. But this criticism is not much better founded than the former. The feelings of suspense and awful attention which she excites, are awakened by means of springs which lie open, indeed, to the first touch, but which are peculiarly liable to be worn out by repeated pressure. The public soon, like Macbeth, become satiated with horrors, and indifferent to the strongest *stimuli* of that kind. It shows, therefore, the excellence and power of Mrs Radcliffe's genius, that she was able three times to bring back her readers with fresh appetite to a banquet of the same description; while of her numerous imitators, who rang the changes upon old castles and forests, and 'antres diro,' scarcely one attracted attention, until Mr Lewis published his *Monk*, several years after she had resigned her pen.

The materials of these celebrated romances, and the means employed in conducting the narrative, are all selected with a view to the author's primary object, of moving the reader by ideas of impending danger, hidden guilt, supernatural visiting – by all that is terrible, in short, combined with much that is wonderful. For this purpose, her scenery is generally as gloomy as her tale, and her personages are those at whose frown that gloom grows darker. She has uniformly (except in her first effort) selected for her place of action the south of Europe, where the human passions, like the weeds of the climate, are supposed to attain portentous growth under the fostering sun; which abounds with ruined monuments of antiquity, as well as the more massive remnants of the middle ages; and where feudal tyranny and Catholic superstition still continue to exercise their sway over the slave and bigot, and to indulge to the haughty lord, or more haughty priest, that sort of despotic power, the exercise of which seldom fails to deprave the heart, and disorder the judgment. These circumstances are skilfully selected, to give probability to events which could not, without great violation of truth, be represented as having taken place in England. Yet, even with the allowances which we make for foreign minds and manners, the unterminating succession of misfortunes which press upon the heroine, strikes us as unnatural. She is continually struggling with the tide of adversity, and hurried downwards by its torrent; and if any more gay description is occasionally introduced, it is only as a contrast, and not a relief, to the melancholy and gloomy tenor of the narrative.

In working upon the sensations of natural and superstitious fear, Mrs Radcliffe has made such use of obscurity and suspense, the most fertile source, perhaps, of sublime emotion; for there are few dangers that do not become familiar to the firm mind, if they are presented to consideration as certainties, and in all their open and declared character; whilst, on the other hand, the bravest have shrunk from the dark and the doubtful. To break off the narrative, when it seemed at the point of becoming most interesting – to extinguish a lamp, just when a parchment containing some hideous secret ought to have been read – to exhibit shadowy forms and half-heard sounds of woe, are resources which Mrs Radcliffe has employed with more effect than any other writer of romance. It must be confessed, that in order to bring about these situations, some art or contrivance, on the part of the author, is rather too visible. Her heroines voluntarily expose themselves to situations, which in nature a lonely female would certainly have avoided. They are too apt to choose the midnight hour for investigating the mysteries of a deserted chamber or secret passage, and generally are only supplied with an expiring lamp, when about to read the most interesting documents. The simplicity of the tale is thus somewhat injured – it is as if we witnessed a dressing up of the very phantom by which we are to be startled; and the imperfection, though redeemed by many beauties, did not escape the censure of criticism.

A principal characteristic of Mrs Radcliffe's romances, is the rule which the author imposed upon herself, that all the circumstances of her narrative, however mysterious, and apparently superhuman, were to be accounted for on natural principles, at the winding up of the story. It must be allowed, that this has not been done with uniform success, and that the author has been occasionally more successful in exciting interest and apprehension, than in giving either interest or dignity of explanation to the means she has made use of. Indeed, we have already noticed, as the torment of romance-writers, those necessary evils, the concluding chapters, when they must unravel the skein of adventures which they have been so industrious to perplex, and account for all the incidents which they have been at so much pains to render unaccountable. Were these great magicians, who deal in the wonderful and fearful, permitted to dismiss their spectres as they raise them, amidst the shadowy and indistinct light so favourable to the exhibition of phantasmagoria, without compelling them into broad daylight, the task were compara-tively easy, and the fine fragment of *Sir Bertrand* might have rivals in that department. But the modern author is not permitted to escape in that way. We are told of a formal old judge before whom evidence was tendered, of the ghost of a murdered person having declared to a witness, that the prisoner at the bar was guilty: the judge admitted the evidence of the spirit to be excellent, but denied his right to be heard through the mouth of another, and ordered the spectre to be summoned into open court. The public of the current day deal as rigidly, in moving for a *quo warranto* to compel an explanation from the story-teller; and the author must either at once represent the knot as worthy of being severed by supernatural aid, and bring on the stage his actual fiend or ghost, or, like Mrs Radcliffe, explain by natural agency the whole marvels of his story.

We have already, in some brief remarks on *The Castle of Otranto*, avowed some preference for the more simple mode, of boldly avowing the use of supernatural machinery. Ghosts and witches, and the whole tenets of superstition, having once, and at no late period, been matter of universal belief, warranted by legal authority, it would seem no great stretch upon the reader's credulity to require him, while reading of what his ancestors did, to credit for the time what those ancestors devoutly believed in. And yet, notwithstanding the success of Walpole and Maturin, (to whom we may add the author of *Forman,*) the management of such machinery must be acknowledged a task of a most delicate nature. 'There is but one step', said Bonaparte, 'betwixt the sublime and the ridiculous', and in an age of universal incredulity, we must own it would require, at the present day, the support of the highest powers, to save the supernatural from slipping into the ludicrous. The *Incredulus odi* is a formidable objection.

There are some modern authors, indeed, who have endeavoured, ingeniously enough, to compound betwixt ancient faith and modern incredulity. They have exhibited phantoms, and narrated prophecies strangely accomplished, without giving a defined or absolute opinion, whether these are to be referred to supernatural agency, or whether the apparitions were produced (no uncommon case) by an over-heated imagination, and the presages apparently verified by a casual, though singular, coincidence of circumstances. This is, however, an evasion of the difficulty, not a solution; and besides, it would be leading us too far from the present subject, to consider to what point the author of a fictitious narrative is bound by his charter to gratify the curiosity of the public, and whether, as a painter of actual life, he is not entitled to leave something in shade, when the natural course of events conceals so many incidents in total darkness. Perhaps, upon the whole, this is the most artful mode of terminating such a tale of wonder, as it forms the means of compounding with the taste of two different classes of readers; those who, like children, demand that each particular circumstance and incident of the narrative shall be fully accounted for; and the more imaginative class, who, resembling men that walk for pleasure through a moonlight landscape, are more teazed than edified by the intrusive minuteness with which some well-meaning companion disturbs their reveries, divesting stock and stone of the shadowy semblances in which fancy had dressed them, and pertinaciously restoring to them the ordinary forms and commonplace meanness of reality.

It may indeed be claimed as meritorious in Mrs Radcliffe's mode of expounding her mysteries, that it is founded in possibilities. Many situations have occurred, highly tinctured with romantic incident and feeling, the mysterious obscurity of which has afterwards been explained by deception and confederacy. Such have been the impostures of superstition in all ages; and such delusions were also practised by the members of the Secret Tribunal, in the middle ages, and in more modern times by the Rosicrucians and Illuminati, upon whose machinations Schiller has founded the fine romance of *The Ghost-Seer*. But Mrs Radcliffe has not had recourse to so artificial a solution. Her heroines often sustain the agony of fear, and her readers that of suspense, from incidents which, when explained, appear of an ordinary and trivial nature; and in this we do not greatly applaud her art. A stealthy step behind the arras, may doubtless, in some situations, and when the nerves are tuned to a certain pitch, have no small influence upon the imagination; but if the conscious listener discovers it to be only the noise made by the cat, the solemnity of the feeling is gone, and the visionary is at once angry with his senses for having been cheated, and with his reason for having acquiesced in the deception. We fear that some such feeling of disappointment and displeasure attends most readers, when they read for the first time the unsatisfactory solution of the mysteries of the black pall and the wax figure, which has been adjourned from chapter to chapter, like something suppressed, because too horrible for the ear. . . .

SOURCE: extract from 'Introduction' to volume on Mrs Radcliffe in *Ballantyne's Novelist's Library* (Edinburgh, 1821–24, 1 September 1824); reproduced in Scott's *Lives of the Novelists* (1825)

NOTE

1. [Ed.] The 'unknown author' is Thomas James Mathias (1754?–1835), a royal librarian. His *Pursuits of Literature* (1794) strongly satirised

contemporary authors. Mathias's allusion to Ariosto is a misquotation, erroneously sourced by Scott or his editor. The lines actually occur in c. XLVI.4. (not 7.) of *Orlando Furioso*, and read:

e la notrita
Damigella rivulzia al sacro speco. (11.3–4)
(*Orlando Furioso*, ed. M. Turchi, Garzanti Editore s.p.a., 1974, 7th ed.
1985, p. 1269)

Ariosto is referring here, amongst references to a whole line of illustrious women, to a historical personage, one Domitilla Trivulzio, a Milanese who was learned in poetry. The reference to the 'sacred cave' ('il sacro speco') is to the cave of Delphi, sacred to Apollo, god of poetry, and this is the real point of Mathias's compliment to Mrs Radcliffe – that he is comparing her, via Ariosto, to the Pythoness, the priestess of Apollo who uttered and perhaps interpreted his oracles. I owe this information to Sharon Sage.

# *James Hogg*  (1826)

'Mrs Radcliffe never introduced . . . any real ghosts'

TICKLER: I never had any professed feeling of the super or preter-natural in a printed book. Very early in life, I discovered that a ghost, who had kept me in a cold sweat during a whole winter's midnight, was a tailor who haunted the house, partly through love, and partly through hunger, being enamoured of my nurse, and of the fat of ham which she gave him with mustard, between two thick shaves of a quartern loaf, and afterwards a bottle of small-beer to wash it down, before she yielded him the parting-kiss. After that I slept soundly, and had a contempt for ghosts, which I retain to this day.
SHEPHERD: Weel, it's verra different wi' me. I should be feared yet even for the ninth part o' a ghost, and I fancy a tailor has nae mair; – but I'm no muckle affecket by reading about them – an oral tradition out o' the mouth o' an auld grey-headed man or woman is far best, for then you canna dout the truth o' the tale, unless ye dout a' history thegither, and then, to be sure, you'll end in universal skepticism.

NORTH: Don't you admire the romances of the Enchantress of Udolpho?

SHEPHERD: I hae nae doubt, sir, that had I read Udolpho and her ither romances in my boyish days, that my hair would hae stood on end like that o' ither folk, for, by nature and education baith, ye ken, I'm just excessive superstitious. But afore her volumes fell into my hauns, my soul had been frichtened by a' kinds of traditionary terrors, and mony hunder times hae I maist swarfed wi' fear in lonesome spats in muirs and woods, at midnicht, when no a leevin thing was movin but mysel and the great moon. Indeed, I canna say that I ever fan' mysel alane in the hush o'darkened nature, without a beatin at my heart; for a' sort o' spiritual presence aye hovered about me – a presence o' something like and unlike my ain being – at times felt to be solemn and nae mair – at times sae awfu' that I wushed mysel nearer ingle-licht – and ance or twice in my lifetime, sae terrible that I could hae prayed to sink down into the moss, sae that I micht be saved frae the quaking o' that ghostly wilderness o' a world that was na for flesh and bluid!

NORTH: Look – James – look – what a sky!

SHEPHERD: There'll be thunder the morn. These are the palaces o' the thunder, and before day-break every window will pour forth lichtnin'. Mrs Radcliffe has weel described mony sic, but I have seen some that can be remembered, but never, never painted by mortal pen; for after a', what is ony description by us puir creturs o' the works o' the Great God?

NORTH: Perhaps it is a pity that Mrs Radcliffe never introduced into her stories any real ghosts.

SHEPHERD: I canna just a'thegether think sae. Gin you introduce a real ghost at a', it maun appear but seldom – seldom, and never but on some great or dread account – as the ghost o' Hamlet's father. Then, what difficulty in makin' it speak with a tomb-voice! At the close o' the tale, the mind would be shocked unless the dead had burst its cearments for some end which the dead alane could have accomplished – unless the catastrophe were worthy of an Apparition. How few events, and how few actors would, as the story shut itself up, be felt to have been of such surpassing moment as to have deserved the very laws o' nature to have been in a manner changed for their sakes, and shadows brought frae amang the darkness o' burial-places, that seem to our imaginations locked up frae a' communion wi' the breathin' world!

NORTH: In highest tragedy, a Spirit may be among the dramatis personae – for the events come all on processionally, and under a feeling of fate.

SHEPHERD: There, too, you see the ghost, and indifferently personated though it may be, the general hush proves that religion is the deepest principle o' our nature, and that even the vain shows o' a theatre can be sublimed by an awe-struck sadness, when, revisiting the glimpses o' the moon, and makin' night hideous, comes glidin' in and awa' in cauld unringin' armour, or unsubstantial vapour, a being whose eyes since saw the cheerfu' sun-light, and whose footsteps since brought out echoes frae the flowery earth.

NORTH: In this posthumous tale of Mrs Radcliffe – I forget the name – a real ghost is the chief agent, and is two or three times brought forward with good effect; but I confess, James, that, agreeably to your excellent observations, I became somewhat too much hand-in-glove with his ghostship, and that all supernatural influence departed from him through too frequent intercourse with the air of the upper world.

TICKLER: Come, James, be done with your palavering about ghosts, you brownie, and 'gie us another sang'. . . .

SOURCE: extract from 'Noctes Ambrosianae' No. XXVII, *Blackwood's* xx (1826) pp. 90–109.

Hogg was among several contributors to the 'Noctes Ambrosianae' series of papers in *Blackwood's*, 1822–35 (others being John Wilson, John Gibson Lockhart and William Maginn) – Ed.]

## *Sir Walter Scott* (1827)

### 'The effect of the supernatural . . . is easily exhausted'

No source of romantic fiction, and no mode of exciting the feelings of interest which the authors in that description of literature desire to produce, seems more directly accessible than the love of the supernatural. It is common to all classes of mankind, and perhaps is to none so familiar as to those who assume a certain degree of scepticism on the subject; since the reader may have often observed in conversation, that the person who professes himself most incredulous on the subject of marvellous stories, often ends his remarks by indulging the company with some well-attested anecdote, which it is difficult or impossible to account for on the narrator's own principles of absolute scepticism. The belief itself, though easily capable of being pushed into superstition and absurdity, has its origin not only in the facts upon which our holy religion is founded, but upon the principles of our nature, which teach us that while we are probationers in this sublunary state, we are neighbours to, and encompassed by the shadowy world, of which our mental faculties are too obscure to comprehend the laws, our corporeal organs too coarse and gross to perceive the inhabitants.

All professors of the Christian Religion believe that there was a time when the Divine Power showed itself more visibly on earth than in these our latter days; controlling and suspending, for its own purposes, the ordinary laws of the universe; and the Roman Catholic Church, at least, holds it as an article of faith, that miracles descend to the present time. Without entering into that controversy, it is enough that a firm belief in the great truths of our religion has induced wise and good men, even in Protestant countries, to subscribe to Dr Johnson's doubts respecting supernatural appearances.

That the dead are seen no more, said Imlac, I will not undertake to maintain against the concurrent and unvaried testimony of all ages, and of all nations. There is no people, rude or learned, among whom apparitions of the dead are not related and believed. This opinion, which perhaps prevails as far as human nature is diffused, could become universal only by its truth; those that never heard of one another could not have agreed in a tale which nothing but experience can make credible. That it is doubted by single cavillers, can very little weaken the general evidence; and some who deny it with their tongues, confess it by their fears.     [from *Rasselas*]

Upon such principles as these there lingers in the breasts even of philosophers, a reluctance to decide dogmatically upon a point where they do not and cannot possess any, save negative, evidence. Yet this inclination to believe in the marvellous gradually becomes weaker. Men cannot but remark that (since the scriptural miracles have ceased,) the belief in prodigies and supernatural events has gradually declined in proportion to the advancement of human knowledge; and that since the age has become enlightened, the occurrence of tolerably well attested anecdotes of the supernatural characters are so few, as to render it more probable that the witnesses have laboured under some strange and temporary delusion, rather than that the laws of nature have been altered or suspended. At this period of human knowledge, the marvellous is so much identified with fabulous, as to be considered generally as belonging to the same class.

It is not so in early history, which is full of supernatural incidents; and although we now use the word *romance* as synonymous with fictitious composition, yet as it originally only meant a poem, or prose work contained in the Romaunce language, there is little doubt that the doughty chivalry who listened to the songs of the minstrel, 'held each strange tale devoutly true', and that the feats of knighthood which he recounted, mingled with tales of magic and supernatural interference, were esteemed as veracious as the legends of the monks, to which they bore a strong resemblance. This period of society, however, must have long past before the Romancer began to select and arrange with care, the nature of the materials out of which he constructed his story. It was not when society, however differing in degree and station, was levelled and confounded by one dark cloud of ignorance, involving the noble as well as the mean, that it need be scrupulously considered to what class of persons the author addressed himself, or with what species of decoration he ornamented his story. 'Homo was then a common name for all men', and all were equally pleased with the same style of composition. This, however, was gradually altered. As the knowledge to which we have before alluded made more general progress, it became impossible to detain the attention of the better instructed class by the simple and gross fables to which the present generation would only listen in childhood, though they had been held in honour by their fathers during youth, manhood, and old age.

It was also discovered that the supernatural in fictitious composition requires to be managed with considerable delicacy, as criticism begins to be more on the alert. The interest which it excites is indeed a powerful spring; but it is one which is peculiarly subject to be exhausted by coarse handling and repeated pressure. It is also of a character which it is extremely difficult to sustain, and of which a very small proportion may be said to be better than the whole. The marvellous, more than any other attribute of fictitious narrative, loses its effect by being brought much into view. The imagination of the reader is to be excited if possible, without being gratified. If once, like Macbeth, we 'sup full with horrors', our taste for the banquet is ended, and the thrill of terror with which we hear or read of a night-shriek, becomes lost in that stated indifference with which the tyrant came at length to listen to the most deep catastrophies that could affect his house.  . . .

[Here Scott follows the authorities of Burke and Milton – Ed.]  . . .

From these sublime and decisive authorities, it is evident that the exhibition of supernatural appearances in fictitious narrative ought to be rare, brief, indistinct, and such as may become a being to us so incomprehensible, and so different from ourselves, of whom we cannot justly conjecture whence he comes, or for what purpose, and of whose attributes we can have no regular or distinct perception.

Hence it usually happens, that the first touch of the supernatural is always the most effective, and is rather weakened and defaced, than strengthened by the subsequent recurrence of similar incidents. Even in *Hamlet*, the second entrance of the ghost is not nearly so impressive as the first; and in many romances to which we could refer, the supernatural being forfeits all claim both to our terror and veneration, by condescending to appear too often; to mingle too much in the events of the story, and above all, to become loquacious, or, as it is familiarly called, *chatty*. We have, indeed, great doubts whether an author acts wisely in permitting his goblin to speak at all, if at the same time he renders him subject to human sight. Shakspeare, indeed, has contrived to put such language in the mouth of the buried majesty of Denmark as befits a supernatural being, and is by the style distinctly different from that of the living persons in the drama. In another passage he has had the boldness to intimate, by two expressions of similar force, in what manner and with what tone supernatural beings would find utterance:

> And the sheeted dead
> Did *squeak* and *gibber* in the Roman streets.

But the attempt in which the genius of Shakespeare has succeeded would probably have been ridiculous in any meaner hand; and hence it is, that, in many of our modern tales of terror, our feelings of fear have, long before the conclusion, given way under the influence of that familiarity which begets contempt.

A sense that the effect of the supernatural in its more obvious application is easily exhausted, has occasioned the efforts of modern authors to cut new walks and avenues through the enchanted wood, and to revive, if possible, by some means or other, the fading impression of its horrors.

The most obvious and inartificial mode of attaining this end is, by adding to, and exaggerating the supernatural incidents of the tale. But far from increasing its effect, the principles which we have laid down, incline us to consider the impression as usually weakened by exaggerated and laborious description. Elegance is in such cases thrown away, and the accumulation of superlatives, with which the narrative is encumbered, renders it tedious, or perhaps ludicrous, instead of becoming impressive or grand.

There is indeed one style of composition, of which the supernatural forms an appropriate part, which applies itself rather to the fancy than to the imagination, and aims more at amusing than at effecting or interesting the reader. To this species of composition belong the eastern tales, which contribute so much to the amusement of our youth, and which are recollected, if not reperused, with so much pleasure in our more advanced life. There are but few readers of any imagination who have not at one time or other in their life sympathized with the poet Collins, 'who', says Dr. Johnson, 'was eminently delighted with those flights of imagination, which pass the bounds of nature, and to which the mind is reconciled only by a passive acquiescence in popular traditions. He loved fairies, genii, giants, and monsters; he delighted to rove through the meadows of enchantment, to gaze on the magnificence of golden palaces, to repose by the waterfalls of Elysian gardens.' It is chiefly the young and the indolent who love to be soothed by works of this character, which require little attention in the perusal. In our riper age we remember them as we do the joys of our infancy, rather because we loved them once, than that they still continue to afford us amusement. The extravagance of fiction loses its charms for our riper judgment; and notwithstanding that these wild fictions contain much that is beautiful and full of fancy, yet still, unconnected as they are with each other, and conveying no result to the understanding . . . .

SOURCE: extract from review article, 'On the Supernatural in Fictitious Composition; and particularly on the works of Ernest Theodore William Hoffmann', in *Foreign Quarterly Review*, I (1827).

# *T. B. Macaulay*   (1833)

## 'Entertainment worthy of a Roman epicure'

. . . What then is the charm, the irresistible charm, of [Horace] Walpole's writings? It consists, we think, in the art of amusing without exciting. He never convinces the reasons, or fills the imagination, or touches the heart; but he keeps the mind of the reader constantly attentive, and constantly entertained. He had a strange ingenuity peculiarly his own, an ingenuity which appeared in all that he did, in his building, in his gardening, in his upholstery, in the matter and in the manner of his writings. If we were to adopt the classification, not a very accurate classification, which Akenside has given of the pleasures of the imagination, we should say that with the Sublime and the Beautiful Walpole had nothing to do, but that the third province, the Odd, was his peculiar domain. The motto which he prefixed to his *Catalogue of Royal and Noble Authors* might have been inscribed with perfect propriety over the door of every room in his house, and on the titlepage of every one of his books; 'Dove diavolo, Messer Ludovico, avete pigliate tante coglionerie?'[1] In his villa, every apartment is a museum; every piece of furniture is a curiosity; there is something strange in the form of the shovel; there is a long story belonging to the bell-rope. We wander among a profusion of rarities, of trifling intrinsic value, but so quaint in fashion, or connected with such remarkable names and events, that they may well detain our attention for a moment. A moment is enough. Some new relic, some new unique, some new carved work, some new enamel, is forthcoming in an instant. One cabinet of trinkets is no sooner closed than another is opened. It is the same with Walpole's writings. It is not in their utility, it is not in their beauty, that their attraction lies. They are to the works of great historians and poets, what Strawberry Hill is to the Museum of Sir Hans Sloane or to the Gallery of Florence. Walpole is constantly showing us things, not of very great value indeed, yet things which we are pleased to see, and which we can see nowhere else. They are baubles; but they are made curiosities either by his grotesque workmanship or by some association belonging to them. His style is one of those peculiar styles by which everybody is attracted, and which nobody can safely venture to imitate. He is a mannerist whose manner has become perfectly easy to him. His affectation is so habitual and so universal that it can hardly be called affectation. The affectation is the essence of the man. It pervades all his thoughts and all his expressions. If it were taken away, nothing would be left. He coins new words, distorts the senses of old words, and twists sentences into forms which make grammarians stare. But all this he does, not only with an air of ease, but as if he could not help doing it. His wit was, in its essential properties, of the same kind with that of Cowley and Donne. Like theirs, it consisted in an exquisite perception of points of analogy and points of contrast too subtle for common observation. Like them, Walpole perpetually startles us by the ease with which he yokes together ideas between which there would seem, at first sight, to be no connexion. But he did not, like them, affect the gravity of a lecture, and draw his illustrations from the laboratory and from the schools. His tone was light and fleering; his topics were the topics of the club and the ballroom; and therefore his strange combinations and far-fetched allusions, though very closely resembling those which tire us to death in the poems of the time of Charles the First, are read with pleasure constantly new.

No man who has written so much is so seldom tiresome. In his books there are scarcely any of those passages which, in our school days, we used to call *skip*. Yet he often wrote on subjects which are generally considered as dull, on subjects which men of great talents have in vain endeavoured to render popular. When we compare the *Historic Doubts about Richard the Third* with Whitaker's and Chalmer's books on a far more interesting question, the character of Mary Queen of Scots; when we compare the *Anecdotes of Painting* with Nichols's *Anecdotes*, or even with Mr [Isaac] D'Israeli's *Quarrels of Authors* and *Calamities of Authors*, we at once see Walpole's superiority, not in industry, not in learning, not in accuracy, not in logical power, but in the art of writing what people will like to read. He rejects all but the attractive parts of his subject. He keeps only what is in itself amusing, or what can be made so by the artifice of his diction. The coarser morsels of antiquarian learning he abandons to others, and sets out an entertainment worthy of a Roman epicure, an entertainment consisting of nothing but delicacies, the brains of singing birds, the roe of mullets, the sunny halves of peaches. This, we think, is the great merit of his romance. There is little skill in the delineation of the charaters. Manfred is as commonplace a tyrant, Jerome as commonplace a confessor, Theodore as commonplace a young gentleman, Isabella and Matilda as commonplace a pair of young ladies, as are to be found in any of the thousand Italian castles in which *condottieri* have revelled or in which imprisoned duchesses have pined. We cannot say that we much admire the big man whose sword is dug up in one quarter of the globe, whose helmet drops from the clouds in another, and who, after clattering and rustling for some days, ends by kicking the house down. But the story, whatever its value may be, never flags for a single moment. There are no digressions, or unseasonable descriptions, or long speeches. Every sentence carries the action forward. The excitement is constantly renewed. Absurd as is the machinery, insipid as are the human actors, no reader probably ever thought the book dull. . . .

SOURCE: review article, 'Walpole's Letters to Sir Thomas Mann', *Edinburgh Review* (Oct. 1833).

NOTE

1. [Ed.] Translatable, perhaps (for polite ears, that is), is 'Where the devil did you drag out all this rubbish, Master Ludovic?'

# Wilkie Collins  (1842)

### 'Such a hash of diablerie, demonology, massacre'

... It turned (it generally somehow does whenever I am in her company) upon literature, and I sat with my back to the window, and my hand in my pocket, freezing my horrified auditors by a varied recital of the most terrible portions of the Monk and Frankenstein. Every sentence that fell from my lips was followed in rapid succession by – 'Lor!' – 'oh!' 'ah!' 'He! He!' 'Good gracious!' etc etc. None of our country relations I am sure ever encountered in their whole lives before such a hash of diablerie, demonology, massacre, with their [?] and bread and butter. I intend to give them another course, comprising, The Ancient Mariner, Jack the Giant Killer, the Mysteries of Udolpho and an inquiry into the life and actions (when they were little girls) of the witches of Macbeth. . . .

Source: extract from letter (25 August 1842) to his father; ALS Pierpoint Morgan Library.

# PART TWO

# Twentieth-Century Studies

# George Saintsbury 'Explained Supernatural' (1916)

. . . Of the terror and mystery novel (the 'novel of suspense', as some call it, adopting from Scott a label doubtfully intended as such) the chief writers – almost the only ones now known, except to special students – were Mrs Radcliffe and 'Monk' Lewis. But in the eighteenth century it enjoyed an enormous popularity, securely registered and irremediably ridiculed in Miss Austen's *Northanger Abbey*.[1] In Lewis's hands (as it had done in those of the Germans) it admitted real *diablerie* and permitted great licence of situation and action; in Mrs Radcliffe's and in most, though not quite all, of her minor followers, it was strictly 'proper', and employed a curious, ingenious, and at the time highly-realised machinery, which has been accurately enough called the 'explained supernatural'. Both these methods of applying the supernatural element were revived in the sensational novels of the third quarter of the nineteenth century and sporadically since. The first is not justly chargeable with what has been perhaps not unjustly called the 'schoolboy naughtiness' and extravagance of *The Monk*. Bulwer and Mrs Oliphant, to name no later writers, showed that conclusively; George Macdonald more than conclusively. But few complete examples exist in which enormous difficulty of handling the pure supernatural in prose and at length has been mastered. The 'explained supernatural', though something not quite unlike it occurs in the work of Wilkie Collins and others, has, since the attraction of its first appearance and its startling contrast to things known and popular passed away, been itself little popular, either with the public or with the critics. Some at least of the former do not like to be cheated of their wonders; many of the latter regard such a much-ado-about-nothing as inartistic. . . .

SOURCE: extract from *The Peace of the Augustans* (1916), pp. 168–9.

NOTE

1. It is said that the apparently burlesque titles (*Horrid Mysteries*, etc.) of the rubbish in which the innocent Catherine and less innocent Isabella

revelled, are certainly genuine in part and probably in whole. The practictioners were extremely numerous; and the practice, even in its original form, continued far into the nineteenth century – almost until the further developments spoken of above. [*Horrid Mysteries* is indeed one of the titles for translation of Grosse's *Genius* – see J. M. S. Tompkins's study, below – Ed.]

## Sigmund Freud     The 'Uncanny'   (1919)

I

. . . [the 'uncanny'] undoubtedly belongs to all that is terrible – to all that arouses dread and creeping horror; it is equally certain, too, that the word is not always used in a clearly definable sense, so that it tends to coincide with whatever excites dread. Yet we may expect that it implies some intrinsic quality which justifies the use of a special name. One is curious to know what this peculiar quality is which allows us to distinguish as 'uncanny' certain things within the boundaries of what is 'fearful'.

As good as nothing is to be found upon this subject in elaborate treatises on aesthetics, which in general prefer to concern themselves with what is beautiful, attractive and sublime, that is with feelings of a positive nature, with the circumstances and the objects that call them forth, rather than with the opposite feelings of unpleasantness and repulsion. . . .

The German word *unheimlich** is obviously the opposite of *heimlich*, *heimisch* – meaning 'familiar', 'native', 'belonging to the home'; and we are tempted to conclude that what is 'uncanny' is frightening precisely because it is *not* known and familiar. Naturally not everything which is new and unfamiliar is frightening, however; the relation cannot be inverted. We can only say that what is novel can easily become frightening and uncanny; some new things are frightening but not by any means all. Something has to be added to what is novel and unfamiliar to make it uncanny.' . . .

[Here Freud quotes numerous examples from German dictionaries of the history of the word's usage – Ed.]

. . . In general we are reminded that the word *heimlich* is not

---

* [Translator's note] Throughout this paper 'uncanny' is used as the English rendering of *unheimlich*: literally 'unhomely'.

unambiguous, but belongs to two sets of ideas, which without being contradictory are yet very different: on the one hand, it means that which is familiar and congenial, and on the other, that which is concealed and kept out of sight. The word *unheimlich* is only used customarily, we are told, as the contrary of the first signification, and not of the second. Sanders tells us nothing concerning a possible genetic connection between these two sets of meanings. On the other hand, we notice that Schelling says something which throws quite a new light on the concept of the 'uncanny', one which we had certainly not awaited. According to him everything is uncanny that ought to have remained hidden and secret, and yet comes to light.

Some of the doubts that have thus arisen are removed if we consult Grimm's dictionary.[1]

We read [Freud's italics at sections 4 and 9]:

*Heimlich*; adj. and adv. *vernaculus, occultus*; MHG. heimelîch, heîmlich.

p. 874. In a slightly different sense: 'I feel *heimlich*, well, free from fear. . . .'

(*b*) *Heimlich*, also in the sense of a place free from ghostly influences . . . familiar, friendly, intimate.

4. *From the idea of 'homelike', 'belonging to the house', the further idea is developed of something withdrawn from the eyes of others, something concealed, secret, and this idea is expanded in many ways.* . . .

p. 876. 'On the left bank of the lake there lies a meadow *heimlich* in the wood.' Schiller, *Tell*. . . . Poetic licence, rarely so used in modern speech . . . In conjunction with a verb expressing the act of concealing: 'In the secret of his tabernacle he shall hide me (*heimlich*).' Ps. xxvii 5 . . . *Heimlich* places in the human body, pudenda . . . 'the men that died not were smitten' (on their *heimlich* parts). i Samuel v 12. . . .

(*c*) Officials who give important advice which has to be kept secret in matters of state are called *heimlich* councillors; the adjective, according to modern usage, having been replaced by *geheim* [secret]. . . . 'Pharaoh called Joseph's name "him to whom secrets are revealed"' (*heimlich* councillor). Gen. xli 45.

p. 878. 6 *Heimlich*, as used of knowledge, mystic, allegorical: a *heimlich* meaning, *mysticus, divinus, occultus figuratus*.

p. 878. *Heimlich* in a different sense, as withdrawn from knowledge, unconscious: . . . *Heimlich* also has the meaning of that which is obscure, inaccessible to knowledge. . . . 'Do you not see? They do not trust me; they fear the *heimlich* face of the Duke of Friedland.' *Wallensteins Lager*, Act 2.

9. *The notion of something hidden and dangerous, which is expressed in the last paragraph is still further developed, so that 'heimlich' comes to have the meaning usually ascribed to 'unheimlich'* Thus: 'At times I feel like a man who walks in the night and believes in ghosts; every corner is *heimlich* and full of terrors for him'. Klinger.

Thus *heimlich* is a word the meaning of which develops towards an ambivalence, until it finally coincides with its opposite, *unheimlich*. *Unheimlich* is in some way or other a sub-species of *heimlich*. . . .

## II

In proceeding to review those things, persons, impressions, events and situations which are able to arouse in us a feeling of the uncanny in a very forcible and definite form, the first requirement is obviously to select a suitable example to start upon. Jentsch has taken as a very good instance 'doubts whether an apparently animate being is really alive; or conversely, whether a lifeless object might not be in fact animate'; and he refers in this connection to the impression made by wax-work figures, artificial dolls and automatons. He adds to this class the uncanny effect of epileptic seizures and the manifestations of insanity, because these excite in the spectator the feeling that automatic, mechanical processes are at work, concealed beneath the ordinary appearance of animation. Without entirely accepting the author's view, we will take it as a starting-point for our investigation because it leads us on to consider a writer who has succeeded better than anyone else in producing uncanny effects.

Jentsch says: 'In telling a story, one of the most successful devices for easily creating uncanny effects is to leave the reader in uncertainty whether a particular figure in the story is a human being or an automaton; and to do it in such a way that his attention is not directly focussed upon his uncertainty, so that he may not be urged to go into the matter and clear it up immediately; since that, as we have said, would quickly dissipate the peculiar emotional effect of the thing. Hoffmann has repeatedly employed this psychological artifice with success in his fantastic narratives.'

This observation, undoubtedly a correct one, refers primarily to the story of 'The Sand-Man' in Hoffmann's *Nachtstücken*,[2] which contains the original of Olympia, the doll in the first act of Offenbach's opera, *Tales of Hoffmann*. But I cannot think – and I hope that most readers of the story will agree with me – that the theme of the doll, Olympia, who is to all appearances a living being, is by any means the only element to be held responsible for the quite unparalleled atmosphere of uncanniness which the story evokes; or, indeed, that it is the most important among them. Nor is this effect of the story heightened by the fact that the author himself treats the episode of Olympia with a faint touch of satire and uses it to make fun of the young man's idealization of his mistress. The main theme of the story is, on the contrary, something different, something which gives its name to the story, and which is always re-introduced at the critical moment: it is the theme of the 'Sand-Man' who tears out children's eyes.

This fantastic tale begins with the childhood–recollections of the student Nathaniel: in spite of his present happiness, he cannot banish the memories associated with the mysterious and terrifying death of the father he loved. On certain evenings his mother used to send the children to bed early, warning them that 'the Sand-Man was coming'; and sure enough Nathaniel would not fail to hear the heavy tread of a visitor with whom his father would then be occupied that evening. When questioned about the Sand-Man, his mother, it is true, denied that such a person existed except as a form of speech; but his nurse could give him more definite information: 'He is a wicked man who comes when children won't go to bed, and throws handfuls of sand in their eyes so that they jump out of their heads all bleeding. Then he puts the eyes in a sack and carries them off to the moon to feed his children. They sit up there in their nest, and their beaks are hooked like owls' beaks, and they use them to peck up naughty boys' and girls' eyes with.'

Although little Nathaniel was sensible and old enough not to believe in such gruesome attributes to the figure of the Sand-Man, yet the dread of him became fixed in his breast. He determined to find out what the Sand-Man looked like; and one evening, when the Sand-Man was again expected, he hid himself in his father's study. He recognized the visitor as the lawyer Coppelius, a repulsive person of whom the children were frightened when he occasionally came to a meal; and he now identified this Coppelius with the dreaded Sand-Man. Concerning the rest of the scene, Hoffmann already leaves us in doubt whether we are witnessing the first delirium of the panic-stricken boy, or a succession of events which are to be regarded in the story as being real. His father and the guest begin to busy themselves at a hearth with glowing flames. The little eavesdropper hears Coppelius call out, 'Here with your eyes!' and betrays himself by screaming aloud; Coppelius seizes him and is about to drop grains of red-hot coal out of the fire into his eyes, so as to cast them out on to the hearth. His father begs him off and saves his eyes. After this the boy falls into a deep swoon; and a long illness followed upon his experience. Those who lean towards a rationalistic interpretation of the Sand-Man will not fail to recognize in the child's phantasy the continued influence of his nurse's story. The grains of sand that are to be thrown into the child's eyes turn into red-hot grains of coal out of the flames; and in both cases they are meant to make his eyes jump out. In the course of another visit of the Sand-Man's, a year later, his father was killed in his study by an explosion. The lawyer Coppelius vanished from the place without leaving a trace behind.[3]

Nathaniel, now a student, believes that he has recognized his childhood's phantom of horror in an itinerant optician, an Italian called Giuseppe Coppola. This man had offered him barometers for sale in his university town, and when Nathaniel refused had added: 'Eh, not barometers, not barometers – also got fine eyes, beautiful eyes.' The student's terror was allayed on finding that the proffered eyes were only harmless spectacles, and he bought a pocket-telescope from Coppola. With its aid he looks across into Professor Spalanzani's house opposite and there spies Spalanzani's beautiful, but strangely silent and motionless daughter, Olympia. He soon falls in love with her so violently that he quite forgets his clever and sensible betrothed on her account. But Olympia was an automaton whose works Spalanzani had made, and whose eyes Coppola, the Sand-Man, had put in. The student surprises the two men quarrelling over their handiwork. The optician carries off the wooden, eyeless doll; and the mechanician, Spalanzani, takes up Olympia's bleeding eye-balls from the ground and throws them at Nathaniel's breast, saying that Coppola had stolen them from him (Nathaniel). Nathaniel succumbs to a fresh attack of madness, and in his delirium his recollection of his father's death is mingled with this new experience. He cries, 'Faster – faster – faster– rings of fire – rings of fire! Whirl about, rings of fire – round and round! Wooden doll, ho! lovely wooden doll, whirl about –', then falls upon the professor, Olympia's so-called father, and tries to strangle him.

Rallying from a long and serious illness, Nathaniel seemed at last to have recovered. He was going to marry his betrothed with whom he was reconciled. One day he was walking through the town and market-place, where the high tower of the Town-Hall threw its huge shadow. On the girl's suggestion they mounted the tower, leaving her brother, who was walking with them, down below. Up there, Clara's attention is drawn to a curious object coming along the street. Nathaniel looks at this thing through Coppola's spy-glass, which he finds in his pocket, and falls into a new fit of madness. Shouting out, 'Whirl about, my wooden doll!' he tries to fling the girl into the depths below. Her brother, brought to her side by her cries, rescues her and hastens down to safety with her. Up above, the raving man rushes round, shrieking 'Rings of fire, whirl about!' – words whose origin we know. Among the people who begin to gather below there comes forward the figure of the lawyer Coppelius, suddenly returned. We may suppose it was his approach, seen through the telescope, that threw Nathaniel into his madness. People want to go up and overpower the madman, but Coppelius laughs and says, 'Wait a bit; he'll come down of himself'. Nathaniel suddenly stands still, catches sight of Coppelius, and with a wild shriek 'Yes! "Fine eyes – beautiful eyes" ', flings himself down over the parapet. No sooner does he lie on the paving-stones with a shattered skull than the Sand-Man vanishes in the throng.

This short summary leaves, I think, no doubt that the feeling of something uncanny is directly attached to the figure of the Sand-Man, that is, to the idea of being robbed of one's eyes; and that Jentsch's point of an intellectual uncertainty has nothing to do with this effect. Uncertainty whether an object is living or inanimate, which we must admit in regard to the doll Olympia, is quite irrelevant in connection with this other, more striking instance of uncanniness. It is true that the writer creates a kind of uncertainty in us in the beginning by not letting us know, no doubt purposely, whether he is taking us into the real world or into a purely fantastic one of his own creation. He has admittedly the right to do either; and if he chooses to stage his action in a world peopled with spirits, demons and ghosts, as Shakespeare does in *Hamlet*, in *Macbeth* and, in a different sense, in *The Tempest* and *A Midsummer Night's Dream*, we must bow to his decision and treat his setting as though it were real for as long as we put ourselves into his hands. But this uncertainty disappears in the course of Hoffmann's story, and we perceive that he means to make us, too, look through the fell Coppola's glasses – perhaps, indeed, that he himself once gazed through such an instrument. For the conclusion of the story makes it quite clear that Coppola the optician really is the lawyer Coppelius and thus also the Sand-Man.

There is no question, therefore, of any 'intellectual uncertainty': we know now that we are not supposed to be looking on at the products of a madman's imagination behind which we, with the superiority of rational minds, are able to detect the sober truth; and yet this knowledge does not lessen the impression of uncanniness in the last degree. The theory of 'intellectual uncertainty' is thus incapable of explaining that impression. . . . [Freud then discusses at length the psychoanalytic connection between the morbid anxiety about the loss of sight expressed in Hoffmann's tale, and the fear of castration – Ed.] . . .

Hoffmann is in literature the unrivalled master of conjuring up the uncanny. His *Elixire des Teufels* [The Devil's Elixir] contains a mass of themes to which one is tempted to ascribe the uncanny effect of the narrative; but it is too obscure and intricate a story to venture to summarize. Towards the end of the book the reader is told the facts, hitherto concealed from him, from which the action springs; with the result, not that he is at last enlightened, but that he falls into a state of complete bewilderment. The author has piled up too much of a kind; one's comprehension of the whole suffers as a result, though not the impression it makes. We must content ourselves with selecting those themes of uncanniness which are most prominent, and seeing whether we can fairly trace them also back to infantile sources. These themes are all concerned with the idea of a 'double' in every shape and degree, with persons, therefore, who are to be considered identical by reason of looking alike; Hoffmann accentuates this relation by transferring mental processes from the one person to the other – what we should call telepathy – so that the one possesses knowledge, feeling and experience in common with the other, identifies himself with another person, so that his self becomes confounded, or the foreign self is substituted for his own – in other words, by doubting, dividing and interchanging the self. And finally there is the constant recurrence of similar situations, a same face, or character-trait, or twist of fortune, or a same crime, or even a same name recurring throughout several consecutive generations.

The theme of the 'double' [*der Doppelganger*] has been very throughly treated by Otto Rank. He has gone into the connections the 'double' has with reflections in mirrors, with shadows, guardian spirits, with the belief in the soul and the fear of death; but he also lets in a flood of light on the astonishing evolution of this idea. For the 'double' was originally an insurance against destruction to the ego, an 'energetic denial of the power of death', as Rank says; and probably the 'immortal' soul was the first 'double' of the body. This invention of doubling as a preservation against extinction has its counterpart in the language of dreams, which is fond of representing castration by a doubling or multiplication of the genital symbol; the same desire spurred on the ancient Egyptians to the art of making images of the dead in some lasting material. Such ideas, however, have sprung from the soil of unbounded self-love, from the primary narcissism which holds sway in the mind of the child as in that of primitive man; and when this stage has been left behind the double takes on a different aspect. From having been an assurance of immortality, he becomes the ghastly harbinger of death.

The idea of the 'double' does not necessarily disappear with the passing of the primary narcissism, for it can receive fresh meaning from the later stages of development of the ego. A special faculty is slowly formed there, able to oppose the rest of the ego, with the function of observing and criticizing the self and exercising a censorship within the mind, and this we become aware of as our 'conscience'. In the pathological case of delusions of being watched this mental institution becomes isolated, dissociated from the ego, and discernible to a physician's eye. The fact that a faculty of this kind exists, which is able to treat the rest of the ego like an object – the fact, that is, that man is capable of self-observation – renders it possible to invest the old idea of a 'double' with a new meaning and to ascribe many things to it, above all, those things which seem to the new faculty of self-criticism to belong to the old surmounted narcissism of the earlist period of all.[4]

But it is not only this narcissism, offensive to the ego-criticizing faculty, which may be incorporated in the idea of a double. There are also all those unfulfilled but possible futures to which we still like to cling in phantasy, all those strivings of the ego which adverse external circumstances have crushed, and all our suppressed acts of volition which nourish in us the illusion of Free Will.[5]

But, after having thus considered the manifest motivation of the figure of a 'double', we have to admit that none of it helps us to understand the extraordinarily strong feeling of something uncanny that pervades the conception; and our knowledge of pathological mental processes enables us to add that nothing in the content arrived at could account for that impulse towards self-protection which has caused the ego to project such a content outward as something foreign to itself. The quality of uncanniness can only come from the circumstance of the 'double' being a creation dating back to a very early mental stage, long since left behind, and one, no doubt, in which it wore a more friendly aspect. The 'double' has become a vision of terror, just as after the fall of their religion the gods took on daemonic shapes.

It is not difficult to judge, on the same lines as his theme of the 'double', the other forms of disturbance in the ego made use of by Hoffmann. They are a harking-back to particular phases in the evolution of the self-regarding feeling, a regression to a time when the ego was not yet sharply differentiated from the external world and from other persons. I believe that these factors are partly responsible for the impression of the uncanny, although it is not easy to isolate and determine exactly their share of it.

That factor which consists in a recurrence of the same situations, things and events, will perhaps not appeal to everyone as a source of uncanny feeling. From what I have observed, this phenomenon does undoubtedly, subject to certain conditions and combined with certain circumstances, awaken an uncanny feeling, which recalls that sense of helplessness sometimes experienced in dreams. Once, as I was walking through the deserted streets of a provincial town in Italy which was strange to me, on a hot summer afternoon, I found myself in a quarter the character of which could not long remain in doubt. Nothing but painted women were to be seen at the windows of the small houses, and I hastened to leave the narrow street at the next turning. But after having wandered about for a while without being directed I suddenly found myself back in the same street, where my presence was now beginning to excite attention. I hurried away once more, but only to arrive yet a third time by devious paths in the same place. Now, however, a feeling overcame me which I can only describe as uncanny, and I was glad enough to abandon my exploratory walk and get straight back to the piazza I had left a short while before. Other situations having in common with my adventure an involuntary return to the same situation, but which differ radically from it in other respects, also result in the same feeling of helplessness and of something uncanny. As, for instance, when one is lost in a forest in high altitudes, caught, we will suppose, by the mountain mist, and when every endeavour to find the marked or familiar path ends again and again in a return to one and the same spot, recognizable by some particular landmark. Or when one wanders about in a dark, strange room, looking for the door or the electric switch, and collides for the hundredth time with the same piece of furniture – a situation which, indeed, has been made irresistibly comic by Mark Twain, through the wild extravagance of his narration.

Taking another class of things, it is easy to see that here, too, it is only this factor of involuntary repetition which surrounds with an uncanny atmosphere what would otherwise be innocent enough, and forces upon us the idea of something fateful and unescapable where otherwise we should have spoken of 'chance' only. For instance, we of course attach no importance to the event when we give up a coat and get a cloakroom ticket with the number say, 62; or when we find that our cabin on board ship is numbered 62. But the impression is altered if two such events, each in itself indifferent, happen close together, if we come across the number 62 several times in a single day, or if we begin to notice that everything which has a number – addresses, hotel-rooms, compartments in railway-trains – always has the same one, or one which at least contains the same figures. We do feel this to be 'uncanny', and unless a man is utterly hardened and proof against the lure of superstition he will be tempted to ascribe a secret meaning to this obstinate recurrence of a number, taking it, perhaps, as an indication of the span of life allotted to him. Or take the case that one is engaged at the time in reading the works of Hering, the famous physiologist, and then receives within the space of a few days two letters from two different countries, each from a person called Hering: whereas one has never before had any dealings with anyone of that name. Not long ago an ingenious scientist attempted to reduce coincidences of this kind to certain laws, and so deprive them of their uncanny effect.[6] I will not venture to decide whether he has succeeded or not.

How exactly we can trace back the uncanny effect of such recurrent similarities to infantile psychology is a question I can only lightly touch upon in these pages; and I must refer the reader instead to another pamphlet, now ready for publication, in which this has been gone into in detail, but in a different connection [Freud's *Beyond the Pleasure-Principle* – Ed.]. It must be explained that we are able to postulate the principle of a *repetition-compulsion* in the unconscious mind, based upon instinctual activity and probably inherent in the very nature of the instincts – a principle powerful enough to overrule the pleasure-principle, lending to certain aspects of the mind their daemonic character, and still very clearly expressed in the tendencies of small children; a principle, too, which is responsible for a part of the course taken by the analyses of neurotic patients. Taken in all, the foregoing prepares us for the discovery that whatever reminds us of this inner *repetition-compulsion* is perceived as uncanny. . . .

There is one more point of general application I should like to add, though, strictly speaking, it has been included in our statements about animism and mechanisms in the mind that have been surmounted; for I think it deserves special mention. This is that an uncanny effect is often and easily produced by effacing the distinction between imagination and reality, such as when something that we have hitherto regarded as imaginary appears before us in reality, or when a symbol takes over the full functions and significance of the thing it symbolizes, and so on. It is this element which contributes not a little to the uncanny effect attaching to magical practices. The infantile element in this, which also holds sway in the minds of neurotics, is the over-accentuation of psychical reality in comparison with physical reality – a feature closely allied to the belief in the omnipotence of thoughts. In the midst of the isolation of war-time a number of the English *Strand Magazine* fell into my hands; and, amongst other not very interesting matter, I read a story about a young married couple, who move into a furnished flat in which there is a curiously shaped table with carvings of crocodiles on it. Towards evening they begin to smell an intolerable and very typical odour that pervades the whole flat; things begin to get in their way and trip them up in the darkness; they seem to see a vague form gliding up the stairs – in short, we are given to understand that the presence of the table causes ghostly crocodiles to haunt the place, or that the wooden monsters come to life in the dark, or something of that sort. It was a thoroughly silly story, but the uncanny feeling it produced was quite remarkable.

To conclude this collection of examples, which is certainly not complete, I will relate an instance taken from psycho-analytical experience; if it does not rest upon mere coincidence, it furnishes a beautiful confirmation of our theory of the uncanny. It often happens that male patients declare that they feel there is something uncanny about the female genital organs. This *unheimlich* place, however, is the entrance to the former *heim* [home] of all human beings, to the place where everyone dwelt once upon a time and in the beginning. There is a humorous saying: 'Love is home-sickness'; and whenever a man dreams of a place or a country and says to himself, still in the dream, 'this place is familiar to me, I have been there before', we may interpret the place as being his mother's genitals or her body. In this case, too, the *unheimlich* is what was once *heimisch*, home-like, familiar; the prefix 'un' is the token of repression. . . .

SOURCE: extracts from article first published (in German) in *Imago*, v (1919); reproduced as 'The "Uncanny" ', translated by Alix Strachey, in *Collected Papers of Sigmund Freud* (London, 1957), pp. 368–9, 370, 375–7, 378–83, 386–91, 397–9.

NOTES

[Reorganised and renumbered from the original – Ed.]

1. Jakob & Wilhelm Grimm, *Deutsches Wörterbuch* (Leipzig, 1877), IV 2, p. 874 et seq.

2. In E. T. W. Hoffmann's *Sämtliche Werke*, Grisebach edn, vol. III.

3. Frau Dr Rank has pointed out the association of the name with 'Copella' – *crucible*, connecting it with the chemical operations that caused the father's death; and also the association with 'coppo' – *eye-socket*.

4. I cannot help thinking that when poets complain that two souls dwell within the human breast, and when popular psychologists talk of the splitting of the ego in an individual, they have some notion of this division (which relates to the sphere of ego-psychology) between the critical faculty and the rest of the ego, and not of the antithesis discovered by psycho-analysis between the ego and what is unconscious and repressed. It is true that the distinction is to some extent effaced by the circumstance that derivatives of what is repressed are foremost among the things reprehended by the ego-criticizing faculty.

5. In Ewers's *Der Student von Prag*, which furnishes the starting-point of

Rank's study on the 'double', the hero has promised his beloved not to kill his antagonist in a duel. But on his way to the duelling-ground he meets his 'double', who has already killed his rival.

6. P. Kammerer, *Das Gesetz der Serie.*

*Joyce M. S. Tompkins*     The Gothic
Romance    (1932)

. . . The castles of Gothic romance, unlike those of medieval romance, are never new. The tale may play in bygone centuries, but they are more ancient still; usually, too, they have at least one ruinous wing, for decay was Gothic and picturesque, and the romance-writers wished somehow to combine in their architecture the attractions of tyrannous strength and of melancholy. Hence all the absurdities of feudal chiefs, who fail to keep their castles in repair, and mansions that fall to ruin in less than twenty years. Ossian's lament for Balclutha rang in the ears of the age, and on some ruined wall in every Gothic domicile the thistle shakes its lonely head and the moss (literally, Mrs Roche assures us) whistles to the wind. The eighteenth century thought much of death and decay, from churchyard-poets to philosophers, who broke open coffins, prized apart ankle-joints with their walking-sticks, and sent minutes of their researches to the *Gentleman's Magazine.* Decay was part of every romantic spell, the noiseless slipping of life into oblivion. It was consonant with the cult of the dim and the half-seen; and, from this angle, the defaced tomb of an unknown knight has superior attractions to the fully-authenticated resting-place of an historical character. When the romantic asks: 'What have these old walls seen?' he does not want too precise an answer.

Mingled with the melancholy and awe, inspired by a Gothic building, was a gentle thrill of complacency. It is not usually explicit in the Gothic romance, for obvious reasons, but it is liberally attested elsewhere. There is a castle in William Hutchinson's pastoral *A Week at a Cottage* (1775), whose 'disconcerted walls stand sullenly and brave the wrath of Time'. It is a record not only of tyranny but of the expiration of tyranny; it is 'an object now for Pleasure's Eye', and its nodding battlements 'now domineer not, but adorn the Place'. To the hero of the Reverend James Thomson's *Denial, or the Happy Retreat* (1790) the ruins of a castle 'demonstrate the stability of the government, the progress of civilization, the security of property and the safety of the subject'. The romantic thrill was superimposed upon this ground-work of complacency; and perhaps not enough has been made, as an ingredient in the attraction of romance, of the charm of recovery, the breaking as well as the binding of the spell, and the return, with full hands, to a familiar world.

The degradation of the Gothic castle, when every hall is the scene of deeds of violence, and the heroine makes her way through dungeons littered with rotting bones, relying on, and inevitably finding, a secret door, need not be illustrated. The dim veils of romance were torn, and the author, often under German influence, set out to hit hard and often. Gothic architecture suffered from over-production, and Mrs Roche in *The Children of the Abbey* (1796) provided no less than four edifices, a Welsh mansion, an Irish castle and convent, and a Scottish Abbey. Mrs Roche and Mrs Isabella Hedgeland imported Gothic scenery and effects into tales (professedly) of contemporary life, but Mrs Hedgeland, at least, fails to keep her footing, and towards the end of *The Ruins of Avondale Priory* (1796) the portcullises thicken, the two guilty dowagers assume a feudal complexion, and we overhear an ancient warder saying 'Methinks'.

Castles and convents (to which we shall presently turn) bring with them the theme of imprisonment, perennially attractive to the romantic mind. What the realist has to say about prisons is soon said, or was, before minute psychology came into fashion. It was said by Smollett when he described Peregrine Pickle after several months in gaol, desperate, squalid and mulish. For the romantic mind, however, the significance of a prison is inexhaustible. It is the dark frame that enhances whatever emotions are displayed within it; it is the supreme test of virtue and the expiation of the penitent; it provides that recess (otherwise sought for on desert islands, in Arcady or the pale allegorical realms), that limited fragment of being, secluded from the complexities of social life, where consciousness is forced back on itself, friends are left alone with their love and enemies with their hatred, criminals with their guilt and saints with their God.[1] It is the instrument of tyranny and the occasion of love's triumph, as King Lear, ceasing to envisage earthly reality, believed; it is the secret altar of resignation and the secret shambles of the butcher, a charnel-house when shame corrupts there, but turned by the breath of the virtuous to an enclosed garden of lilies. The romantic minds of the eighteenth century made little use of the advantages of a prison in shaping a plot, and did not much study the ingenuities of escape. Their style was broadly emotional; prison and prisoner were not so much the factors of a problem as a symbolic picture. Godwin's *Caleb Williams* (1794) is the first novel to give a circumstantial account of an escape. Before writing it he had prepared his mind by reading criminal literature and, without sacrificing the symbolic quality of the situation – indeed, in him it is stronger than ever, reinforced as it is by his social theories – he imported into it a keen interest in the practical aspects of escape. There is more than a suggestion of this double appeal in Holcroft's precise account of the conditions of Frank Henley's imprisonment in *Anna St Ives* (1792), but Frank does not contrive to break prison; and we see the influence of both models in George Walker's description of his hero's imprisonment in a madhouse in *Theodore Cyphon; or, the Benevolent Jew* (1796), and of the persistence, ingenuity and suspense of his flight. These stories pleased the philosophers because they illustrated the power of mind over circumstance, and they pleased the public because of their strong narrative interest. It is, however, only at the end of our period that the attention of the novelist was turned to the prison-breaker; the early romance writers, who were mostly women, saw in the prisoner one more example of their favourite virtue, patient fortitude.

Contemporary events reinforced the imprisonment theme. The philanthropy of the eighteenth century cast an eye of curious horror at those grim dungeons which Europe had not yet fully outgrown. Prison conditions in England were bad enough, worse in some cases, as John Howard declared, than the corresponding conditions abroad, but the treatment meted out to serious criminals, more particularly state offenders, was nothing like so atrocious. The English public was kept in mind of the happy contrast. From time to time the *Gentleman's Magazine* overflowed with revolting details of foreign judicial procedure, while the reviewers of the *Monthly* and the *Critical* are sure to quote similar accounts in full, whenever it falls to their lot to review a book of travel. Thus English readers learned that, in Denmark, Count Struensee and Count Brand lay for weeks, weighted with iron, on the stone floor of their cells. They heard of Frederick the Great's punishment of Baron Trenck, and were soon to read in Trenck's own memoirs of the Saxon fortress of Königstein, and of the disloyal secretary who had languished there for thirty years, without seeing the light of day. They turned to Spain and saw the Inquisition re-established and the enlightened Count Olivadez a prisoner in its dungeons, and found later in Trenck's memoirs the passage where Olivadez, escaped into safety at Paris, shows the author the marks of the torture on his body. In Portugal the fall of the Marquis of Pombal not only consigned members of his party to ingeniously hideous deaths, but raised as from the dead their long-imprisoned predecessors, clothed in rags and half-starved, together with a son of the Marquis of Tavora, who had grown up in solitary imprisonment since he was five years old, knew no language and was 'in every respect in a pure state of nature'.[2] In France, meanwhile, a few miles away, not yet abolished if largely disused, were *lettres de cachet*,[3] oubliettes, monastic prisons, seigneurial rights over body and life, and, summing up this whole world of abused power in two thunderous syllables, the Bastille, of whose rigours they learnt much from such books as the highly-coloured *French Inquisition* (1715) of Constantin de Renneville and the more sober and recent *Memoirs of the Bastille* (1783) of Linguet, on which Mrs Radcliffe seems to have based the manuscript of the prisoner in *The Romance of the Forest*.[4] There were descriptions of Russian punishments, illustrated at times with plates at which the reviewer's heart sickened, anecdotes of the slave-trade, and, to fill in any possible gap, such revivals of the bloody past as Lithgow's account of his experiences in the hands of the Inquisition at Malaga, reprinted by the *Gentleman's Magazine* in 1776. And presently came the Terror to provide sensation hot and hot.

It will be readily seen how all this material lent itself to the purposes of the terror-monger, whose dreadful compositions in dripping dungeons, stained instruments, and putrid or mangled flesh increase in number and violence as the public temperature rises with the insecurity and excitement of the French Revolution.[5] But physical horror was not the emotion that the first Gothic romance-writers tried to raise. They had to preserve the dignity of the human body and bear witness to the supremacy of the soul. With the selective licence of romance, they left dirt and vermin out of account, ignored tedium, and defied the power of unremitting oppression to produce imbecility of mind. The secretary, of whom Trenck tells, was more like a wild beast than a man after his thirty years' imprisonment, but the Marchesa Mazzini [in Radcliffe's *A Sicilian Romance* (1790)] walks out of her subterranean cell with collected piety, and, for all we hear to the contrary, as neat as a new pin. Prolonged imprisonment in secret vaults occurs often in these books, and once more contemporary journalism provides sources and illustrations of this theme. Louis XVI released an unhappy prisoner, whose guilt was having spoken ill of the late king, from a forty years' captivity in the Bastille.[6] The reverberating fall of that fortress[7] set other rumours afloat, and Lord Massereene, an Irish peer, who had been imprisoned for debt in the Châtelet, in the first place, and, on attempting to escape, transferred to a dungeon under the Seine, where 'his beard grew to a most immoderate length', landed at Dover, and, jumping out of the boat, fell on his knees, kissed the ground thrice, and exclaimed: 'God bless the land of liberty'.[8] In fiction, the victim of such an imprisonment is usually presumed dead by the world, and the tyrant has thus a free field for his revenge or his lust. We are not to imagine, however, that ten years or so can weaken the divine authority of virtue, and Stephen Cullen, who exposes the hero's mother to the solicitations of an Abbot for nearly twenty years, preserves her unsullied to the end.[9] 'The patience of this lover we cannot but admire', said the *Critical.*

It was the Marchesa Mazzini who set the fashion in England for these returns from the dead, but an earlier example is found in the history of the Duchess of C—— in Mme de Genlis's *Adèle et Théodore* (1782).[10] Mme de Genlis declares in a footnote that this story of a jealous husband who imprisoned his wife for nine years in a subterranean cavern, without light, is true in its essentials, and that she has met the lady. However this may be, she alone makes some faint attempt to trace the effects of such an imprisonment. The Duchess cannot bear the slightest light, and has almost forgotten how to read and write; her greatest consolation has been the weak whisper of thunder that penetrated to her during the heaviest storms. Mrs Radcliffe did not repeat the extravagant situation; in her next book she resisted the temptation to resurrect Adeline's father, and thus left unspoilt the authentic, if rhetorical, pathos of the manuscript which his daughter finds. She had set a fashion, however, and it was followed to such an extent that the experienced reader of the Gothic Romance hesitates to believe in the death of anybody, especially if it be a parent or a wife. Yet Mme de Genlis's suggestions were not taken up, and no attempt was made to procure the willing suspension of our disbelief until 1798, when Harriet Lee, according to the *Critical*, judiciously varied the trite incident by the derangement of the sufferer.[11] This 'decline of intellect is finely conceived', wrote the reviewer; 'it is the probable effect of long and solitary confinement'. It is; but nothing illustrates more clearly the wilfulness of eighteenth-century romance than its reluctance to consider the fact.[12]

A similarly wilful bias, this time in the direction of melodrama, is obvious whenever the story approaches a convent. The dealings of the literary men of Protestant England in the eighteenth century with the institutions of the Romance Catholic Church are a little disingenuous. They are very conscious of the picturesque attractions of convents, vows of celibacy, confession and penance; they are seduced by the emotional possibilities of the situations that can be based on these usages; but they seldom fail to make it quite clear that they regard the usages as superstitious and irrational, and, if they did, there was not wanting a critic to blame this 'attempt to gloss over the follies of popery, or to represent its absurdities as sacred'.[13] Thus Mrs Radcliffe, having introduced a monk's tomb as a picturesque property in *The Romance of the Forest*, is careful to express through the mouth of Louis La Motte her real opinion of monasticism. 'Peace be to his soul', soliloquizes the young man; 'but did he think a life of mere negative virtue deserves an eternal reward? Mistaken man! reason, had you trusted its dictates, would have informed you, that the active virtues, the adherence to the golden rule, "Do as you would be done unto", could alone deserve the favour of a Deity, whose glory is benevolence.' From Addison's *Theodosius and Constantia*, however, to Jerningham's *Death of Arabert, Monk of La Trappe* (1771), the conflict of love and vows was a recognized source of pathos, and Mrs Radcliffe seized on it in *A Sicilian Romance* when she made the nun Cornelia die at the high altar in her lover's presence, in 'a fine devotional glow'.[14] Mrs Radcliffe's convent is one of those odd affairs, imagined by Gothic romancists, where monks and nuns in adjacent buildings are shepherded by an abbot. Jerningham, who, as a Catholic, should have had more discretion, yet introduces Arabert's mistress into La Trappe, where she lives as a monk, unknown to her lover.[15] Ignorance enhanced the charm of this material. There were no convents in England, and though a certain number of English girls attended French convent-schools, where there were also to be found poor Englishwomen living cheaply as parlour-boarders, such information as they could supply did not seriously affect the readiness of the novel-reading public to believe that any extravagance could happen in such a setting;[16] moreover, to set against authentic accounts, such as Father Isla's *Fray Gerundo de Campazos* (translated in 1772), there were the secret violences divulged by Baculard d'Arnaud and Jean Gaspard Dubois-Fontenelle. Out of two pictures, both hailing from Catholic countries, the Protestant public were bound to choose the more lurid, thus providing themselves not only with emotional excitement, but with a thrill of that warm complacency which always stole through a British bosom when meditating Continental tyrannies.

Dubois-Fontenelle's *Effects of the Passions, or Memoirs of Floricourt*, translated in 1788, though written some twenty years before, was a fine anthology of monastic horrors for the nascent Gothic Romance to draw on. The author, who had failed to get his anti-ecclesiastical drama *La Vestale* past the censor, but had nevertheless seen it enjoy a good circulation, packed into his novel as many strong situations as it would hold. We begin with Floricourt's beloved, Julia, who has been forced into a convent by her father. The lovers meet and plight their troth in the burial vaults under the church; their attempted escape, however, is frustrated, for Floricourt is late at his grisly trysting-place, and Julia, having dropped her lamp and overcome by terror, is on the point of death when he finds her, and expires in his arms. The second volume shifts to secular prisons, but the third presents us with the story of M. and Mme Vareuil. Vareuil, made a monk at fourteen, is detected in lewd offences, subjected to inhuman discipline and finally immured for life in a secret and devilishly ingenious dungeon (the monastery possessed at least four of these). The walls are undermined by flood, and he escapes and marries in England, but years later is lured back and recaptured. His wife follows him into the monastery, where she lives disguised as a monk, and at length effects his escape from a subterranean iron cage, only to see him die in her arms of exhaustion. These are the effects of the passions of love and cruelty, and for all the theatrical extravagance of the story, there is in it a sense of frenzied beating against the bars, of possible agonies and possible perversions of the human mind, which differentiates it from the English treatments of such themes. Some vestige of reality, some trace of true indignation, are discernible under these hyperboles; but they are not discernible in the *Monk*.

It was the asceticisms of conventual life that attracted the English imagination, and now the range was extended from Addison's melancholy resignation, which by no means fell out of use, to include these French savageries. An alternative line of treatment – the ribald – is perennial and universal, and hardly needs comment, except to observe that, when the salt of humour evaporated, the lasciviousness of priests, monks and nuns added an ugly ingredient to the hellish brew of the sensational writer. In the 1770s a recalcitrant daughter is often imprisoned in a nunnery, and exposed to the unkindness of a bigoted, venal abbess; but by the 'nineties she is exposed to much more than that.[17] 'Nunnery-tale books' had been a well-known class before the Gothic Romance came to give the material a more picturesque turn. They had been, as a rule, scandalously indecent; but the union of lasciviousness and terror, outlined in many anecdotes, recorded in travel-books and made current by the reviews, was first thoroughly worked by M. G. Lewis in *The Monk* (1795). This scandalous book ('Yes! the author of the Monk signs himself LEGISLATOR', wrote Coleridge in the *Critical*; 'we stare! and tremble') is pervaded by a sort of excitable heat. Lewis lets his fancy dwell on amorous encounters among the corruptions of burial vaults, on an imprisoned mother, caressing her putrid babe, on the forcing of innocence and the state of a man after torture. He acknowledged that he was inspired by *The Mysteries of Udolpho*, and Mrs Radcliffe must have felt that he had both stolen and debased her thunder. She had herself touched on monastic themes in her early work, *A Sicilian Romance*, and in Germany, whither she went to look for copy for a new book, she had caught impressive glimpses of conventual life – a nun in prayer under a pointed arch, black-cowled monks striding under the cliffs at Boppart – which she still wished to embody in it; she had also, it seems, read *Herman of Unna*, and seen in the baldly-described incident of a girl's captivity in a mountain-convent an opportunity for her picturesque pen. Whether or no the further stimulus of Lewis's *Monk* was needed to complete *The Italian*, at all events in that, the last romance published in her lifetime, she made a gallant attempt to redeem the subject of monastic tyranny, and to treat it in a manner that should be quite terrible and yet consistent with perfect delicacy. In *The Italian* there is no lust and no luxurious cruelty; in place of them there is bigotry and ambition. There are no scenes of blood, but there is that 'dreadful hieroglyphic', the straw mattress of the unknown dead nun. The lovers break no vows, for Mrs Radcliffe did not care for rebels, and turned aside from the criminal, unless uncommonly majestic. But there is the Church of the Dominican Convent, with Schedoni in silent penance; and there is San Stefano, that stately nightmare among the Apennines, with its airy prison, its secret cells and the gorgeous pomp of its pilgrimage shrine. There is also, towards the end of the story, a good abbess who governs her convent in enlightened fashion, and this, no doubt, Mrs Radcliffe felt, kept the balance true. The material is carried to the highest pitch of the picturesque. It has, of course, no religious bearing, for what religion there is in *The Italian* – and Mrs Radcliffe, reticent as she is, sometimes lets her quiet faith become apparent – is undogmatic and uninstitutional. Nor does she develop the psychological aspects of her subject, in which direction alone there was a possibility of advance. Failing this, it hovered in other hands between the picturesque and the sensational. It did not lose favour, however. In particular, the living tomb of the unchaste nun continued to provide a 'grateful horror', and was handled by Sir Walter Scott in *Marmion* in the best romantic manner.[18] He knew better, however, than to introduce it into a novel, and the *Monastery* is a human place.

The display of ecclesiastical tyranny in *The Italian* is not completed until Vivaldi has been led through the dungeons of the Inquisition at Rome, and has stood trembling among masked familiars before his judges in their black-draped hall. And here we have to record one small but delightful act of defiance on the part of the Shakespeare of Romance-writers. Grosley's *New Observations on Italy and its Inhabitants* had been Mrs Radcliffe's stand-by in certain sections of *The Mysteries of Udolpho*, and still, apparently, lingered in her mind. But Grosley had belittled the power of the Roman Inquisition in the most unromantic way; for over a hundred years, he said, it had passed no capital sentence; 'everything there is transacted in private by spiritual and pecuniary penalties'. Now Grosley was in Rome in 1758, and it was in that very year – for she dates *The Italian* with superfluous exactness – that Vivaldi heard the groans of the tortured and was himself bound on the rack.[19] It was inevitable that the Gothic Romance and the later Tale of Terror should turn to the Inquisition for material. It had always filled a large place in the English imagination, which was familiar with its outer forms, its espionage system, the silent removal of its victim by night, the black-hung torture-chamber, the great crucifixes, the candles and the hooded attendants. From being the object of Protestant abomination it had become the object of philosophic disapproval; or, rather, both emotions combined in the eighteenth century to make this theme an eminently lively one. The picaresque found room for it,[20] and in 1771 there came out a book which in its subject-matter though not in its treatment anticipates some of the most thrilling features of the Gothic Romance. This is the *Adventures of a Jesuit*; and the noticeable thing about it is that, in the character of Don Bertram de Torres, it provides an early sketch of the powerful, ubiquitous man of mystery, who thrusts himself into the hero's life to act in some sort as his guardian, and after assuming a variety of disguises, turns out to be a familiar of the Inquisition. The tale is a puzzle rather than a mystery, for the author does not know his own mind, and misses opportunities all through the book; but the material was there, and it needed only the romantic vision to colour it. Here, as in many other cases, the curiosity of the eighteenth century had peered into a subject which the romance-writers were to commandeer; they knew the facts, but limited their imaginative participation, and kept their defences up; whereas the romance-writers first filled these terrors with life, and then deliberately exposed their sensibilities to them.

One need not assume that Mrs Radcliffe knew *The Adventures of a Jesuit*, although in *The Italian* she does link the Inquisition – not, it is true, very closely – with the figure of a man of mystery, the confessor, Schedoni. The plan of that book, the first half of which is dominated by Schedoni, who, in the second, summons up the dread society to fill the scene, and himself shrinks before it, is much closer to the plan of certain German romances, which became known in England between 1794 and 1796, namely, Schiller's *Ghost-Seer, or Apparitionist*, Cajetan Tschink's *Victim of Magical Delusions, or the Mystery of the Revolution in P——l, a magico-political tale*, and Marquis Grosse's *Genius*, on the second translation of which was bestowed the famous title *Horrid Mysteries*. To these we may add, though the likeness is not so close, Benedicte Naubert's *Herman of Unna*.[21] All four concern the activities of powerful secret societies (if the Inquisition may be included, for the sake of expediency, in such a description), and in the first three the appearance of the society is heralded by that of a mysterious, austere and yet attractive man, who ultimately proves to be an associate of the society. The pattern was Schiller's,[22] and the theme, with its political and magical ingredients, was of common interest to Western Europe. At the end of the eighteenth century, rumours of secret societies and widespread conspiracies flew thick. Great changes were in progress, and men of liberal sympathies and men tenacious of ancient forms of life were alike prone to see something monstrous and abnormal in each other's activities. Many strands went to form this web, which shimmers with different colours as it is viewed from different angles. The Jesuits, whose Order had been suspended by the Pope in 1773, had found refuge in Prussia, where Protestant imaginations credited them with persistent activity. The Spanish Inquisition, reduced at one time to a mere College of Inquiry, had been re-established in its full powers some five years later. This was an ominous sign of the gathering strength and oblique methods of the forces of reaction. On the other hand, Conservatives saw in philosophers and reformers banded conspirators against Church and State, and their apprehension increased to panic under the pressure of the French Revolution. A fantastic element enriched the confusion in the stories of occult powers, their practitioners and the discipline required for initiation. Here we are on debatable ground, on the confines of magic and science, of moral idealism and charlatanry, of all that is most seductive to the imagination of man and most perilous to his reason. Cagliostro might grow old in his Italian prison, but the philosopher's stone did not lose its attractive power. Rosicrucianism was a beneficent mystery or a sinister deceit. Freemasonry either liberated the spirit of man and forwarded the era of his perfection, or, by relaxing moral restraints, plunged him into cynical debauchery. The enthusiasts for hidden wisdom do not express themselves through the novel – or, at least, no such novels reached England before the turn of the century; rather, we find the skilled intriguer, making use of this false glamour to lure an ardent young man to initiation in order that he may commit his will and all his resources to the service of the society. Freemasonry and Illuminism were constantly associated with infidelity and political liberalism, but the attractions of natural magic, the mummery of magic-lanterns, explosive powders and combined mirrors, could be adapted equally well to the purposes of the reactionary party. We have thus a shifting phantasmagoria of bewitchment, from which there emerges the notion of some widely-ramified secret society, subversive in its aims and formidable in its strength, wielding or simulating occult powers by means of which its ignorant tools are controlled, but in its ultimate nature, when the last grades are passed, sceptical and anarchic. Germany, which, owing to the tolerance of Frederick the Great and the tyranny of other governments, seethed with societies, where prophets appeared who practised animal magnetism, professed to raise the dead, or to live a thousand years upon a tea,[23] was a fruitful bed for these fantastic ideas, but even in England, where elemental spirits and natural magic were not taken very seriously, the disturbed atmosphere of the revolutionary period caused the idea of a grand political conspiracy to take root, though in shallow soil, and to bear some astounding fruits. Thus there were found English adherents to the theories of Abbé Barruel, who, in his *Memoires pour servir à l'histoire du Jacobinisme* (1797–8), maintains that the French Revolution was due to a threefold interacting conspiracy of the philosophers against religion, the Freemasons against kings, and the Illuminists (an inner ring of sceptics, using the superstitious lower grades to further their secret aim) against organized society. This theory gave the Jacobins an ancestry reaching back through the Knights Templar to the Manichees; and certainly, in comparison with bearing blame oneself, it must have seemed almost tolerable to have been undone by so far-reaching, long-prepared, diabolically ingenious a conspiracy. We had also extravagances of native growth, for John Robison, Professor of Natural Philosophy at Edinburgh, produced *Proofs of a Conspiracy against all the Religions and Governments of Europe, carried on in the Secret Meetings of Free Masons, Illuminati and Reading Societies* (1797), which proofs are adduced in favour of the same contentions as Barruel's. We need enter no further into these superficially intricate, but really oversimplified, explanations of a vast political change. Barruel's and Robison's books were published just after the translations of the German stories, but they serve to show how receptive the reading public was to this new form of romantic terror.

SOURCE: extract from chapter, 'The Gothic Romance', in *The Popular Novel in England, 1770–1800* (London, 1932), pp. 267–84.

NOTES

[Reorganised and renumbered from the original – Ed.]

1. Cf. Chaucer's treatment of the prison in *The Knight's Tale*.
2. Cf., e.g., *Gentleman's Magazine* (1773), p. 515; *Scots Magazine*, 1772, p. 161, and 1777, p. 217; the account of the Venetian dungeons where prisoners stand twelve days up to the knees in putrid water among corpses in Helenus Scott's *Adventures of a Rupee* (1782); *The Memoirs of Henry Masers de la Tude, during a confinement of thirty-five years in the State Prisons of France* (1787); Trenck's *Memoirs*, translated by Holcroft (1788) among others; Helen Maria Williams's account in her *Letters written in France* (1790) of the discovery at the Bastille of chained skeletons in subterranean dungeons, to which, or to similar material, we may trace the irrelevant chained skeletons in, e.g., *The Castle of Count Roderick* (1794); and the extract from Mariana Starke's *Letters from Italy* in the *Critical*, 1800, retailing the anecdote of the French soldiers, during the siege of Mantua, who found a nun fettered in a dungeon under a deserted convent. It is unnecessary to remark that it is not the authenticity of these tales that matters, but their imaginative effect.
3. Very frequent in English novels that deal with French parental tyranny, e.g. Mrs Smith's *Celestina* (1791).
4. See, especially the disappointment of both prisoners that the high window, to which they manage to climb, gives only a blank wall. With so much material, however, one cannot venture a definite ascription.
5. Cf. Lewis's *Monk*, and, for a more moderate treatment of the theme, Ann Yearsley, the Bristol milkwoman's *Royal Captives* (1795), a story of real power and deep feeling, though both naïve and melodramatic in expression. The plot is founded on the mystery of the Man in the Iron Mask.
6. See *Scots Magazine* (1774), p. 321.
7. In 1789, *The Memoirs of Charles Townly, written by himself*, appeared, containing a good section on the hero's imprisonment in the Bastille; before the end of the year, the book was provided with a new title-page, *The Bastille; or the History of Charles Townly*.
8. See *Gentleman's Magazine* (1789), pp. 66 & 752.
9. See *The Haunted Priory: or, the Fortunes of the House of Rayo. A Romance founded partly on historical facts* (1794). This book was published anonymously. In 1796 appeared *The Castle of Inchvally: a Tale alas! too true. By Stephen Cullen, Author of the Haunted Priory.*
10. *Adèle et Thèodore, ou Letters sur l'Education* (1782), translated in 1783 as *Adelaide and Theodore; or, Letters on Education.*
11. See Harriet Lee *Canterbury Tales*, vol. I, *The Frenchman's Tale. Constance* (1797).

12. Ellis Cornelia Knight in her optimistic continuation of *Rasselas*, *Dinarbas* (1790), devotes Rasselas to solitary confinement for months, without books or conversation. He sustains himself by studying the scenery.

13. See *Critical* (March 1792), on Mrs Mary Robinson's *Vancenza*. Mrs Robinson, who was liberal and 'philosophic' in her sympathies, was very careful to make this clear in her next romance, *Hubert de Sevrac* (1796). Critics sometimes refused to accept an author's premisses, if these were based on Catholic usages; thus the *Critical*, reviewing Mrs Bennett's *Agnes de Courci* (1789), denied the enormity of a breach of celibacy. There is in some novels a mild plea for a 'Protestant nunnery' (e.g. *Indiana Danby*, 1765), but the motive is not so much religious as social; such an institution would be a centre of good works and a means of disposing unmarried women.

14. On the other hand, the Catholic Mrs Inchbald dealt with the theme in *A Simple Story* (1791) discreetly and delicately. Dorriforth, though charmed, does not love till released from his vows; it is the Protestant girl, unaccustomed to associate a sacred prohibition with any man, who is enmeshed.

15. Jerningham was educated at Douai, though he later became a Protestant. La Trappe captured English imaginations; cf. George Keate's *Sketches from Nature* (1779). There were also French handlings of the subject; see Baculard d'Arnaud's *Comte de Comminges*.

16. A few quietly-authentic convent settings can be found, though the story they enclose is frequently improbable. This is the case with *Anecdotes of a Convent* (1771) by the author of *Memoirs of Mrs Williams*; here the plot is concerned with a boy bred up in a convent as a girl, and believing himself to be one; the author declares that the story is true.

17. For priestly villainy, see *Santa Maria, or the Mysterious Pregnancy* (1797) by Joseph Fox. A priest, now penitent, confesses to drugging and violating nuns and then suffering them to be buried in a state of trance.

18. The convent scenes of *Marmion* are very like those in Mrs Isabella Hedgland's *Baron's Daughter* (1802), which also play at Lindisfarne; but the material was common.

19. See J. M. S. Tompkins, 'Ramond, Grosley and Mrs Radcliffe', *Review of English Studies* (July 1929).

20. See, for example, Charles Johnstone's *Chrystal; or, the Adventures of a Guinea*.

21. The order of translation was: *Herman of Unna* (1794), ascribed to Professor Cramer; *The Ghost-Seer* (1795); *The Victim of Magical Delusions*, by P. Will (1795) and *The Genius*, which was twice translated in 1796, as *The Genius: or the Mysterious Adventures of Don Carlos de Grandez*, by Joseph Trapp, and as *Horrid Mysteries* by P. Will. Only the first half of *The Ghost-Seer* was translated in 1795.

22. No connection with *The Adventures of a Jesuit* need be supposed. Such resemblances as can be detected are inherent in the subject.

23. Cf. Lady Craven's *Memoirs* (1826).

# *Eleanor M. Sickels*    King Death    (1932)

... the intensity of belief and emotion which we have lost for ourselves we not infrequently seek to regain through vicarious experience – nor are fear, remorse and despair by any means exceptions to this rule. This might be done the more shamelessly in the period we are studying because of the growing ideal of sensibility with its tendency to sentimentalism, which frankly cultivates emotion for its own sake. And here was the whole world of the bygone Age of Faith being opened up by scholars and antiquaries; a world in which religious terror was by no means confined to a far-distant *dies irae*, but was a very present reality, compounded of strange asceticisms and secret ecclesiastical lusts, of ghost-lore, necromancy, and contracts with the Devil. This world arose on the imagination, furthermore, against a background of those ruined castles and abbeys, those twilight churchyards and midnight charnels, already connected in life and in literature with religious musing and half-superstitious fears. What wonder that religious terror, dying out as a living subjective force in most breasts, should flame anew in the vicarious terrorism of 'Gothic' romance?

That such a psychological connection between religious and romantic terror is not altogether fanciful is indicated by the early association of the 'graveyard' mood and paraphernalia with the Gothic. We found this association already illustrated in 'The Pleasures of Melancholy,' 'The Enthusiast', and other selections in Dodsley's *Collection*; and the suggestion was then made that the mere propinquity of the graveyard to the Gothic church, and the Gothic connotations of ruins, might help to account for it. But what country churchyard but has its ghostly or Satanic legends? What charnel house but holds the possibility, nay the probability, of superstitious as well as religious terrors? What monastic ruin but may suggest to a poet not only philosophical reflections on the power of time, but all the strange and passionate and teeming life that once peopled it? And what easier than to pass from horrified Protestant meditations on that ancient life, such as were not infrequent in the ruin-elegies, to a fascinated analysis of its romantic crimes and austerities and the half-forgotten beliefs on which it rested?

As for the connection between superstitious beliefs and black melancholy, the odes to superstition have hinted at it. According to

Charles Churchill, Credulity is 'the child of Folly, Begot on cloister'd Melancholy'. According to Anna Seward, 'grim Superstition' is 'Demon of the Night', before whose 'baseless terror' she prays she may not resign her peace. Henry Headley, in his 'Invocation to Melancholy', tells of standing aghast under the moon by Superstition's antique shrines. John Gilbert Cooper had thought of a convent as the kingdom of 'frozen chastity and Horrour' and of 'Melancholy, daughter of Despair', and in 'The Power of Harmony' (1745) had associated black melancholy, superstition, guilt and death together as fit frequenters of a funeral place of cypress, poison yews, and ruined tombs. It needs only the change of attitude already partly accomplished in Headley and others, from pious horror or complacent superiority to imaginative or even morbid sympathy, to give us *The Monk* or *The Italian*, with their correspondent poetic phenomena.

Indeed the elements which terror-romanticism took from the medieval revival were the very elements which it had in common with black religious melancholy. It took the backgrounds of dim cathedrals, midnight churchyards, ghastly charnel houses and gloomy monastic ruins. It took the death theme, and embroidered it with all the terrors of physical corruption and special visitation. It took the theme of sin, and added domestic and exotic demonology, age-old tales of contracts with Satan, and the expiatory sufferings of the Wandering Jew. And out of the theme of sin, which is never far from the theme of death, it built its arch-types – the criminal monk, the tyrant, the strong dark hero inwardly consumed by remorse. It is not suggested, of course, that the graveyard verse was solely responsible for the elements of black melancholy in the Gothic tales or in the Byronic hero-type; but that there is a real connection, and that it has deep psychological as well as accidentally literary roots, I am convinced is true.

Some idea of the extent to which the graveyard horrifics, largely inherited, as has been said, from seventeenth-century religious melancholy, and further popularized by the mid-century masterpieces of black melancholy, were disseminated through eighteenth-century verse waiting to be assimilated by the Gothic revival, must already have been gained in the course of the discussions of the odes and the elegies. That this material came to be thought of as an essential ingredient of the poetic education may be inferred from a passage in James Beattie's account of the growth of his Edwin's soul:

> Then would be dream of graves, and corses pale,
> And ghosts that to the charnel-dungeon throng,
> And drag a length of clanking chain, and wail,

Till silenced by the owl's terrific song,
Or blast that shrieks by fits the shuddering aisles along.

[*The Minstrel*]

Illustrations of the incidental occurrence of the mood or the paraphernalia might be given *ad infinitum*. But space presses. One or two striking examples of the fusion of the graveyard and Gothic material toward the close of the century, we must, however, examine. One of these is an 'Ode to Fantasy' (1798), 'by the scholar and traveller, John Leyden. The ode was 'written during an attack of ague' and is in consequence sufficiently dismal. In Miltonic octosyllabics, the sick man cries avaunt to the singing lark and cheerful village throngs, and imagines himself in succession watching a funeral, sitting at midnight on the haunted grave of a suicide, listening to lost and wailing ghosts by a winter torrent, working lonely spells on St John's Eve, watching all night by the tortured bed of a dying murderer, braving horrid spectres in some Gothic hall, voyaging over far enchanted deeps, whirling through the air with the fairies, and then – suddenly – witnessing the resurrection of the dead and hearing their shrieks of despair.

The other example, but two years earlier in date, is much more elaborate. When Coleridge and Southey first planned 'Joan of Arc', the poem was fitted with allegorical trappings, which Southey later removed. The longest allegorical interlude, however, he made into a separate poem, which he later published under the title of 'The Vision of the Maid of Orleans'. It is a dream-allegory or vision-poem in three books, the first of which is introduction in graveyard-Gothic style, the second a miniature *Purgatorio*, and the third a miniature *Paradiso*. While practically worthless as poetry, it is thus an amalgam of literary and philosophical influences – Spenser, Dante, Milton, the melancholy tradition white and black, and the thought of the French Revolution and the rationalists being all distinctly discernible.

Falling to sleep at Orleans in somber mood because of her fore-knowledge of her tragic death, Joan dreams that she goes across a moor

Barren, and wide, and drear, and desolate,

through a tempestuous night under a Miltonic moon which intermittently makes 'the moving darkness visible'. She comes to a stagnant water, and steps into a boat driven by a moaning melancholy wind and guided by a wan and hollow-cheeked female figure whose half-hid breast is gnawn by serpents (like that of the allegorical figure of

Despair in James Scott's ode). There are bats and ravens and a 'hollow blast'. Joan leaps to shore at last, to find the orthodox ruin surrounded by 'dark yew' and 'melancholy cypress' and mounds of half-demolished graves. Moonlight filters through the 'fretted window'. Within, fearfully following a wavering blue light, she comes upon an old man, sitting on a mouldering monument half covered with 'wither'd yew-leaves and earth-mouldering bones'. It is Despair.

> The tomb-fires on his face
> Shed a blue light; his face was of the hue
> Of death; his limbs were mantled in a shroud.

As he welcomes her and leads her further into the ruins, the descriptive details are those of the ruin-literature, but darkened, as is usual in the Gothic tales, by midnight, tempest, and superstitious terror. The moon looks through the broken roof, there is ivy about the dismantled columns, there are mutilated sacred statues and fallen crucifixes –

> Meanwhile overhead
> Roar'd the loud blast, and from the tower the owl
> Scream'd as the tempest shook her secret nest.

Despair drags the Maid into the charnel house, and in that dank and fetid air, amid the gruesome, 'fragments of the dead', he repeatedly tempts her to suicide. When even the vision of the livid corpse of her dead lover cannot move her virtue or her logic, he puts her in a coffin and she is dragged towards the bowels of the earth by ghouls, past troops of their breathren feasting on the dead. In the vast 'dome of death' to which they bring her, she sees the Fates (originally classical), and Superstition (perhaps originally Spenserian, certainly rather Gothic). But buoyed up by her eighteenth century arguments, even then she will not strike. This closes Book I.

At this point all the terror paraphernalia of the first vision vanishes, exorcised, one gathers, by the steady virtue of the Maid. Theodore, the beloved, appears to her in the guise of an angel, and is her Virgil throughout this book and her Beatrice throughout the third. Book II is particularly interesting as an illustration of that humanizing of the idea of punishment suggested above. For it is not really an Inferno at all, but a Purgatorio, since none of the punishment need be everlasting if the afflicted soul will repent and be cleansed. The descriptions are an odd melange of Dante, Spenser, *Vathek* and the French Revolution. Two characteristic types of punishment, proportioned and fitted to the crime, may be given:

lewd poets (so early did the future laureate put morals above art!) lie like rotting corpses until their works shall cease to lead men astray on earth; and in a Hall of Glory reminiscent of *Vathek*, ambitious kings sit with burning crowns on their brows until men shall realize the wickedness of royal ambition and 'form one brotherhood' (the future laureate, though moral, was still a radical). Book III, after *Paradiso*, need not detain us here. It is full of Arcadian love in distant stars and the sort of social philosophy we are more used to finding in Shelley.

This poem of Southey's, besides giving a further idea of the paraphernalia of the literature we are studying, and serving as an example of the blending of religious and romantic themes, may stand also as an illustration of the complexity of currents and cross-currents with which we have to do. In truth, the streams which fed the river were very many. So many aspects of the movements which contributed to the satanic and the macabre in romanticism lie outside of our purpose, and so often the satanic and the macabre themselves are dissociated from melancholy, that it will happily be possible to be very brief. Yet something must be said of the most important of these newer influences.

We may speak first of the ballad revival. Macpherson's *Ossian* had been partly based on Highland ballads. But it took over little of the popular superstitious material; Macpherson's ghosts are after all pale and watery beings, completely stripped of terror, and ministering rather to that vague elegiac atmosphere of which we have spoken than to even a temporary black melancholy. To the popularity of the Ossianic poems is probably traceable the romantic partiality for meteors as a sign of terror – meteors are extraordinarily plentiful in *Ossian* – and also something of the partiality for whirlwinds and blasted heaths and tempestuous nights. But when Percy's *Reliques* (1765) and the various other collections containing folk poetry had made available the ballads themselves (or only slightly 'refined' versions of them) there was turned into the stream of English poetry a torrent of new terror material – primitive fears and superstitions, witches and bleeding ghosts and haunted glens and palpable fiends, not excluding Satan himself. These things, being originally to a great extent the outgrowth of religious fear, may naturally be added to the churchyard paraphernalia, or the old paraphernalia may fit easily into the descriptions of ballad situations.

Thus in William Mickle's 'Cumnor Hall' we have bell, raven and howling dog, plus the eerie suggestion of an 'aerial voice' and the mystic medieval 'thrice':

The death-bell thrice was heard to ring,
An aerial voice was heard to call,
And thrice the raven flapp'd its wing
Around the towers of Cumnor Hall.

The mastiff howls at village door . . .

This is a fairly early specimen (about 1777). What could be done with much the same sort of material in a ballad-like tale by a great romantic genius may be seen in Coleridge's 'Christabel'. In the famous and exquisite opening of this poem, the atmosphere of faerie is built up of such familiar elements as a clock striking midnight, hooting owls, a mastiff, the suggested legend of a shrouded ghost, and a chilly moonlit night; and what would the tale itself be without its medieval witch-doctrines and its superstitious omens and marvels? Professor Lowes has taught us to see in 'The Ancient Mariner' the apotheosis rather of the Renaissance voyage-books and of treatises on occult lore than of the ballad revival. But the form and movement at least were borrowed from the ballads. It is worth remembering too that there were in the original draft two or three stanzas, later omitted, which described the figures of the phantom ship quite in the graveyard style. The reader should at this point also be reminded of Keats's 'La Belle Dame Sans Merci'.

Nor did the demonic and macabre elements in popular tradition lack more authentic imitators. All the Scotch poets who busied themselves collecting the traditional material tried their hands now and again at imitation. Burns's were mostly songs, and when he used the supernatural in 'Tam O'Shanter' it was for humorous effect. Scott used native and imported themes indiscriminately in his early ballads and 'tales of wonder'. The influence of the German is discernible in the technique of the first native piece, 'Glenfinlas' (1799), wherein the simple tale of the seduction of a young hunter by a fiend masquerading as a fair maiden is tricked out in all the Gothic paraphernalia of chill death-damps, dancing corpse-lights, and loud bursts of ghastly laughter amid howling whirlwinds and a shower of bleeding human fragments. The 'Eve of St. John' (1799), also written for *Tales of Wonder*, concerns a rendezvous with a murdered man, and the 'sable score' of his burning fingers left on door and wrist when he comes to warn his lady and his murderer (her husband) of the consequences of sinful lust and bloody deeds. The fragment called 'The Shepherd's Tale' (1799) is apparently a legend of border warfare; it has an enchanted cavern in the bowels of the earth – a very popular folk-motif as we have already seen – and a whole army of knights in enchanted slumber. 'Cadyow Castle'

(1801) is a tale of border revenge, but has no supernatural machinery. Scott used ballad themes often enough later, and his work with ballads has been credited with inspiring all his long tales. In several of these he makes effective use of the macabre traditional material: he uses the legends of the sorcerer Michael Scott in 'The Lay of the Last Minstrel', the eerie prophetic visions of the Hermit Monk in 'The Lady of the Lake', and a glen popularly supposed to be haunted in 'Rokeby'. The fearful scenes in the convent vaults in 'Marmion', like the conception of the hero in the same tale, are closer to the main Gothic tradition.

Scott's associates in ballad-collecting, John Leyden and James Hogg, and his follower, William Motherwell, all wrote ballads attaining a fearful and gloomy tone by the use of native superstitions. The best of Leyden's ballads is 'The Elfin King'. It makes fine and restrained use of the macabre:

> And the windlestrae, so limber and grey,
>   Did shiver beneath the tread
> Of the courser's feet, as they rushed to meet
>   The morrice of the dead.

>       .    .    .    .    .    .    .

> Then Sir Geoffry grew pale as he quaffed the ale,
>   And cold as the corpse of clay;
> And with horny beak the ravens did shriek,
>   And fluttered o'er their prey.

>       .    .    .    .    .    .    .

> With panting breast as he forward pressed,
>   He trod on a mangled head;
> And the skull did scream, and the voice did seem
>   The voice of his mother dead . . .

As for the Ettrick Shepherd, [Hogg] was at the height of his by no means despicable powers as soon as he started to write about the popular superstitions of his native land. He was not a gloomy person, and his taste ran fully as much to humorous or pleasant use of the supernatural as to the grim and grisly. Doubtless his finest poem is 'Kilmeny', the Thirteenth Bard's Song from the 'Queen's Wake' (1813); it catches with exquisite grace an eerie and estatic supernaturalism. But there are macabre passages in two or three of the other bardic tales from the 'Queen's Wake', and those among the best: in 'The Abbot M'Kinnon', which tells how, in retribution for ecclesiastical wickedness, St Columba sank the Abbot's ship off the shore of the Isle of Staffa, whereon is the Cave of Fingal; and in 'The Fate of Macgregor', which is told by a bard who has listened to a Spectre's Cradle Song far in the midnight mountains, and which itself concerns a man carried off by an avenging spectre in a 'barge of hell'. Hogg has also a ballad based on 'The Twa Corbies', and macabre traditional tales about a murdered pedlar whose little finger bone bled to reveal the doer of the deed, about a criminal priest who, to feed his lust, made a contract with the fiend, and about the murder of the pious mother of a famous warlock by a rout of witches gathered at midnight in a church. No wonder, when it had so inspired his muse, that Hogg wrote a poem to defend superstition against its detractors! Motherwell, too, sometimes treats such themes of unnatural crime and death: the 'dark Syr Hew' meets a horrible and supernatural death for parricide; a girl finds she has unwittingly married 'the Ettin stark' who 'rules the Realms of Fear'; a woman who has murdered her lover is dragged to a watery grave by his outraged ghost. The best of these ballads and bardic tales manage to effect a dismal and eerie atmosphere by means of a certain naïve simplicity, and use the paraphernalia of terror with restraint.

Not so the more specifically 'Gothic' tales. In them mingle the influence of the lurid melodramatic terrorism from Germany and that of the native graveyard-Gothic tradition. To speak of the Gothic school in England is to think of the novelists – Walpole, Clara Reeve, Ann Radcliffe, M. G. Lewis, Maturin – and it is true that Gothic tales in verse are for the most part but pale reflections of the movement in prose. Yet a brief reference to them is essential.

The classics of the type are M. G. Lewis's *Tales of Terror* (1799) and *Tales of Wonder* (1801), to which Leyden and Scott both contributed. Reference has already been made to Scott's share in these volumes [in a section not included here – Ed.], and perhaps little more need be said of it. In most of the tales, especially Lewis's own, there is really little left of melancholy, black or white. There is rather a lusty delight in superstitious horrors alternating with wild parodying of the same tales seriously presented a few pages back. An excellent idea of Lewis's conception of romance may be gained by reading the Prologue of his *Castle Spectre* (1797). Therein Romance is described as the 'moonstruck child of genius and of woe', a 'lovely maniac' who haunts new-open graves and tempestuous headlands, and is frequently seen fleeing in trembling terror.

> As if from murderous swords of following fiends she fled!

Others besides 'Monk' Lewis – from the Della Cruscans to Joanna

Baillie – told tales in verse about this fearful maid. The very youthful verse of Shelley – to say nothing of those queer concoctions, his schoolboy novels – is Gothic in the extreme. He (or perhaps it was his sister Elizabeth) even plagiarized a whole poem of Lewis's for the *Original Poetry of Victor and Cazire*. . . .

> SOURCE: extract from chapter, 'King Death', in *The Gloomy Egoist: Moods and Themes of Melancholy from Gray to Keats* (New York, 1932), pp. 158–70.

# *Mario Praz*   The Metamorphoses of Satan   (1933)

. . . 3. Towards the end of the eighteenth century Milton's Satan transfused with his own sinister charm the traditional type of generous outlaw or sublime criminal. Schiller's *Räuber* Karl Moor (1781) is an angel-outlaw in the manner of Milton's and of those of his German imitator Klopstock; he had in him the stuff of a Brutus, but unfavourable circumstances had made him into a Catiline. Schiller also, following Milton's example, speaks of the 'majesty' of his Robber, of 'the honourable malefactor, the majestic monster' (*Ungeheuer mit Majestät*). In a scene which was suppressed later Karl Moor says to Spiegelberg:

> 'I do not know, Maurice, if you have read Milton. He who could not endure that another should be above him, and who dared to challenge the Almighty to a duel, was he not an extraordinary genius? He had encountered the Invincible One, and although in defeat he exhausted all his forces, he was not humiliated; eternally, even to the present day, he makes new efforts, and every blow falls back again on his own head, yet still he is not humiliated. . . . An intelligent mind, which neglects mean duties for a more exalted purpose, will be eternally unhappy, whereas the knave who has betrayed his friend and fled before his enemy ascends to Heaven, thanks to an opportune little sigh of repentance. Who would not prefer to roast in the furnace of Belial with Borgia and Catiline, rather than sit up above at table with that vulgar ass? It is he at whose name our gossips make the sign of the cross.'

Karl Moor is compared to 'that first wicked leader who urged thousands of innocent angels into the fire of revolt and dragged them with him into the deep abyss of damnation' [II iii]; he proclaims himself to be [III ii] 'a howling Abaddon among the flowers of a happy world' (here the allusion is to Klopstock's poem *Messias*); Amalie throws herself on his neck [v ii] crying 'Assassin! Demon! I cannot do without you, angel!', and Karl exclaims, 'See, see, the sons of light weep in the arms of a weeping Demon'. From crime to crime Karl rushes into the abyss of despair, till finally the harmony of the moral law is re-established in the Christian ending: through pain the robber is brought back to the path of sacrifice and virtue.

4. Rebels in the grand manner, grandsons of Milton's Satan and brothers of Schiller's Robber, begin to inhabit the picturesque, Gothicized backgrounds of the English 'tales of terror' towards the end of the eighteenth century. The little figures of banditti, which formed pleasing decorative details in the landscapes of the Salvator Rosa school then in fashion, came to life in the writings of Mrs Ann Radcliffe, 'the Shakespeare of romance writers',[1] and took on gigantic and Satanic proportions, becowled and sinister as Goya's bogeys. Montoni, the scoundrel and adventurer of the *Mysteries of Udolpho* (1794), takes pleasure in the violent exercise of his passions; the difficulties and storms of life which ruin the happiness of others stimulate and strengthen all the energies of his mind.

Mrs Radcliffe's masterpiece is the character of Schedoni in *The Italian, or the Confessional of the Black Penitents* (1797). At that time the chief source of mysterious crimes (that source of evil actions in which the British public is forced to believe by its innate Manicheism, whether it be a Machiavellian monster, as in the Elizabethan period, or a double-dyed criminal, as in the detective novels of to-day) was to be found in the Spanish and Italian Inquisition. Illuminism had pointed to the Roman Catholic monk as an infamy which must be crushed, and the recent campaign of the states of Europe against the Society of Jesus had disclosed a sinister background of material interests. Schedoni, therefore, is a monk; when he comes on the scene he appears as a man of unknown origin, but suspected to be of exalted birth and decayed fortunes. Severe reserve, unconquerable silence, love of solitude, and frequent penances, were interpreted by some as the effect of misfortunes preying upon a haughty and disordered spirit, by others as the consequence of some hideous crime which filled his troubled conscience with remorse.

His figure was striking . . . it was tall, and, though extremely thin, his limbs were large and uncouth, and as he stalked along, wrapt in the black garments of his order, there was something terrible in its air; something almost superhuman. His cowl, too, as it threw a shade over the livid paleness of his face, encreased its severe character, and gave an effect to his large melancholy eye, which approached to horror. His was not the melancholy of a sensible and wounded heart, but apparently that of a gloomy and ferocious disposition. There was something in his physiognomy extremely singular, and that cannot easily be defined. It bore the traces of many passions, which seemed to have fixed the features they no longer animated. An habitual gloom and severity prevailed over the deep lines of his countenance; and his eyes were so piercing that they seemed to penetrate, at a single glance, into the hearts of men, and to read their most secret thoughts; few persons could support their scrutiny, or even endure to meet them twice.

Certain qualities can be noticed here which were destined to recur insistently in the Fatal Men of the Romantics: mysterious (but conjectured to be exalted) origin, traces of burnt-out passions, suspicion of a ghastly guilt, melancholy habits, pale face, unforgettable eyes. Decidedly there is something of Milton's Satan in this monk, whose 'whole air and attitudes exhibited the wild energy of something not of this earth'. There is something also of Shakespeare's King John [IV ii]:

> The image of a wicked heinous fault
> Lives in his eye; that close aspect of his
> Does show the mood of a much troubled breast.

His rare smiles are as the smiles of Cassius (*Julius Caesar*, I ii):

> Seldom he smiles, and smiles in such a sort
> As if he mock'd himself and scorn'd his spirit
> That could be mov'd to smile at any thing.

The horror he inspires is not unaccompanied by a certain degree of pity, as in the case of Richard III [V iii]:

> . . . There is no creature loves me;
> And if I die, no soul shall pity me:
> Nay, wherefore should they, since that I myself
> Find in myself no pity to myself?

In other ways Schedoni is reminiscent of the Machiavellians and Jesuits who had been among the abiding features of the English theatre of the seventeenth century:

He cared not for truth, nor sought it by bold and broad argument, but loved to exert the wily cunning of his nature in hunting it through artificial perplexities. At length, from a habit of intricacy and suspicion, his vitiated mind could receive nothing for truth, which was simple and easily comprehended. . . . Notwithstanding all this gloom and austerity, some rare occasions of interest had called forth a character upon his countenance entirely different; and he could adapt himself to the tempers and passions of persons, whom he wished to conciliate, with astonishing facility, and generally with complete triumph.

5. It is possible that the influence of *The Monk*, by Matthew Gregory Lewis, published the year before, in 1796, had also contributed towards the formation of the character of Schedoni. . . . of this immensely successful novel . . . let me point out that it has been noticed that both Schedoni and Lewis's monk Ambrosio are first seen in the full odour of sanctity, then commit the most horrible crimes, and both end as victims of the Inquisition. Lewis, in fact, did little but clothe in a monastic habit a figure which already existed – existed, indeed, actually in Mrs Radcliffe's own repertory, for Lewis asserts that he had read with enthusiasm *The Mysteries of Udolpho* on their first appearing: now the character of Montoni in *The Mysteries of Udolpho* already foreshadowed that of the monk Ambrosio.

Lewis, on the other hand, was acquainted with the German villains put into circulation by the 'Stürmer und Dränger', following the example of Schiller's *Räuber*; in his *Bravo of Venice* (1805) he was merely translating *Aballino, der grosse Bandit*, by Heinrich Zschokke (1794). This Schilleresque romance by Zschokke – later converted into a play – played no little part (in Lamartelière's version, 1801) in making known in France the figure of the 'noble brigand'; it contained, among other things, one curious detail which Sue and other writers of the *roman-feuilleton* did not forget, that of the protagonist's double personality.

Abellino is the assumed name under which an unfortunate nobleman, Flodoardo, becomes a brigand. As Flodoardo he courts the niece of the Doge, Rosamunde, and gives up the brigands to justice; as Abellino he pretends to put himself at the service of the enemies of Venice, and gets rid of the Doge's friends and counsellors. Finally the Doge consents to give his niece's hand to Flodoardo if the latter can deliver up to him within twenty-four hours Abellino, dead or alive. At the hour agreed upon Flodoardo reveals the double part he has played, unmasks the enemies of the Republic, produces the Doge's friends safe and sound, and obtains the hand of Rosamunde. There is no happy ending, however, to *Jean Sbogar*, the novel by Charles Nodier (1818), who, following in Zschokke's footsteps, also confers double personality upon his bandit, who in many respects resembles the bandits of Byron.

SOURCE: sections 3–5 of chapter, 'The Metamorphoses of Satan', in *The Romantic Agony* (London, 1933; 2nd edn, 1970), pp. 59–63 (of 2nd edn).

NOTE

1. [Ed.] The expression is Joyce M. S. Tompkins's, occurring in the extract from her study reproduced in our selection.

*André Breton*     'English *Romans Noirs* and Surrealism'    (1937)

. . . The 'fantastic', which the application of a watchword such as socialist realism excludes in the most radical manner and to which Surrealism never ceases to appeal, constitutes in our view the supreme key to this latent content, the means of fathoming the secret depths of history which disappear beneath a maze of events. It is only at the approach of the fantastic, at a point where human reason loses its control, that the most profound emotion of the individual has the fullest opportunity to express itself: emotion unsuitable for projection in the framework of the real world and which has no other solution in its urgency than to rely on the eternal solicitation of symbols and myths. In this connection it has always appeared to me that nothing could be more opportune than to call attention to that extraordinary efflorescence of English novels at the end of the eighteenth century, known in France as the *romans noirs*. When we consider, at the present time, this literary style now forgotten or in disrepute, we cannot fail to be struck, not only by its prodigious success, but also by the very singular fascination it exercised for some time upon the most critical minds. One of the heroes of Ann Radcliffe, Schedoni, appears without doubt to be the character upon which Byron modelled himself; Thomas Moore frequently evokes with fervour the beautiful diaphanous maidens who come and go in the glades full of birds of the *Forest Romance*. The first novels of Victor Hugo (*Bug-Jargal, Han d'Islande*) as well as those of Balzac (*l'Héritière de Birague, le Centenaire ou les deux Béringheld*, etc.) are directly inspired by the *Monk* of Lewis and the *Melmoth* of Maturin, this same *Melmoth* which Baudelaire was to remember for so long and which, in conjunction with Young's *Night Thoughts*, was to be the most vital source for the all-powerful inspiration of Lautréamont. Such a career, both public and private, in contrast with the extreme discredit to which such works have since been generally condemned, can only be explained by the inference that they were a perfect adaptation of a certain historical situation. The truth, which the Marquis de Sade was the first to disentangle in his *Idée sur les romans*, is that we find ourselves in the presence of a style which, for the period in which it was produced, illustrates 'the indispensable fruit of the revolutionary upheaval to which the whole of Europe was sensitive'. Let us realise the importance of this fact. The attention of humanity in its most universal and spontaneous form as well as in its most individual and purely intellectual form, has here been attracted not by the scrupulously exact description of exterior events of which the world was the theatre, but rather by the expression of the confused feelings awakened by nostalgia and terror. The pleasure principle has never avenged itself more obviously upon the principle of reality. The ruins appear suddenly so full of significance in that they express the collapse of the feudal period; the inevitable ghost which haunts them indicates a peculiarly intense fear of the return of the powers of the past, the subterranean passages represent the difficulty and periods of the dark path followed by each individual towards the light; in the stormy night can be heard the incessant roar of cannon. Such is the turbulent background chosen for the appearance of the beings of pure *temptation*, combining in the highest degree the struggle between the instinct of death on the one hand, which, as Freud has shown, is also an instinct of preservation, and, on the other, Eros who exacts after each human hecatomb the glorious restoration of life. I insist on the fact that the substitution of one kind of scenery for another (scenery of the romantic type for realist scenery) has in no way been determined by the authors of the *romans noirs* and still less contrived by mutual consent. Their undoubted innocence in this respect gives even greater importance to their sensitive testimony. '*Udolpho*', writes Mme de Chastenay, its French translator, '*Udolpho* gave my imagination a shock from which my reason was incapable of shielding it. The menacing voices, the prolonged gloom, the fantastic effect of its terrors overwhelmed me once more like a child and without my being able to discover the cause.' A work of art worthy of the name is one which gives us back the freshness of the emotions of childhood. This can only happen on the express condition that it does not depend directly on the history of current events whose profound echoes in the heart of man can only make themselves felt by the systematic return to fiction.

No attempt at intimidation will cause us to abandon this self-allotted task, which, as we have already made clear, is the elaboration of the *collective myth* belonging to our period in the same way that, whether we like it or not, the style of the *roman noir* may be considered as pathognomonic of the great social troubles in which Europe was enveloped at the end of the eighteenth century. It is not without interest to observe that the initiator of the above style in 1764 was Horace Walpole, a man who, owing to his rank and early experience in public life, was very well informed as to the actual political situation of the time, a man who a year later was to attract the wholehearted attention of Madame du Deffand until her death – Madame du Deffand, who was the intimate friend of the French encyclopaedists, that is to say of those intellectuals who were by definition most hostile to a literary conception such as is revealed in the *Castle of Otranto*. The production of such a work, about which we have the good fortune to have information, approaches, indeed, nothing less than the *surrealist method* and adds once more to its complete justification. A quotation from a letter dated 9 March 1765, from Horace Walpole to William Cole appears to me all the more natural since it reads as though, in the *Manifeste du Surréalisme*, I had only paraphrased and generalised without knowing the affirmations which it contains:

> Shall I even confess to you, what was the origin of this romance? I waked one morning in the beginning of last June, from a dream, of which, all that I could recover was, that I had thought myself in an ancient castle (a very natural dream for a head filled like mine with Gothic story), and that on the uppermost banister of a great staircase I saw a gigantic hand in armour. In the evening I sat down, and began to write, without knowing in the least what I intended to say or relate. The work grew on my hands, and I grew fond of it – add that I was very glad to think of anything, rather than politics – in short, I was so engrossed with my tale, which I completed in less than two months, that one evening, I wrote from the time I had drunk my tea, about six o'clock, till half an hour after one in the morning, when my hand and fingers were so weary, that I could not hold the pen to finish the sentence. . . .

This account shows that the message obtained, the future model of so many others, highly significant in their cumulative effect, must be put to the credit of *dreams* and of the employment of *automatic writing*. Can it in addition help us to determine an important point, which hitherto has been left obscure: are there given places particularly suitable for the manifestation of this kind of sensibility? Yes, there must be observatories of the inner sky. I mean, naturally, observatories already existing in the outer world. This we may describe from the surrealist point of view as the *castle problem*: 'A considerable part of his youth', a biographer says of Lewis, 'was spent in a very old manor house.' . . .

SOURCE: extract from 'Limites non frontières du Surréalisme', *Nouvelle Revue Française*, 48, I (1937); translated as 'Limits not Frontiers of Surrealism', in Herbert Read (ed.), *Surrealism* (London, 1936), pp. 106–11.

## *Samuel Kliger*    The 'Goths' in England    (1945)

It is common knowledge that throughout the eighteenth-century discussions of aesthetic taste the term 'Gothic' was in prevailing usage a *Modewort* or cliché of very wide currency and that, as applied to literature and the fine arts, the same term was used with both eulogistic and disparaging connotations. What is not common knowledge, however, is that the real history of the Gothic begins not in the eighteenth but in the seventeenth century, not in aesthetic but in political discussion; stale platitudes drawn from the classic-romantic dichotomy made familiar by the simpler sort of literary textbooks simply do not suffice to explain the full phenomenon of the Gothic vogue.

Writing in 1648, Nicholas Bacon avers that English laws are largely Gothic in origin: 'Nor can any nation upon earth shew so much of the ancient Gothique law as this Island hath.' In 1672, Sir William Temple calls the English a Gothic people: 'The Saxons were one branch of those Gothic Nations, which, swarming from the Northern Hive, had, under the conduct of Odin, possessed themselves anciently of all those mighty tracts of Land that surround the Baltick Sea.' In the essay 'Of Poetry', Temple refers a second time to 'the ancient Western Goths, our Ancestors.'[1] In 1694, Robert Molesworth [writing on Denmark] argues that England's government in its origins was Gothic and Vandalic: 'The Ancient Form of Government here was the same which the Goths and Vandals established in most if not all Parts of Europe whither they carried their conquests, and which in England is retained to this day for the most part.' According to Swift, writing in 1719, parliaments are a peculiarly Gothic institution, implanted in England 'by the Saxon princes who first introduced them into this island from the same original with the other Gothic forms of government in most parts of Europe.'[2] John Oldmixon, writing in 1724, also assimilates Gothic to English history: 'No Nation has preserv'd their Gothic Constitution better than the English.' Bolingbroke, similarly, sees Goths on the horizon of England's foundation: 'Tho the Saxons submitted to the yoke of Rome, in matters of Religion, they were far from giving up the freedom of their Gothic institutions of government.' Perhaps most strikingly of all, Harrington referred in 1656 to those 'inundations of Huns, Goths, Vandals, Lombards, Saxons, which breaking the Roman Empire, deformed the whole world'; but, notwithstanding the subordination of the Goths in this passage, he nevertheless, in another context, establishes the principle of 'Gothic ballance' as universally embodied in the land reforms effected as a result of *all* the migrations of the Germanic conquerors of Rome.[3]

In view of this varied usage of the term 'Gothic', the primary problem in the investigation of the origins of the Gothic vogue in England must be semantic. Historically, the word 'Gothic' describes only a single Germanic tribe out of many who crossed the Danube in AD 376, and it is by no means so clear as the writers quoted would have their readers believe that the English are a Gothic folk and that 'Gothic' as a name is applicable universally to all the Germanic tribes. The questions, then, are two: 1. How did this extraordinary expansion in the usage of the word take place? 2. What hint does its semantic history in the seventeenth century supply toward establishing a relationship with the eighteenth-century usage in aesthetic discussions, which denoted, as is well known, almost everything primitive which was Germanic in origin and almost everything which was medieval?

A widespread interest in what might be called 'speculative geography' was responsible for one use of the term 'Gothic' to denote all the German tribesmen; political exigency, on the other hand, determined the second use to denote the English people and English government in particular and hence supplied the basis for such assertions as those made by Bacon, Temple, Molesworth and the others.

The speculative geographers were interested in tracing the origins of the people of the world to an ultimate beginning. The Bible, in part, supplied answers to their inquiries; either the Deluge and the subsequent spread of Noah's progeny over the earth or the Babel episode offered a starting-point. Trojan history and the flight of the descendants of Aeneas subsequent to Troy's fall appealed to other writers. But a growing awareness of the large admixture of fable with fact in these stories turned research into other channels. Earlier than the seventeeth century – in fact, in the sixteenth century – an important group of geographers in the Scandinavian countries, particularly a circle of scholars centered at Upsala University, led by a nationalistic interest in the origin of their countries, evolved a theory of a *vagina gentium*, a 'womb of nations', which, on the authority of Jordanes, sixth-century historian of the Goths, they placed in Scandinavia, or Scandza, as Jordanes called it.

The history of the Goths, their conquests, their gradual spread over Europe, which to the unbiased student of history is a sordid account of plunder and betrayal, was to Jordanes a magnificent record of Gothic greatness.[4] Jordanes's main purpose was to glorify the eastern Getes from whom he sprang so as to show them worthy of alliance with the Romans under the rule of Justinian. His first move, therefore, was to relate the Getes to the more splendid Gothic tribe by identifying the Getes as Goths. Following Orosius's statement, 'Getae illi qui et nunc Gothae', Jordanes says that 'the Getae we have proved in a previous passage to be Goths, on the testimony of Orosius Paulus'.[5] This identification of the Getes with the Goths, as we shall presently see, was one of the determining factors in the process which, in the view of seventeenth-century writers, domiciled the Goths in England; to modern scholarship the whole theory belongs to fabling and ethnic confusion.

The primary importance of Jordanes for the modern revival of interest in Gothic antiquity rests on the credence he gave to the theory that all the German tribesmen were generally 'Goths', all stemming from the group which, migrating from Scandza in the north, peopled Europe. In Jordanes's own words:

> The same mighty sea has also in its arctic region, that is, in the North, a great island named Scandza, from which my tale (by God's grace) shall take its beginning. For the race whose origin you ask to know burst forth like a swarm of bees from the midst of this island into the land of Europe. But how or in what wise we shall explain hereafter, if it be the Lord's will.

Returning later to the subject of Scandza, he explains, as he had promised, how 'from this island of Scandza, as from a hive of races or a womb of nations, the Goths are said to have come forth long ago under their king, Berig by name'. The Goths, consequently, are, in Jordanes's theory, the aboriginal folk who spread over Europe and Asia and, dividing into two large branches – the Visigoths and the Ostrogoths – were also known in later history by their various separate names, Huns, Vandals, Lombards, etc. Thus the application of the term 'Gothic' to denote all Germans seemed entirely appropriate to the Renaissance geographers. In order to account for the implantation of Gothic institutions and government in the north, these scholars argued, on the basis of Jordanes's account, that the Goths returned in a second great wave of migrations, repopulating Europe and the north. In a burst of nationalistic pride, Rudbeck, Joannes and Olaus Magnus and others declared that Sweden was Jordanes's Scandza or cradle of nations.[6]

In England the starting-point of speculation about Jordanes's Scandza theory was inevitably the barbarian *adventus* in England, traditionally dated in Bede and the *Anglo-Saxon Chronicle* in 449. From Bede downward, the Angles, Saxons and Jutes were recognized as a Germanic folk. Within Jordanes's agglutinative Gothic tradition it was possible to describe the barbarian invaders as 'Goths' and their institutions as 'Gothic'. Thus there came about the predominance of the term 'Gothic' to describe almost everything primitive which was Germanic and also to indicate almost everything which was medieval (since Roman culture was first recovered in the Renaissance, everything preceding the recovery was non-Roman). Norse poetry, ballads, cathedrals, native common law, parliaments (known as the modern form of the ancient Germanic tribal assemblies described in Tacitus's *Germania*) – all were 'Gothic' in this sense.

At the same time, a second set of circumstances was operating to bring the Goths into English history. The tradition formed in Bede and the *Anglo-Saxon Chronicle* with respect to the Germanic conquest of England was the determining factor which reinforced and was mutually reinforced by the influence previously described.

Bede [in his *Historia Ecclesiastica Gentis Anglorum*, i 15] says distinctly (departing from his source, Gildas, to supply his own knowledge) that England was colonized by three Germanic tribes – Angles, Saxons, Jutes . . .

[He speaks of the Jutes as settling in Kent and the Isle of Wight, and of a 'Jutish nation' controlling the area opposite Wight on the 'West Saxon' mainland – Ed.]

Bede remarks that the German forces were captained by Hengist and Horsa; . . . without stating explicitly that Hengist and Horsa were Jutes, he rather implies that they were. At any rate, what is certain is that, as the seventeenth century read Bede, the Jutes were given a predominance in the invasion and in the subsequent political history of England in such a way as to establish the term 'Gothic' to denote the origins of the English people and their culture.

The 'Alfredian' translation of Bede's Latin text supplies the key to this most important development in the Gothic cult in England. On strict linguistic grounds, the Latin of Bede's *Iutis, Iutarum* when

translated into any of the dialects of Old English cannot possibly
be identical with a *Gēat*-form:

| Northumbrian | :Īote, Īotan |
| Mercian | :Ēote, Ēota |
| Early West Saxon | :*Īete, *Īetan |
| Late West Saxon | :Ȳte, Ȳtan |

Nevertheless, within two centuries after Bede, the 'Alfredian' translation does supplant the normal Old English equivalent of Latin
*Iuti* with a *Gēat*-form:

Comon hi of þrim folcum ðam strangestan Germanie þæt [is] of
Seaxum and of Angle of Geatum. Of Geata fruman syndon Cantware and
Wehtsætan. ... [i 15][7]

It is interesting that in a second passage the same 'Alfredian'
translation inconsistently renders *Iutorum* as *Eota*: 'in þa neahmægðe,
seo is gecegd Eota lond in sume stowe seo is nemned Aet Stane'.[8]
Is the scribe correcting his error of i 15, or is he employing both
forms as equivalents? Modern scholarship can only conjecture, but
what is certain is that, as the seventeenth century read Bede, not
only were 'Jute', 'Eota', and 'Geata' taken as equivalents but 'Goth'
as well. It was this identification (or confusion, as modern scholarship
would call it) which established the term 'Gothic' to denote the
origin of the English in the Jutes. A double-text edition of Bede, in
both Old English and Latin, was made available to the seventeenth
century by Abraham Wheloc, probably the greatest Old English
scholar of his day.[9] Wheloc follows the inconsistency of the 'Alfredian'
scribe. The seventeenth-century evidence is clear beyond cavil, but
the mutual support of Bede and Jordanes must be recognized. The
point to observe is that the Latin authorities also confused Gete
with Goth. Jordanes, himself a Gete, tells the history of the Goths
but calls his history *Getica*. Orosius remarks: 'Getae illi, qui et nunc
Gothi', and this passage is cited, as will be shown, by Sheringham,
who identifies them further by adding 'Jute' to the equation, Goth
= Gete.

The first Old English dictionary, compiled by William Somner,
states the identification in the plainest terms. Under *Geatar*, we find
the simple definition: *Jutae, Getae, Gothes*.[10] The identification is,
apparently, well established; but for a fuller account which brings
out the role of the Jutes in the conquest, we must go back to Kentish
political history.

Written in 1570 but first published in 1576, Lambarde's *Perambulation of Kent* states:

The Saxons, Iutes, and Angles, were the Germaines that came over (as we have said) in aide of the Britons, of which the first sort inhabited Saxonie: the second were of Gotland, and therfore called Gutes, or Gottes. The third were of Angria, or Anglia, a countrie adioning to Saxony.[11]

Camden (1586) treats the three terms as equivalents but cautiously does not assume responsibility for the identification: 'The Jutae, who are by many supposed to be named the Gutae, Getae, or Goths (for a certain MS reads Geatun) are known to have inhabited the upper part of the Cimbrica Chersonesus, still called by the Danes Jutland.'[12] Speed's *Historie* (1611) in discussing 'The Saxons Original', identifies the Jutes as Goths: 'These Iutes, Gutes, Getes, or Gothes, or (as Beda calls them Vites) gave names to those parts of Britaine which they inhabited.'[13] Sir Henry Spelman's *Glossarium Archaeologicum* (1626) also makes the identification. Under *Guti*, the *Glossary* identifies Jute, Gete and Goth. The statement is headed by a distich:

Gothorum variam appelationem
Cantiarios et Vectuarios nostros ab iisdem emanesse.

The definition itself reads in part: '*Guti*. Idem sunt qui Gotti, Gothi, & Goti: quibusdem Jutae & Jutones: Romanis Getae, Anglo-Saxonibus geatas.'[14] The definition cites the law of Edward the Confessor which recognized the Jutes as possessing denizen rights in England . . . .

Robert Sheringham controverts Cluverius, who participated in the Continental discussion of Jordanes by pointing to Jordanes's error in confusing Getes with Goths. Sheringham asserts that they are the same. Chapter IX of his book *De Anglorum Gentis Origine Disceptatio* (1670) is entitled 'Getas Gothosque unam fuisse gentem ostenditur'. He cites Orosius as authority for the identification: 'Getae illi, qui et nunc Gothi' and brings together all the variant names of Goths: 'Populi isti in legibus Edwardi Confessoris Gutae, & Annalibus Petroburgensibus Geatuni, ab aliis Jotuni & Jetae, a Scriptoribus Danicis Jutae & Juitae nominantur; nam Getae & Giotae, & Jotae, & Gutae, & Geatuni, & Jotuni, & Jetae & Jutae & Juitae unum idemq; nomen est.'[15] Aylett Sammes (1676) asserts positively the identity of Jutes, Getes, and Goths: 'Getae, Jetae, Jutae, Juitae, Gutae, Giotae, Jotae, Geotuni, Jotuni, are all the same names, differing only in termination and writ after various orthography.'[16] Laurence Echard's *History of England* follows its predecessors in identifying the Jutes as Goths:

There came great Numbers of People [in response to Hengist's and Horsa's call for reinforcements] of three Nations of Germany, namely, Saxons, Jutes, and Angles, which with those who were here before made up a compleated Army. These two latter People are suppos'd to be Branches of the Saxons, both inhabiting the Cimbrian Chersonese, from whom we have still the names of Juteland and Anglen; the former being call'd Jutes from the Word Goth, and the latter Angles from the Word Angulus or Corner.[17]

The quaint etymologizing of the seventeenth-century writers, however, hardly tells the whole story. The tendency clearly was to establish the term 'Gothic' as descriptive of the Jutes, *one* of the three Germanic tribes which invaded England. But account must also be taken of a second tendency to connect Gothic history with a national apotheosis of democracy in England. In a word, the political institutions which were implanted in England by the 'Gothic' invaders in 449 were thought to be 'free' or 'democratic'; furthermore, the 'Gothic' free institutions were thought to have had a continuous development in England despite the successive Danish and Norman invasions. Bolingbroke, we recall, definitely characterizes Gothic government as free: 'Though the Saxon submitted to the yoke of Rome, in matters of religion, they were far from giving up the freedom of their Gothic institutions of government.'[18] In fact, it is precisely out of such a contrast between Gothic freedom and Roman tyranny that the eighteenth century derived the term 'Gothic' on one side of the antithesis to denote the 'enlightened', the 'liberal', and similar meanings. Thus a preference for the Gothic style in architecture might be characterized as a Whiggish taste; as we shall presently see, William Whitehead, the Tory, attacked the taste for the new-fangled style in architecture and suggested a parallel between the moral turpitude underlying Whig principles of popular government and the debased Gothic taste in the fine arts. Unless the term 'Gothic' had been established as a trope for the 'free' and the 'enlightened', Whitehead could not have been able to point out the parallel. In another passage Bolingbroke makes the contrast between Gothic freedom and Roman tyranny even more vivid.* Criticizing Bayle, who claimed that the barbarian invaders of Rome were destitute of government, Bolingbroke asks:

How barbarous were those nations, who broke the Roman empire,

---

* [Ed.] Albeit a Tory, Bolingbroke is taking here a 'Whig' historical view coincidentally favourable to his party-political critique of the 'tyranny' of Walpolean government, itself based on the identification of the Whig interest with the Hanoverian exclusion of the Stuart claim to the throne.

represented to be, the Goths, for example, or the Lombards? And yet when they came to settle in Italy, and to be better known, how much less barbarous did they appear, even than the Greeks and the Romans? what prudence in their government? what wisdom in their laws?[19]

[Nathaniel] Bacon, whom we have observed designing English law as 'Gothic' in origin, calls the barbarian founding fathers a free people: 'The people were a free people, governed by laws, and those made not after the manner of the Gauls (as Caesar noteth) by the great men, but by the people; and therefore called a free people, because they were a Law to themselves.' Temple describes Gothic government as 'invented by the sages of the Goths, as a government of freemen'. He continues, describing the English constitution as Gothic, pointing out that 'I need say nothing of this our constitution, which is so well known in our island', but he goes on, nevertheless, for a full page, in which he heaps praises on the constitution:

However it be, this constitution had been so celebrated, as framed with great wisdom and equity, and as the truest and justest temper that has ever been found out between dominion and liberty; . . . This seems to have been intended by these Gothic institutions, and by the election and representation of all that possessed lands.[20]

In view of these descriptions of 'Gothic' free institutions, it will become clearer why the Jutes, or Goths, as the seventeenth century denominated them, had a greater effect on English political history than the mere account in Bede would bear out. The role of the Jutes in English history, as the seventeeth century read it, was to create a psychological predisposition in Kentishmen (of Kent, the county where the Jutes planted their seat) ever since 449 to be fiercely liberty-loving. Furthermore, so determined were the Kentishmen to preserve their legacy of liberty from their Jutish forefathers that no conqueror, not even the Norman, could destroy their legacy. In other words, Jutish free institutions (their favorite example was *gavelkynd*) had a continuous history despite the various conquests. A curve of history bound England's future, as Temple, Bolingbroke and Bacon saw it, to England's Gothic past.

The tradition of Kentish valor and love of freedom was so proverbial that it appeared as a commonplace, apparently, in the drama of the period:
Middleton, *The Roaring Girl*

MOLL: The purity of your wench I would fain try – she seems like Kent unconquered.  [II i]

Peele, *Jests*

The fruitful country of Kent ... a climate as yet unconquered. ('How George read a play-book')

Middleton, *Hubburd*

My honest nest of ploughmen! The only Kings of Kent.

Shakespeare, *Henry VI, Part III.*

YORK: In them [Kentishmen] I trust; for they are soldiers, witty, courteous, liberal, full of spirit. [i ii]

Shakespeare, *Henry VI, Part II*

> Kent in the Commentaries Caesar writ,
> Is term'd the civil'st place of all this isle:
> Sweet is the country, because full of riches;
> The people liberal, valiant, active, wealthy. [iv viii]

Thomas Fuller's *Worthies* (1662) includes in its description of the county of Kent an account of the Kentishman's proverbial love of liberty:

> *Kent. Proverbs of Kent:* 'A man of Kent': This may relate either to the liberty or to the courage of this country man; liberty, the tenure of villanage (so frequent elsewhere) being here utterly unknown, and the bodies of all Kentish persons being of free condition. Insomuch that it is holden sufficient for one to avoid the objection of bondage, to say 'that his father was born in Kent!' Now seeing 'servi non sunt viri, quia non sui juris' (a bond-man is no man because not his own man); the Kentish for their freedom have achieved to themselves the name of men.[21]

The dramatic story of William's submission to the Kentish demands for liberty was repeated in many chronicles of the Norman Conquest and in the same context of discussion with a description of Kentish psychology or in a discussion of *gavelkynd*, a free institution as the seventeenth century saw it, planted by the Jutes on English soil in Kent and unbroken in its development. Richard Grafton in his *Chronicle* (1569), for example, tells the story well. Flushed with victory, William moved on toward Kent. Archbishop Stigand of Canterbury aroused the Kentishmen, 'and the whole people rather desyring to ende their haplesse lyfe, then to beare the unaccustomed yoke of servitude, with a comon consent decreed to meete Duke William, & to fight with him for their auncient lawes and libertyes.'

The Kentishmen ambushed William's forces at Swanscombe by the trick of moving boughs. William agreed to their demands, and the story concludes:

> . . . and so the auncient liberties of Englishmen, and their Countries lawes and customes, which before the comming of William Duke of Normandy, were equally held through the whole realm of England, now was onely in the Countie of Kent . . . and is unto this day inviolably observed and kept, that tenure which at this day is called Gavell kynde.[22]

This concluding passage is curious because it implies that *gavelkynd* is not strictly Jutish; it is a native, non-Roman, that is, a free, institution; but apparently it once extended over all England. The Jutish Kentishmen, then, were apparently the most determined and most successful of Englishmen in preserving their original liberties.

Camden, who, as we have seen, identified the Jutes as Goths, also tells the Swanscombe story to the effect that Kent is unconquerable: 'Their Country was never Conquer'd as was the rest of England but surrender'd itself to the Conqueror's power upon Articles of Agreement, by which it was provided that they should enjoy all their liberties and free customs which they then had, and us'd.'[23] John Rastell's law dictionary (1567) describes *gavelkynd* as a Kentish institution but as ultimately Germanic, in itself a clear indication of the overlapping or shift between the terms 'Germanic' and 'Gothic,' the particular denoting the general:

> Gavel-kinde est un Custome annexe & currant ove terres en Kent, appel Gavel kindeterres. Et est pense per les erudite en Antiquities, destre appel Gavel-kinde de *Give all kine*, cest adire, a touts les kinne en un line, accordant come est use enter les Germans, de que nous Anglais, & especialement de Kent, venomns.[24]

Drayton's *Polyolbion* indites a song to 'noble Kent':

> Who, when the Norman first with pride and honor sway'd,
> Threw'st off the servile yoke upon the English lay'd;
> And with a high resolve, most bravely didst restore
> That libertie so long enioyed by thee before.
> Not suffring forraine Lawes should thy free Customes bind,
> Then only showd'st thyselfe of th'auncient Saxon kinde,
> Of all the English shires be thou surnam'd the Free.   ['18th Song on Kent]

It should again be noted how the terms have shifted. Drayton describes Kentish freedom as of the 'auncient Saxon kinde', despite the clear statement in Bede that the Saxon seat in England was elsewhere than in Kent. But the poem stresses the essential ideas of freedom, its source in valorous character, and the continuity in

England (or at least in Kent) of free institutions despite despots. Thus the tradition of Kentish valor and love of freedom became synonymous with the Gothic tradition in England through the intermediary of the etymologizing which brought about the identification of Kentish Jutes and Goths; Nathaniel Bacon states the matter succinctly:

> Another custom of descent remaineth, and that is to the children indifferently, and it is called Gavel-kind or Gave-all kind. . . . It seemeth to be first the laws of the Goths or Jutes.[25]

The terms 'Germanic', 'Jutish' and 'Gothic' shift, but the meaning of 'Gothicism' remained fixed to describe (1) primitive Germanic culture and (2) the medieval in the sense of the stream of history outside of the classic Roman stream, which was recovered in the Renaissance. These two meanings remained appropriate and, in fact, were the reasons for the transfer to aesthetic discussion in the eighteenth century of the term 'Gothic' to describe cathedrals, ballads, Norse poetry, and even Arthurian legend; in the latter case, even if a dim awareness existed that its materials were Celtic and not Germanic, the Arthurian tales were still in these two meanings – (1) primitive, (2) medieval – in the sense that they were clearly segregated from the stream of classical civilization; as a result, Warton and Hurd wrote critiques of Spenser's 'Gothic' *Faerie queene*, whose Arthurian materials, according to modern knowledge, could not conceivably be Germanic.

Jordanes's Scandza-theory and the importance given to the Jutish colonization of Kent explain, consequently, the domiciliation of the 'Goths' in England. The actual facts of the historical Gothic conquest of mighty Rome and the Gothic *Völkerwanderungen* are never so strange as the peregrination which in the minds of the seventeenth-century English writers brought the 'Goths' to England's shores. Their veneration of the Goths of antiquity was profound precisely because they could appreciate Gothic history as a phase of England's cultural, political, and moral evolution.[26]

The aura of Gothic 'freedom' as enshrined in England's Gothic laws arises unmistakably from eighteenth-century discussions of the Gothic. Neo-classic standards of Greco-Roman symmetry and purity of style notwithstanding, not only was it possible to admire the Gothic style in architecture, but a very special taste of the 'constitutional sort' was required to appreciate it:

> Methinks there was something respectable in those old hospitable Gothick halls, hung round with the Helmets, Breast-Plates, and Swords of our

Ancestors; I entered them with a Constitutional Sort of Reverence and look'd upon those arms with Gratitude, as the Terror of former Ministers, and the Check of Kings. Nay, I even imagin'd that I here saw some of those good Swords, that had procur'd the Confirmation of Magna Charta, and humbled Spencers and Gavestons. And when I see these thrown by to make Way for tawdry Gilding and Carving, I can't help considering such an Alternation as ominous even to our Constitution. Our old Gothick Constitution had a noble Strength and Simplicity in it, which was well enough represented by the bold Arches, and the solid Pillars of the Edifices of those Days. And I have not observed that the modern Refinements in either have in the least added to their Strength and Solidity.[27]

This was the Whig taste in the fine arts; *per contra*, from the Tory point of view the Whig taste for the Gothic was as abominable as the Whig clamor for popular government was politically irresponsible. According to William Whitehead, Tory spokesman:

> From a thousand instances of our imitative inclinations I shall select one or two, which have been, and still are, notorious and general. A few years ago everthing was Gothic; our houses, our beds, our book-cases, and our couches, were all copied from some parts or other of our old cathedrals. The Grecian architecture, where, as Dryden says.
>
> > Firm Doric pillars formed the lower base
> > The gay Corinthian holds the higher space,
> > And all below is strength, and all above is Grace,
>
> that Architecture, which was taught by nature and polished by the graces, was totally neglected. Tricks and conceits got possession everywhere. . . . This, however odd it might seem, and however unworthy of the name of Taste, was cultivated, was admired and still has its professors in different parts of England. There is something, they say, in it congenial to our old Gothic constitution, which allows everyone the privilege of playing the fool, and of making himself ridiculous in whatever way he pleases.[28]

Thus the term 'Gothic' appears on both sides of an antithesis, e.g., it is used in praise or in censure. Party politics was intervening to condition the critic's taste in the arts. It is, however, a curious feature of the eighteenth-century discussion of the 'Gothic' that it is possible to find within the same context of discussion the 'Gothic' both condemned and praised. Thomson's *Liberty* affords an excellent example, one among many.

That its ideas were not lightly considered may be gathered from the fact that Thomson thought the poem *Liberty* (1735–36) to be his greatest work. In the poem the sight of Rome's ruins fills Thomson with a nostalgic longing for the grandeur of the past and he invokes the spirit of Liberty to give him an account of the causes underlying Rome's decline. Liberty delivers a lengthy monologue, explaining that Rome's liberty departed when the Empire suffered military reverses, but fundamentally the true cause was the spiritual corruption of the Romans which made them an easy prey to the invading barbarian armies. Liberty then traces its migrations, and in Book IV, the climax of the monologue, Liberty describes its happiest of all homes in England. It is understandable how Thomson could have persuaded himself that *Liberty* was his greatest poem. Thomson's imagination was afire with the spectacle of the valorous, liberty-loving men of the north because he could appreciate their history as a phase of England's moral and political growth. The poem could be considered great because its theme – the increment of history turned back to enrich the lives of England's humblest citizens – was great.

The Goths, in Thomson's account, are the original democrats of the world. Rome once had liberty but lost it in spiritual decay. Happily, the Gothic invaders brought about a rebirth of liberty, for,

> Long in the barbarous heart the buried seeds
> Of freedom lay, for many a wintry age.
>
> [*Liberty*, III 539–40]

Liberty fled to the north, as a stopover on its way to England:

> Thence, the loud Baltic passing, black with storm,
> To wintry Scandinavia's utmost bound –
> There I the manly race, the parent hive
> Of the mixed kingdoms, formed into a state
> More regularly free.  [IV 370–4][29]

The 'yellow-haired, blue-eyed Saxon' [IV 670] brought with him to England the gift of Gothic free institutions:

> untamed
> To the refining subleties of slaves,
> They brought a happy government along;
> Formed by that freedom which, with secret voice,
> Impartial nature teaches all her sons,
> And which of old through the whole Scythian mass
> I strong inspired.  [IV 680–95][30]

Another passage describes the Gothic gift of liberty to England:

> that general liberty
> . . .
> I through the northern nations wide diffused.
> Hence many a people, fierce with freedom, rushed
> From the rude iron regions of the north.  [IV 798, 801–3]

Inconsistently, however, the same poem condemns Gothic architecture. Describing Greece, Thomson says: 'In architecture too thy rank supreme!' Gothic architecture violates the rules:

> Such thy sure rules that Goths of every age,
> Who scorned their aid, have only loaded earth
> With laboured heavy monuments of shame.

[II 373, 377–9]

Inconsistency both in ideas and in the usage of terms is no rare phenomenon in intellectual history; it is true even of philosophers and, still more, of popular writers. The inconsistent use of the term 'Gothic' simultaneously in both eulogistic and dyslogistic senses is only one part of the history, still to be told in its entirety, of the curious entanglement of ideas about the 'Gothic' in the seventeenth and eighteenth centuries.

SOURCE: article, 'The "Goths" in England: An Introduction to the Gothic Vogue in Eighteenth-Century Aesthetic Discussion', *Modern Philology* (November 1945), pp 107–17.

NOTES

[Reorganised and renumbered from the original – Ed.]

1. 'Of Poetry', in J. E. Spingarn, *Critical Essays of the Seventeenth Century* (Oxford, 1909), III, p. 86.

2. Jonathan Swift, 'Abstract of the History of England' (1719); in Bohn (ed.), *Prose Works of Swift* (London, 1897–1908), x, p. 225.

3. Sir James Harrington, *The Commonwealth of Oceana* (1656); in J. Toland (ed.), *The Oceana and Other Essays* (London, 1737), p. 37. For discussion of the Gothic balance, see pp. 39 ff. Cf. also Liljegrens edn (Heidelberg, 1924), p. 42, and his notes, which do not, however, explain the Gothic balance.

4. Jordanes, *De Origina Actibusque Getarum* (AD 551), text edited by Mommsen in the *Monmenta Germaniae Historia* – 'Auctores Antiquissimi', v (Berlin, 1882). The English translation, *The Gothic History of Jordanes*, is by Charles C. Mierow (Princetown, N. J. 1915). Following Mommsen's usage, the text is referred to briefly as the *Getica*.

5. Ibid., ix 58; in Mierow, p. 66. There is no 'previous passage', but in v 40 (Mierow, p. 61) Jordanes uses 'Goth' interchangeably with 'Gete'. For Orosius, see his *History against the Pagans*, trans. with notes by I. W. Raymond (New York, 1936), i 16 – p. 64.

6. The Upsala circle of scholars is described by Thor J. Beck, *Northern Antiquities in French Learning and Literature, 1755–1855: A Study in Pre-Romantic Ideas* (New York, 1934). Ethel Seaton has described the trade channels and

diplomatic and scholarly correspondence, which extended knowledge of the Upsak discussions to England, in *Literary Relations of England and Scandinavia in the Seventeeth Century* (Oxford, 1935). F. E. Farley's *Scandinavian Influences in the English Romantic Movement* (Boston, Mass., 1903) is a valuable bibliographical guide.

7. *The Old English Bede*, Early English Texts Society, old series, xcv, p. 52.

8. Bedes original (*Historia Ecclesiastica* . . ., iv 16) reads: 'In proximam Iutorum prouinciam translati . . . in locum, qui vocatur Ad Lapidem.'

9. Published in Cambridge in 1644. This double-text edition of Bede included portions of the *Chronicle*. The monumental work of Abraham Wheloc and his associates has been reverently described by David C. Douglas, *English Scholars* (London, 1939).

10. William Somner, *Dictionarium Saxonico-Latino-Anglicum* (Oxford, 1649), *s.v.* 'Geatar'.

11. William Lambarde, *A Perambulation of Kent* (1576; reprinted London, 1826), p. *xiii*.

12. William Camden, *Britannia* (1586). Philemon Holland published an English translation in 1610; the text cited here is from Edmund Gibson's version (2nd edn, London, 1722), p. *civii*.

13. John Speed, *Historie of Great Britaine* (1611; 3rd edn, London, 1632), p. 199.

14. Either Jordanes or Orosius (or both) is in all probability the source of the statement 'Romanis Getae'.

15. Sheringham, op. cit. (Cambridge, 1670), p. 36.

16. Aylett Sammes, *Britannia Antiqua Illustrata* (London, 1676) p. 417.

17. Laurence Echard, *History of England*, 3rd edn. (London, 1720), p. 17.

18. Henry St John, Viscount Bolingbroke, 'Remarks on the History of England' (1730–31); included in *Works*, 5 vols (London, 1754), I, p. 315.

19. Bolingbroke, 'Fragments or Minutes of Essays', in *Works*, op. cit., v, p. 111.

20. William Temple, 'Introduction to the History of England (1672), in *Works* (London, 1720), II, p. 537.

21. Thomas Fuller, *The Worthies of England* (post-humous publication, 1662; reprinted in 3 vols, London, 1840), II, p. 122.

22. Richard Grafton, *Chronicle* (1569; reprinted in 2 vols, London, 1809), I, pp. 154–6.

23. Camden, op. cit. (1722 edn), p. 218.

24. John Rastell, *Les Termes de la Ley* (1567; reprinted London, 1721), *s.v.* 'Gavel-Kinde'.

25. Nicholas Bacon, *Historical and Political Discourse of the Laws and Government of England* (London, 1648), p. 96.

26. The specific equation Gothi = Getae is present in the writings of the Continental Gothicists – Rudbeck, Verelius, the Magnus brothers, Worm and Bartholin – since they all draw on the classical writers who first made the erroneous identification. Naturally, however, they do not add Jutae to the equation, since as Swedish patriots they were interested in tracing Jordanes's Scandza to Scandinavia. Consequently, they attach merely a

toponymic significance to the name Gothae by identifying them as residents originally of the island of Gotland (cf. Beck). On the other hand, George Hickes, England's greatest Anglo-Saxon scholar and author of the monumental *Theaurus*, does not appear in our account simply because he refrained from fanciful etymologizing. Richard Verstegen, whose book, *Restitution of Decayed Intelligence* (1605), imparted widely to English readers knowledge of northern antiquities, is interested in maintaining a Saxon origin of the English people, deriving then from the Asiatic Sacae. Verstegen dismissed the Jutish-Gothic identification (p. 125): 'Some will have them called Juites, and not Wites, and others will have them called Jeates, or rather Gothes, but these latter meane not to meddle, for that they over-shoote the marke too far, and so will never hit it.'

27.  Unsigned contribution in *Common Sense*, 150 (15 Dec. 1739); also reproduced in the *Gentleman's Magazine*, IX (1739), p. 641.

28.  William Whitehead, *World*, 12 (22 March 1753).

29.  Jordanes's 'officina-gentium', the cradle of nations of Scandza, is obviously the source of Thomson's reference to a 'parent hive'.

30.  Scythia, in Jordanes's account, was the Asiatic home of the Goths after they left Scandza. By bringing the Goths to Asia, Jordanes introduced an oriental element into the Gothic tradition. This fact was of considerable importance in the eighteenth-century discussion of the 'Gothic'. Because of the prevailing notion that people of the north were deficient in imagination –

> True wit in northern climes will not grow
> Except like orange trees 'tis housed from snow

– and, conversely, the Asiatics had lively imaginations, it was possible on the basis of Jordanes's description of the Gothic migration to Asia, followed by a second remigration to the north, to account, for example, for the diverse elements in the Ossianic poems. The setting of the poems (*le paysage ossianique*) was clearly northern, picturing gloomy skies, stormy scene etc.; but its expression was biblical in its intensity. Both of its elements were accounted for by the Scandza-theory; the tribal folk-memory preserved characteristics of both their northern and their Asiatic homes.

## *Leslie Fiedler*    'The Substitution of Terror for Love'   (1960)

. . . Just as the Richardsonian novel soon became the contested heritage of two conflicting parties, philistine and anti-bourgeois, so the gothic novel was fought for. But even as the sentimental novel seems essentially genteel, and is only exploited against the grain for anti-philistine ends, so the gothic romance is fundamentally anti-bourgeois and can only with difficulty be adapted to the needs of the sentimental middle classes. Nonetheless, it was a 'female scribbler', Ann Radcliffe, celebrated by her bourgeois admirers as the 'Shakespeare of the Romance writers', who first managed to make a success of gothic fiction. Her books, which appeared between 1789 and 1797, are all much alike, variations on the archetypal theme which she found in Walpole and made her own.

Through a dream landscape, usually called by the name of some actual Italian place, a girl flees in terror and alone amid crumbling castles, antique dungeons and ghosts who are never really ghosts. She nearly escapes her terrible persecutors, who seek her out of lust and greed, but is caught; escapes again and is caught; escapes once more and is caught (the middle of Mrs Radcliffe's books seem in their compulsive repetitiveness a self-duplicating nightmare from which it is impossible to wake); finally breaks free altogether and is married to the virtuous lover who has all along worked (and suffered equally with her) to save her. In the end, all the ghosts that have terrorized her are explained as wax-works or living men in disguise, the supernatural appearances that have made her enemies seem more than human revealed as mere mechanical devices, etc.

Mrs Radcliffe's most successful version of her single theme is found in *The Italian*, which appeared in 1797; and, indeed, it is Italy, the Mediterranean South with its overtones of papistry and lust, that is the true ghost, never quite exorcized by the fables of the more genteel gothicists. That symbolic Italy represents only one of their debts to Restoration drama, from whose stock of sensational effects the gothic novelists rifled whatever seemed to them of use. If the gothic romance seems in certain regards more theatrical than the sentimental novel, whose beginnings after all were model letter books for the uncultured, this is because many of its devices were to begin with stage properties, and Walpole himself the author of *The Mysterious Mother* as well as *The Castle of Otranto* – in Byron's words, of 'the last tragedy' as well as the 'first Romance' of European literature. The basic fable of the gothic novel, however, at least as defined by Mrs Radcliffe, seems actually derived from such books as *Clarissa*. Schedoni, the sinister male protagonist of *The Italian*, pursues his victim, just as Lovelace once pursued Clarissa; and at the center of the story appears that girl on the run, the Persecuted Maiden who, under one name or another, had been fleeing violation ever since Angelica took off at high speed through the pages of *Orlando Furioso*. There are, nonetheless, notable differences between the Richardsonian and Radcliffean treatments of the pursuit of the Maiden.

First of all, there is the matter of setting. The flight of Clarissa, however mythic in its implications, takes place in society – in a real, contemporaneous world of fashion, friends, parents, parties and business. The flight of the gothic heroine is out of the known world into a dark region of make-believe, past the magical landscapes of a legendary Italy, along the shadowy corridors of the haunted castle, which is to say, through a world of ancestral and infantile fears projected in dreams. The sentimental heroine confronts the dangers of the present, that is, of life as recorded in the newspaper; the gothic heroine evades the perils of the past, that is, of life as recorded in history.

There is, moreover, a question of tone and emphasis. However melodramatic or even tragic the implications of the sentimental fable, its intent is to reveal the power of light and redemption, to insist that virtue if not invariably successful is at least always triumphant. The gothic fable, on the other hand, though it may (in its more genteel examples) permit the happy ending, is committed to portraying the power of darkness. Perhaps another way to say this is that the fully developed gothic centers not in the heroine (the persecuted principle of salvation) but in the villain (the persecuting principle of damnation.) The villain-hero is, indeed, an invention of the gothic form, while his temptation and suffering, the beauty and terror of his bondage to evil are among its major themes.

Finally, there is the matter of the archetypal function of the basic gothic story; for such a function it must have or it could not have persisted as it did. The Clarissa-Lovelace archetype expresses, as we have seen, the sense of their own innocence possessed by the classes for whom the novel was produced. The myth of *The Castle of Otranto*, on the other hand, projects a sense of guilt and anxiety, the guilt of the Break-through, as dimly perceived by the bourgeoisie – and especially by the intellectuals who were its sons. 'What is this secret sin; this untold tale, that art cannot extract, nor penance cleanse?' asks the question quoted from Walpole's *The Mysterious Mother* by Mrs Radcliffe in *The Italian*. The answer in the original play is incest – incest of brother and sister-daughter bred out of an original incest of mother and son – the breach of the primal taboo and the offence against the father! In more general terms, the guilt which underlies the gothic and motivates its plots is the guilt of the revolutionary haunted by the (paternal) past which he has been striving to destroy; and the fear that possesses the gothic and motivates its tone is the fear that in destroying the old ego-ideals of Church and State, the West has opened a way for the inruption of darkness: for insanity and the disintegration of the self. Through the pages of the gothic romance, the soul of Europe flees its own darker impulses.

These deeper implications are barely perceptible in the gently spooky fiction of Mrs Radcliffe, in which terror is allayed by the final pages, all inruptions of the irrational rationally explained away. Indeed, so polite does horror become in her novels, that it seems to a modern palate insipid. But in the single volume of another gothic fictionist, the Walpolean fable takes on a significance that evaded Mrs Radcliffe's total body of work; and all its absurdity, its outrageous violence is released. That writer is the *enfant terrible* Matthew Gregory Lewis, who at the age of twenty wrote in three weeks the four hundred pages of *The Monk*, by which name he insisted on being called forever after ('a two-fold barbarity, Madam'). It is a fantastic, amusing, horrifying book, this shrill *tour de force* produced at top speed by an English boy to support his deserted mother. Actually composed in Weimar, it benefits perhaps by approaching the tradition of *The Castle of Otranto* as developed in German horror fiction rather than in the novels of English gentlewomen.

At any rate, the appearance of *The Monk* in 1796 made its author a showpiece at all the literary parties of that London season, though it also shocked the official guardians of morality so deeply that for perhaps a hundred years it remained bootleg reading. 'A romance, which if a parent saw it in the hands of a son or daughter, he might reasonably turn pale', one of its shocked readers called it; 'a poison for youth and a provocative for the debauchés'. One considerate bookseller was reported to have underlined all 'the worst parts for a sixteen year old subscriber, so that she might skip them!' And it was, perhaps, in a similarly marked copy that Byron browsed among its more scandalous passages, emerging with the horrified (and somewhat improbable) comment that they represented the 'philtered ideas of a jaded voluptuary'. The book seems inoffensive enough nowadays, though occasionally melodramatic to the point of howling absurdity; but it was obviously intended to offend and disturb the right-minded bourgeoisie, which in its own day rose satisfactorily to the bait. . . .

By the time Lewis is through with [his] sadist farrago, the major symbols of the gothic have been established, and the major meanings of the form made clear. In general, those symbols and meanings depend on an awareness of the spiritual isolation of the individual in a society where all communal systems of value have collapsed or have been turned into meaningless clichés. There is a basic ambivalence in the attitude of the gothic writers to the alienation which they perceive. On the one hand, their fiction projects a fear of the solitude which is the price of freedom; and on the other hand, an almost hysterical attack on all institutions which might inhibit that freedom or mitigate the solitude it breeds. Chief of the gothic symbols is, of course, the Maiden in flight – understood in the spirit of *The Monk* as representing the uprooted soul of the artist, the spirit of the man who has lost his moral home. Not the violation or death which sets such a flight in motion, but the flight itself figures forth the essential meaning of the anti-bourgeois gothic, for which the girl on the run and her pursuer become only alternate versions of the same plight. Neither can come to rest before the other – for each is the projection of his opposite – *anima* and *animus*, actors in a drama which depends on both for its significance. Reinforcing the meaning of the haunted victim and the haunted persecutor (each the other's obsession) is the haunted countryside, and especially the haunted castle or abbey which rises in its midst, and in whose dark passages and cavernous apartments the chase reaches its climax. Symbols of authority, secular or ecclesiastic, in ruin – memorials to a decaying past – such crumbling edifices project the world of collapsed ego-ideals through which eighteenth-century man was groping his proud and terrified way. If he permitted himself a certain relish in the contemplation of those ruins, this was because they were safely cast down, and he could indulge in nostalgia without risk. If he was terrified of them, dreamed supernatural enemies lurking in their shadows, it was because he suspected that the past, even dead, *especially* dead, could continue to work harm. Even as late as Henry James, an American writer deeply influenced by gothic modes was able to imagine the *malaria*, the miasma which arises from decaying ruins, striking down Daisy Miller as she romantically stands at midnight in the Coliseum. . . .

The primary meaning of the gothic romance, then, lies in its substitution of terror for love as a central theme of fiction. The titillation of sex denied, it offers its readers a vicarious participation in a flirtation with death – approach and retreat, approach and retreat, the fatal orgasm eternally mounting and eternally checked. More than that, however, the gothic is the product of an implicit aesthetic that replaces the classic concept of nothing-in-excess with the revolutionary doctrine that nothing succeeds like excess. Aristotle's guides for achieving the tragic without falling into 'the abominable' are stood on their heads, 'the abominable' itself being made the touchstone of effective art. Dedicated to producing nausea, to transcending the limits of taste and endurance, the gothic novelist is driven to seek more and more atrocious crimes to satisfy the hunger for 'too-much' on which he trades.

It is not enough that his protagonist commit rape; he must commit it upon his mother or sister; and if he himself is a cleric, pledged to celibacy, his victim a nun, dedicated to God, all the better! Similarly, if he commits murder, it must be his father who is his victim; and the crime must take place in darkness, among the decaying bodies of his ancestors, on hallowed ground. It is as if such romances were pursuing some ideal of absolute atrocity which they cannot quite flog their reluctant imaginations into conceiving. For the abominable, to be truly effective, must remain literally unspeakable; and where – as in the case of *The Monk* – it has adapted itself to the censor and the mode, become respectable and chic, it ends by seeming ridiculous. The abominable as an absolute leads to either sickness or silliness, betraying the man who is obsessed by the horror he evokes or the one who plays at it merely to shock and succeed.

Some would say, indeed, that the whole tradition of the gothic is a pathological symptom rather than a proper literary movement, a reversion to the childish game of scaring oneself in the dark, or a plunge into sadist fantasy, masturbatory horror. For Wordsworth, for instance, heir of the genteel sentimentality of the eighteenth century, gothic sensationalism seemed merely a response (compounding the ill to which it responded) to the decay of sensibility in an industrialized and brutalized world – in which men had grown so callous that only shock treatments of increasing intensity could move them to react. Yet there is more than this even to *The Monk*. If Lewis writes in one sense what he must and in another what he hopes will sell, he also writes for a more conscious and respectable end: to shake the philistines out of their self-satisfied torpor. *Épater la bourgeoisie*: this is the secret slogan of the tale of terror; and it remains into our own time a not-so-secret slogan of much highbrow literature, particularly of such spectacular bourgeois-baiting movements as Dada, Surrealism and Pop Art. . . .

Beside the good old word 'hell', however, is placed the newer word 'history', equally important to an understanding of the form; for behind the gothic lies a theory of history, a particular sense of the past. The tale of terror is a kind of historical novel which existed before the historical novel (the invention of Walter Scott) came into being. The Richardsonian novel of contemporary life had discovered the present for fiction, made time a medium in which characters moved. The social meanings of the Lovelace-Clarissa story assume a clear-cut conception of a differing Then and Now. Richardson claimed for his own province the Now, in which a servant could marry her employer's son; but by implication he has already defined a Then, in which that son would have taken such a girl whenever he desired her and on whatever terms his own whim prompted. This Then, the gothic novel claimed for its province, making of the past an essential subject of fiction for the first time. Shakespeare had, to be sure, written historical plays; but how ahistorical they, in fact, were: assuming a past indistinguishable from the present in all things (in costume, in speech, in moral attitudes) except for certain recorded events which happened to have happened then instead of now.

The gothic felt for the first time the *pastness* of the past; and though it did not, like the later novels of Manzoni and Scott, attempt with scholarly accuracy to document that difference, it tried to give some sense of it: the sense of something lapsed or outlived or irremediably changed. It is no accident that Horace Walpole was an 'antiquary', a researcher into ancient modes and styles, who lived in a reconstructed 'gothic' villa. The very adjective, which gave to both the home he designed and the fictional tradition he founded a name, implies a certain attitude toward the past. Originally 'gothic' was a thoroughly pejorative word, applied not only to whatever belonged in fact to rude 'medieval' times, i.e., any period before the sixteenth century, but also to any surviving mode of speech or behaviour considered unworthy of enlightened modernity. Duelling, for instance, is referred to by one eighteenth-century critic as a 'gothic custom', while another makes a fictional character condemn 'husband' as a 'gothic word'. Rousseau, on the other hand, modestly describes his own novel, *La Nouvelle Héloïse*, as 'gothic', meaning presumably that it possesses a certain antique simplicity and an unsophisticated style.

By and large, however, the writers of gothic novels looked on the 'gothic' times with which they dealt (and by which, despite themselves, they were fascinated) as corrupt and detestable. Their vision of that past was bitterly critical, and they evoked the olden days not to sentimentalize but to condemn them. Most gothicists were not only avant-garde in their literary aspirations, but radical in their politics; they were, that is to say, anti-aristocratic, anti-Catholic, anti-nostalgic. They liked to think that if their work abounded in ghosts, omens, portents and signs, this was not because they themselves were superstitious, but because they were engaged in exposing 'that superstition which debilitates the mind, that ignorance which propagates error, and that dread of invisible agency which makes inquiry criminal'. Beneath the spectacular events of the tale of terror, the melodramatic psychology and theatrical horror, rings the cry. '*Écrasez l'infâme!*' The spirit of Voltaire broods over the haunted castle; and ghosts squeak eerily that they do not exist.

Yet the authors of gothic novels, followers of Voltaire though they were and exponents of the Enlightenment, were plagued by a hunger for the inexplicable, a need of the marvellous which they could neither confess nor escape. At a moment when everywhere rationalism had triumphed in theory and madness reigned in fact, they were especially baffled; and they ended by compounding the hypocrisy of their times with a corresponding hypocrisy of their own. In the name of optimism, they exploited melancholy; in the name of light, they paid tribute to darkness; in the name of history, they yielded themselves up to fancy.

Their attitude toward Catholicism is a case in point. Like most other classic forms of the novel, the gothic romance is Protestant in its ethos; indeed, it is the most blatantly anti-Catholic of all, projecting in its fables a consistent image of the Church as the Enemy; we have already noticed how standard and expected were the character of the depraved monk, the suborned Inquisitor, the malicious abbess. Yet the gothic imagination feeds on what its principles abhor, the ritual and glitter, the politics and pageantry of the Roman Church. The ideal of celibacy and its abuses particularly intrigue the more prurient gothic fictionists, as do the mysteries of the confessional, where for ages – into the ear of God knows what lustful priest – was whispered 'this secret sin, this untold tale', which they had made subject of their art. Sixty years after *The Monk*, Nathaniel Hawthorne was still playing fast and loose with Catholicism, sending his Puritan protagonists into the very heart of Saint Peter's, into the confessional booth itself – only to withdraw them at the last possible moment, resolutely anti-Papist after all. The conversion of Hawthorne's own daughter to Catholicism and her entry into a convent mark a final consummation (achieved by history in despite of art) of the gothicists' long, absurd flirtation with the Church they presumably abhorred.

The contradictions between the liberal uses and demonic implications, the enlightened principles and reactionary nostalgia of the tale of terror by no means exhaust the ambiguities at its heart. A further conflict arises out of an attempt to solve the earlier ones by passing off the machinery of horror essential to the form as mere 'play', 'good theatre', which demands not credence but the simplest suspension of adult disbelief. Far from satisfying the gothic writers, this device leaves them with the annoying sense that the kind of novel they produce presumably for high-minded ends is really no more than a lowbrow amusement, a literary vice (like the detective story and science fiction which are its heirs). Why, they are driven to ask themselves, do they indulge in the child's game of make-believe unless to titillate their own jaded sensations and those of their readers? But to *play* with horror, no matter what one's declared intent, is to pander to the lowest, darkest impulses of the mind.

Certain devices are built into the gothic from the start to help resolve its contradictions. There is, for instance, the convention of treating magic as science and thus reclaiming it for respectability in the Age of Reason; the magician Faust in his black robes becomes the scientist in his white coat (Dr Frankenstein is a transitional figure on the way), and no good reader of newspapers cavils at him as improbable or outmoded. At first the sciences favored by the gothic romancers are those of the gothic past, astrology and alchemy; and such ancient symbolical dreams as the universal solvent and the elixir of life (in the works of Hawthorne, for instance, and those of E. T. A. Hoffmann) possess the imagination. Later, these are replaced or reinforced by the bourgeois pseudo-sciences of mesmerism, phrenology, ventrilocution – in the novels of Charles Brockden Brown and, once more, those of Hawthorne [in America]; and finally, in our own age, they are largely abandoned for popularized versions of modern physics. . . .

. . . The device of the explained supernatural is as useful for the reader as for the writer, enabling him to get his thrills and keep his self-respect; but it does more than that. It embodies in the very technique of fiction a view of the world which insists that though fear is real, its causes are delusive; that daylight reveals to us the essential goodness of a universe to which the shadows of night had given a false aspect of evil.

Like other self-protective devices of the gothic, the explained supernatural poses new problems as it solves old ones, leaving some readers at least with the sense of having been shamefully hoaxed, betrayed into responding with pity and terror to a mere bag of tricks. What is the point of horror that is not in some sense real? Only Hawthorne, of all writers who insist on casting a new light in their final pages on what they have all along presented in quite another, manages to leave us satisfied and unashamed; for he developed in his novels and tales a method of 'alternative explanations' that permits us at the end of an action to throw back over it the interpretation that suits our temperament best. He gives us the choice of many readings: magical, mechanical, psychological; and even allows us not to make a choice at all, but like him to endure them all, to emerge from his story not with some assured insight into the causes of human depravity but only with a confirmed sense of the ambiguity of life.

Implicit in the gothic novel from the beginning is a final way of redeeming it that is precisely opposite in its implications to the device of the explained supernatural, a way of proving not that its terror is less true than it seems but more true. There *is* a place in men's lives where pictures do in fact bleed, ghosts gibber and shriek, maidens run forever through mysterious landscapes from nameless foes; that place is, of course, the world of dreams and of the repressed guilts and fears that motivate them. This world the dogmatic optimism and shallow psychology of the Age of Reason had denied; and yet this world it is the final, perhaps the essential, purpose of the gothic romance to assert. . . .

SOURCE: extracts from chapter, 'Charles Brockden Brown and the Invention of the American Gothic', in *Love and Death in the American Novel* (New York, 1960; revised edn 1967), pp. 127–30, 131, 134–5, 136–9, 139–40 (excerpted from 1967 version).

## *Robert Kiely*    'Lewis's *The Monk*: A Brutal Revolt against the Limits of Human Nature'    (1973)

. . . The moral, it would seem, is obvious – so much so that it hardly carries any force at all when Lewis states it. Ambrosio's sin is pride which eventually leads him to the excesses of lust and wrath. A moral (and sensible) man would be humbler, avoid extremes in all things, and distrust the snares of art. Yet, *The Monk* is not finally a drama of moral alternatives. Indeed, like a great many later romantic heroes, Ambrosio is a being for whom reform and salvation are unthinkable. He has most of the attributes of a conventional hero – beauty, strength, intelligence – but they are inhibited by the circumstances of his life, by the monastery cell, the forbidden bedchamber, the magic circle. What assumes central importance in the novel is the spectacle of energy imprisoned, given hope of escape, and then disappointed. In Ambrosio's case, moral culpability is admitted, but the fact that nearly all the characters in the novel – innocent and guilty alike – suffer the same fate casts some doubt on its relevance.

All who reach out for a life beyond their own – even by means of unselfish love – are greeted by a nightmare and thrust into

confinement, darker and more isolated than the prison they had
originally sought to escape. Thus, in the subplot of Raymond and
Agnes, though the young lovers are guilty of no crime other than
their desire to be together, they encounter supernatural as well as
mudane obstacles of the most gruesome sort. When Raymond
arranges to meet his mistress at midnight, he finds himself embracing
a vision of death: 'I beheld before me an animated corse. Her
countenance was long and haggard; her cheeks and lips were
bloodless; the paleness of death was spread over her features . . .
My blood was frozen in my veins . . . My nerves were bound up in
impotence, and I remained in the same attitude inanimate as a
statue.' An elaborate explanation about the origins of this ghost is
given, but it adds almost nothing to the psychological pattern of the
narrative. What is more to the point is that the beautiful Agnes is
very nearly turned into a living corpse because of her attempt to
run off with her lover. Her family consigns her to a convent where,
when it is discovered that she is pregnant, she is locked in the vault
under the statue of St Clare. There her baby dies and there she is
eventually found by her brother, 'a creature stretched upon a bed
of straw, so wretched, so emaciated, so pale, that he doubted to
think her a woman'. Lewis permits Agnes to recover and marry
Raymond in the end, but not without repeating in a minor key the
basic theme found in the narrative of Ambrosio.

Whereas Raymond and Agnes are primarily victims of circumstance, Ambrosio is both victim and victimizer. He embraces a body
which becomes a corpse on his first visit to the lovely Antonia's
bedchamber, though this is no spectre but Elvira, the girl's mother,
whom he murders when she discovers him about to rape her
daughter. Ambrosio arrives in the room imagining Antonia's
youthful beauty and suddenly, as in a nightmare, finds himself
wrestling with an aged demon: 'He dragged her towards the bed
. . . and pressing his knees upon her stomach . . . witnessed without
mercy the convulsive trembling of her limbs beneath him . . . Her
face was covered with a frightful blackness . . . her hands were stiff
and frozen.' Ambrosio's reaction is much like Raymond's. He is not
sufficiently sadistic to be stimulated by his crime, but, on the
contrary, suffers from it almost as though he had been his own
victim: 'He staggered to a chair, and sank into it almost as lifeless
as the unfortunate who lay extended at his feet . . . He had no desire
to profit by the execution of his crime. Antonia now appeared to
him as an object of disgust.'

Two patterns are woven through the different accounts of these
strange embraces. One is the reversal of the medieval tale of the

'loathly lady' in which the courage and fidelity of a young knight married to an old hag are rewarded when the bride turns into a beautiful damsel. True beauty is seen not only as the prize of virtue but as a durable quality which may be veiled but not defeated by ugliness. The union of the real and the ideal is possible. In *The Monk*, beauty, physical and spiritual, is a deception, an apparition as unattainable and incredible as a stock Gothic ghost. The only reality outside the self is seen in the second pattern, in which the sexual drive ends in an act of murder. Sex, no more than religion, can provide the self with a route to transcendence. The reality beyond the sex act, like that beneath the church floor, is a tomb.

All of the encounters with female corpses are, in addition to their intrinsic unpleasantness, stylistically striking. Lewis's touch is nearly always lighter and surer than Mrs Radcliffe's, but for the most part he shows a similar reliance on Latinate abstractions, circumlocutions, euphemism, and a connotative rather than a denotative vocabulary. Nearly every page contains such sentences as, 'Her distress was beyond the power of description' or 'Excessive was the universal grief at hearing this decision'. Yet in the scenes where a desirable sexual partner is replaced by a dead body, irony and euphemism vanish, and a sudden specificity of language brings the scene into shocking focus. The blackened face of Antonia's mother has a substantiality lacking in the 'ivory' arms, the 'coral' lips, the 'inexpressibly sweet' smiles of the living heroines, and in the 'bloodless cheeks' of ghosts.

It is Ambrosio and his surrogate Raymond in the subplot who give credence to what they see. The reaction to the vision of death is a trance in which the human witness becomes like the thing he sees. But Lewis takes his protagonist beyond the ephemeral confusion of Walpole's heroes of the hysterical paralysis of Mrs Radcliffe's heroines. True, Ambrosio is a confused hero, subject to contradictory impulses, desirous of obtaining incompatible goals, but his solution to complexity is violence. Strangely enough, despite his reputed intelligence and emotional strength, Ambrosio is a character who seems to have almost no capacity to assimilate change. Every new and unexpected idea or event makes him flutter and reel. It is perhaps natural enough that his original discovery that his attentive novice is a beautiful woman should bring on the confusion of 'a thousand opposing sentiments', but this is by no means the last of Ambrosio's nervous palpitations. At Matilda's first advances, he is 'confused, embarrassed, and fascinated'; at first sight of Antonia, 'a thousand new emotions' sprang into his bosom 'and he trembled to examine into the cause which gave them birth'; when unable to seduce Antonia in the conventional ways, he is filled with shame and 'the most horrible confusion'; when Matilda promises to help him by means of black magic, 'his hand trembles as she leads him toward the vaults'; and, finally, when apprehended by Elvira by the side of her daughter's bed, he is struck 'by terror, confusion, and disappointment'.

Still, despite certain resemblances in sensibility, Ambrosio is no Emily St Aubert, nor is he merely the buffoon seducer caught without his trousers (except for a brief moment when he stands 'pale and confused, the baffled culprit' trembling before his victim's mother). Fearing humiliation and scandal, Ambrosio breaks out of both roles, adopts 'a resolution equally desperate and savage', and 'turning around suddenly, he grasp(s) Elvira's throat'. Lewis's language as well as Ambrosio's behavior is suddenly simplified. The author cannot release his protagonist from all convention; murder, under such circumstances, is not unprecedented in history and literature. But he can release him from impotence, confusion, and triviality. He can keep him from being altogether ridiculous by making him momentarily and believably monstrous. The impostor monk makes life conform to his will by destroying it.

In a Gothic distortion of the tomb scene in *Romeo and Juliet*, the drugged Antonia is presumed dead and brought to rest near the remains of her murdered mother in the vaults under the convent of St Clare. There Ambrosio pursues her, wakens, rapes and kills her in an insane frenzy which repeats not only the violence of his previous murder but of another which is occurring simultaneously in the streets of Madrid. Stopped while leading a religious procession, the abbess of St Clare is accused of murdering Agnes and is torn to pieces by a furious mob. Lewis, who often finds more commonplace events 'indescribable', once again chooses his words with apparent ease:

They tore her one from another, and each new tormentor was more savage than the former. They stifled with howls and execrations her shrill cries for mercy, and dragged her through the streets, spurning her, trampling her, and treating her with every species of cruelty which hate or vindictive fury could invent. At length a flint, aimed by some well-directing hand, struck her full upon the temple. She sank upon the ground bathed in blood, and in a few minutes terminated her miserable existence. Yet though she no longer felt their insults, the rioters still exercised their impotent rage upon her lifeless body. They beat it, trod upon it, and ill used it, till it became no more than a mass of flesh, unsightly, shapeless, and disgusting.

In a novel in which so much is theatrical and ornamentally grotesque, these scenes of violence possess an energy and realism for which the reader is not fully prepared. The abbess is without question presented as a wicked woman, but, like Elvira in the role of interfering parent, she is an uninteresting caricature *except* at the moment of her terrifying death when she becomes for a brief time the vivid image of a tormented human being. It is almost as though Lewis had played an unfair trick on the reader by endowing his Gothic stereotypes with life at unexpected and fatal moments.

When we speak of 'realism' or truth to life in a novel like *The Monk*, it is not a Defoe-like accumulation of detail that is meant, but a contrast between static and stylistically formal scenes and short episodes of concrete action, presented in relatively straightforward language. The murder of Elvira follows the long, elaborate, and ritualistic conjuring scene in the sepulcher; the mutilation of the abbess interrupts a slow, stately procession described with almost Spenserian solemnity. Lewis displays a detachment and control over his mode, first, by means of the amusing ironical aside and, increasingly and more effectively, by means of the pathetic aside, the quick glimpse at pain as inflicted and felt. From one point of view, conventional Gothic cruelty is too preposterously exaggerated, and therefore laughable. From the other, it does not go nearly far enough; it is only a weak charade when compared with human brutality and suffering as they really are.

What seems to have held Lewis's imagination more than institutional despotism was the more intimate and essentially psychological subjugation of one individual by another. Unlike Walpole's caricatures, his characters do relate to one another, but primarily as slaves to masters or victims to tormentors. The conventional pairs of lovers, Raymond and Agnes, Lorenzo and Antonia, are kept apart during most of the narrative, whereas emphasis is given to Ambrosio's contact with Matilda, Elvira, and Antonia, all of whom he presumes to overpower while, in another sense, he is himself being overpowered.

It is precisely this question of power – the conditions under which it increases and those under which it is transferred from one individual to another – which seems to have fascinated Lewis and led him to the rigidities and excesses of Gothic fiction. He appears to have recognized that the one could not exist without the other; that excess of any kind could not tolerate contradiction or complexity, and that excess of individual freedom thrives on the potential subjugation of everything but the self. The combination of the extreme gesture of release from convention, on the one hand, and the imposition of an absurdly rigid reductionism on the other, defines a human predicament as well as a peculiar stage in the history of the novel.

It is often said that in Gothic fiction there are either no believable characters at all or else there is one so monstrously absorbent as to make the form seem a kind of obscene exhibitionism. There is nothing between the cipher and the creature of gargantuan potency in an empty world. If this is not true of *The Monk* from the beginning, it becomes true in time. As Ambrosio casts off old roles, he deserts simplicity, bypasses complexity, and finds contradiction and confusion the corollaries of uninhibited power. The history of his personality is not one of growth, but one of painful constriction alternating with disastrous expansion.

Turning for the last time to the scene in the monastery garden where the young novice reveals he is a woman, we can learn something of Lewis's attitude toward personality. When Walpole engineers an unmasking, the onlookers gape and bless themselves and that is the end of it. But Lewis's Gothic disguises tend to have consequences. The sudden external change of sex signals the beginning not only of a breakdown in the conventional distinction between the strong and aggressive male and the weak and submissive female but a generalized blurring of gender and temperament. If Rosario begins as the too delicate and graceful novice, the transformation into Matilda does not bring about a more stable gender:

> But a few days had passed, since she appeared the mildest and softest of her sex, devoted to [Ambrosio's] will, and looking up to him as a superior being. Now she assumed a sort of courage and manliness in her manners and discourse . . . She spoke no longer to insinuate, but command.

Simultaneously, Ambrosio, for a while, loses his masculine assertiveness along with his chastity and self-command. What is important is not that this is some sort of transvestite game, but that it shows human personality as essentially unstable, inconsistent, capable of so much that it is often productive of nothing. Lewis does not treat Ambrosio as Sade might have done – as a simple lecher in monkish habit. In attempting to escape one confining role, Ambrosio discovers his 'true' self is some combination of lecher-virgin-saint-murderer-man-woman-rapist-victim – with no stress and no stability in any one part.

The nightmare of this novel is the spectacle of a creature whose nature dilutes and immobilizes itself. Where is a hero, a man in control of his own power, in a world of mannish women, effeminate men, servile masters, commanding slaves, where the dead often

seem more animated than the impotent, rigid, terrified living? How
does one wake up from the double nightmare of a realm of excessive
and inhibiting classification which gives way to one of vanishing
distinctions? Though Lewis's symbolism is largely sexual and
sepulchral, the questions have obvious political, social, philosophical,
and aesthetic applicability.

And so too do the outbursts of physical violence. For Ambrosio,
having at last had enough of half-measures, can, when everything
else fails, summon up the power to destroy. His murder of Elvira, if
not the explicit cause of all the other destruction in the novel, is
nonetheless quickly followed by the mutilation of the abbess, the
burning of the convent, the rape and murder of Antonia, and finally
his own death, which seems to put the order of Genesis itself into
reverse. Having been seized by the devil and thrown from a 'dreadful
height', he 'rolled from precipice to precipice, till, bruised and
mangled, he rested on the river's banks . . .'

Six miserable days did the villain languish. On the seventh a violent storm
arose: the winds in fury rent up rocks and forests: the sky was now black
with clouds, now sheeted with fire: the rain fell in torrents; it swelled the
stream; the waves overflowed their banks; they reached the spot where
Ambrosio lay, and, when they abated, carried with them into the river the
corse of the despairing monk.

In no other scene is Lewis's language so charged, his rhythm so
insistent, his feelings so obviously engaged, as in this last, where he
smashes his own creation. Righteous anger against the sinning
monk? Perhaps, in some measure, but, more fundamentally, he
seems to be taking over the work of his own protagonist by revealing
his greatest strength in a brutal revolt against the limits of human
nature and the myth of an orderly universe. Lewis's final vision is
of a chaos which neither man nor art has the capacity to control or
avoid. Indeed, uncontrollable energy would seem to be the only
energy there is in the world of *The Monk*. The artist, like the monk
who seeks liberation from lifeless conventions, is apt to find himself
unexpectedly on the side of the flood.

Source: sections 5 and 6 of chapter on *The Monk*, in *The Romantic Novel in England* (Cambridge, Mass., 1973), p. 111–17.

Coral Ann Howells      'Fictional Technique in
Radcliffe's *Udolpho*'    (1978)

... What Mrs Radcliffe aimed to provide was a stimulus to
her reader's imagination freed from the restrictiveness of rational
definition – a 'negative' as she called it in her essay on the
Supernatural in Poetry: 'Obscurity, or indistinctness, is only a
negative; which leaves the imagination free to act upon the few hints
that truth reveals to it.' Her fictional technique is very close to the
'judicious obscurity' in literature which Edmund Burke praised so
highly in his treatise on the Sublime. [See Part One above – Ed.] It
has been remarked that Mrs Radcliffe is similar to Burke in her
treatment of sublimity and doubtless she was working within a
framework of contemporary aesthetic assumptions. I think their
affinity rests on something more radical, however, and that is their
shared recognition of the fundamental importance of imagination,
those powers which, as Burke says, 'captivate the soul before the
understanding is really able either to join with them or oppose
them'. Burke analysed sublimity in his treatise and Mrs Radcliffe
dramatised his analysis in her fiction, adding narrative interest to
aesthetic speculation. Her novels are pervaded by sublime images
closely associated with feelings of fear and a kind of elation won
through acute tension and anxiety. The affective power of mountain
landscapes and dim twilit perspectives would have struck an
answering chord in her eighteenth-century readers, and while their
impact on us has lost some of its force through long usage there is
still enough stimulus generated by vast dim images for us to feel
disconcerted as Mrs Radcliffe harasses her characters and her
readers alike.

Mrs Radcliffe's method of presenting her material is a complex
mixture of external and internal techniques. Sometimes she works
entirely by externals, describing characters, situations and scenery
to the reader so that we may react to a concrete series of images in
the way we might react to paintings in a gallery. At the other
extreme she may use her own modified version of indirect interior
monologue, showing how a character's mind and emotions are
interacting in the very process of registering experience and compelling the reader's imaginative participation by the intensity of focus

on one point of view. More frequently she combines internal and external methods so that scenery or incidents arouse the reader's emotions while at the same time they reflect the feelings of characters involved and allow the author yet another voice, discreet yet distinctly evaluative. Mrs Radcliffe moves deftly from one point of view to another, stimulating and guiding her reader's expectations and responses, while managing to preserve the illusion of imaginative freedom.

The variety and subtlety of Mrs Radcliffe's technique can be seen most clearly in her scenic descriptions and especially in her treatment of architecture. The description of the castle of Udolpho is a typical example of Radcliffian Gothic. It is a long description but, as Sir Walter Scott said when quoting it in his Memoir, 'so beautiful a specimen of Mrs Radcliffe's talents that we do not hesitate to insert it'.

Towards the close of day, the road wound into a deep valley. Mountains, whose shaggy steeps appeared to be inaccessible, almost surrounded it. To the east, a vista opened, that exhibited the Apennines in their darkest horrors; and the long perspective of retiring summits, rising over each other, their ridges clothed with pines, exhibited a stronger image of grandeur, than any that Emily had yet seen. The sun had just sunk below the top of the mountains she was descending, whose long shadow stretched athwart the valley, but his sloping rays, shooting through an opening of the cliffs, touched with a yellow gleam the summits of the forest, that hung upon the opposite steeps, and streamed in full splendour upon the towers and battlements of a castle, that spread its extensive ramparts along the brow of a precipice above. The splendour of these illumined objects was heightened by the contrasted shade, which involved the valley below.

'There', said Montoni, speaking for the first time in several hours, 'is Udolpho.'

Emily gazed with melancholy awe upon the castle, which she understood to be Montoni's; for, though it was now lighted up by the setting sun, the gothic greatness of its features, and its mouldering walls of dark grey stone, rendered it a gloomy and sublime object. As she gazed, the light died away on its walls, leaving a melancholy purple tint, which spread deeper and deeper, as the thin vapour crept up the mountain, whilethe battlements above were still tipped with splendour. From those too, the rays soon faded, and the whole edifice was invested with the solemn duskiness of evening. Silent, lonely and sublime, it seemed to stand the sovereign of the scene, and to frown defiance on all, who dared to invade its solitary reign. As the twilight deepened, its features became more awful in obscurity, and Emily continued to gaze, till its clustering towers were alone seen rising over the tops of the woods, beneath whose thick shade the carriages soon after began to ascend.

The extent and darkness of these tall woods awakened terrific images in her mind, and she almost expected to see banditti start up from under the trees. At length the carriages emerged upon a healthy rock, and, soon after, reached the castle gates, where the deep tone of the portal bell, which was struck upon to give notice of their arrival, increased the fearful emotions, that had assailed Emily.                                              [II v 226-7]

The first paragraph is one of the purple passages of Gothic scenic description, an imaginative re-creation in prose of a typical Salvator Rosa painting, with the physical features of sublimity carefully arranged in a deliberately aesthetic description: in the foreground the rugged mountains surrounding and dominating a deep valley, then the 'vista' of the landscape opening out into a 'perspective' of the Apennines whose 'darkest horrors' carried specific emotional and aesthetic connotations for those familiar with the ethos of the Grand Tour. Mrs Radcliffe stresses the emotional power of the visual impression by a brief shift to Emily's point of view, 'it all exhibited a stronger image of grandeur than any Emily had yet seen'. Emphasis on light and dark, the play of sunlight and shadow, follows Burke's strict caution 'against anything light and *riant*'. The sun is setting and as the valley is plunged in shadow, the last rays of sunshine stream through an opening in the cliffs to highlight a castle built above on a precipice. This now becomes the focus of attention; in its splendour, it both satisfies us aesthetically and stimulates our emotions, like an exclamation mark on the landscape. The castle is high up, lit by the sun, while the valley below is in shadow.

'Below' is an important word, not only in the aesthetic patterning of the passage but in its emotional patterning as well, for a great deal of the force of the castle as an image derives from its position 'above' the travellers. We have the sense of winding down into a dark enclosed space: a Gothic road is never straight, and the valley into which it leads is 'surrounded' by 'steeps' which are 'inaccessible'; the labyrinthine quality of the place is hinted at in the description of the valley as 'involved' in shade (surely a word with Miltonic overtones for Mrs Radcliffe). If we look carefully at the syntax we notice a very odd thing: the subject of every sentence and clause is non-human. It is a road, mountains, vistas, the sun, or indeed the castle – there are no human agents here at all. The environment is supreme and things have an active life of their own, imposing their own conditions upon the human beings who come there. This is more than the effect of impressionistic description; it is basic to the Gothic heroine's experience of the world.

Once, it is true, we have a reference to Emily 'seeing' and that is her only response, a passive private registration. 'Seeing' and 'gazing' can be purely aesthetic activities too, closely related to late eighteenth-century experience of the sublime and the picturesque – what Dr Johnson called 'a voluntary agitation of the mind' – though sublime emotions can be rapidly transformed by a change in perspective into something much more disturbing for the beholder. This is precisely Emily's experience when Montoni announces that the splendid castle belongs to him. His speech astonishes the reader too, for his is the first human voice to break the silence of contemplation as with his terse comment he dissipates the aesthetic illusion. Now that the castle has a name and an owner it ceases to be merely a sublime object and its attributes of power and magnificence are brought uncomfortably close. His statement is the shock technique which destroys the 'delightful horror' of aesthetic distance and awakens a very real sense of menace.

In the next paragraph there is a shift to Emily's point of view, but the quality of her gazing has been altered by her knowledge that Udolpho belongs to Montoni. Now gazing with 'melancholy awe' she sees its sublimity as 'gloomy', while the onset of darkness is described in words evocative of her own feelings: the 'melancholy' purple tint spreads 'deeper and deeper', describing not only colour and density but also harking back to the 'depths' of the first paragraph. In the 'solemn' duskiness, the castle takes on an 'awful' power as it rises 'silent, lonely, and sublime', a presence which 'frowns defiance'. The adjectives and the personification of the castle show the curious fusion that has taken place in Emily's mind between the attributes of the edifice and its owner, so that by the time the light fades there is no separation between the outer world and Emily's inner world; the 'terrific images' of sublimity have multiplied and transformed themselves in her imagination so that she 'almost expected' to see banditti rise up as fearful presences in a nightmare landscape. Her fears may have had some rational basis in sixteenth-century Italy, but Emily's reaction is primarily an imaginative one, more likely based on an authorial memory of Salvator Rosa's paintings than on anything in actuality. Udolpho has become for her the symbol of dread and everything associated with it shares the attributes of danger, so that even the 'deep' tone of the portal bell increases her 'fearful emotions'. These fears are exaggerated to such a pitch that she sees her arrival at Udolpho as her entry into a prison.

At this point Mrs Radcliffe quietly comments: '. . . her imagination, ever awake to circumstance, suggested even more terrors than her reason could justify'. It is the first remark the author has permitted herself since the point of view became Emily's. As frequently happens in *Udolpho*, the heroine's feelings have been presented in such detail and the reader's identification with those feelings so encouraged that we find we are accepting something as fact which is, or could be, merely a projection of the character's imagination. The author's balanced comment at the end of the paragraph is likely to be missed, quietly stated as it is within the context of Emily's fears. I think this is intentional: Mrs Radcliffe wanted to exploit the emotional possibilities of the scene, but her rational comment is there too, posing the antithesis between the suggestions of imagination and the justifications of reason, implying that there may be other ways of judging than the one chosen by the heroine and unobtrusively keeping the way open for a return via commonsense to the familiar world. (For the wittiest appreciation of Mrs Radcliffe's virtuoso performance we must turn to Jane Austen's *Northanger Abbey* where in the frustration of Catherine's hopes in her approach to Northanger there is a recognition both of the emotional power of the description and of its dimension of conscious artificiality.) . . .

SOURCE: extract from chapter on *The Mysteries of Udolpho* in *Love, Mystery and Misery: Feeling in Gothic Fiction* (London, 1978), pp. 32–7.

## *Sandra M. Gilbert & Susan Gubar* Mary Shelley's Monstrous Eve (1979)

. . . Many critics have noticed that *Frankenstein* (1818) is one of the key Romantic 'readings' of *Paradise Lost*. Significantly, however, as a woman's reading it is most especially the story of hell: hell as a dark parody of heaven, hell's creations as monstrous imitations of heaven's creations, and hellish femaleness as a grotesque parody of heavenly maleness. But of course the divagations of the parody merely return to and reinforce the fearful reality of the original. For by parodying *Paradise Lost* in what may have begun as a secret, barely conscious attempt to subvert Milton, Shelley ended up telling, too, the central story of *Paradise Lost*, the tale of 'what misery th' inabstinence of Eve / Shall bring on men'.

Mary Shelley herself claims to have been continually asked 'how I . . . came to think of and to dilate upon so very hideous an idea' as that of *Frankenstein*, but it is really not surprising that she should have formulated her anxieties about femaleness in such highly literary terms. For of course the nineteen-year-old girl who wrote *Frankenstein* was no ordinary nineteen-year-old but one of England's most notable literary heiresses. Indeed, as 'the daughter of two persons of distinguished literary celebrity', and the wife of a third, Mary Wollstonecraft Godwin Shelley was the daughter and later the wife of some of Milton's keenest critics, so that Harold Bloom's useful conceit about the family romance of English literature is simply an accurate description of the reality of her life.

In acknowledgment of this web of literary/familial relationships, critics have traditionally studied *Frankenstein* as an interesting example of Romantic myth-making, a work ancillary to such established Promethean masterpieces as Shelley's *Prometheus Unbound* and Byron's *Manfred*. ('Like almost everything else about [Mary's] life', one such critic remarks, *Frankenstein* 'is an instance of genius observed and admired but not shared.') Recently, however, a number of writers have noticed the connection between Mary Shelley's 'waking dream' of monster-manufacture and her own experience of awakening sexuality, in particular the 'horror story of Maternity' which accompanied her precipitous entrance into what Ellen Moers calls 'teen-age motherhood'. Clearly they are articulating an increasingly uneasy sense that, despite its male protagonist and its underpinning of 'masculine' philosophy, *Frankenstein* is somehow a 'woman's book', if only because its author was caught up in such a maelstrom of sexuality at the time she wrote the novel.

In making their case for the work as female fantasy, though, critics like Moers have tended to evade the problems posed by what we must define as *Frankenstein*'s literariness. Yet, despite the weaknesses in those traditional readings of the novel that overlook its intensely sexual materials, it is still undeniably true that Mary Shelley's 'ghost story', growing from a Keatsian (or Coleridgean) waking dream, is a Romantic novel about – among other things – Romanticism, as well as a book about books and perhaps, too, about the writers of books. Any theorist of the novel's femaleness and of its significance as, in Moers's phrase, a 'birth myth' must therefore confront this self-conscious literariness. For as was only natural in 'the daughter of two persons of distinguished literary celebrity', Mary Shelley explained her sexuality to herself in the context of her reading and its powerfully felt implications.

For this orphaned literary heiress, highly charged connections between femaleness and literariness must have been established early, and established specifically in relation to the controversial figure of her dead mother. As we shall see, Mary Wollstonecraft

Godwin read her mother's writings over and over again as she was growing up. Perhaps more important, she undoubtedly read most of the reviews of her mother's *Posthumous Works*, reviews in which Mary Wollstonecraft was attacked as a 'philosophical wanton' and a monster, while her *Vindication of the Rights of Woman* (1792) was called 'A scripture, archly fram'd for propagating w[hore]s'. But in any case, to the 'philosophical wanton's' daughter, all reading about (or of) her mother's work must have been painful, given her knowledge that that passionate feminist writer had died in giving life to *her*, to bestow upon Wollstonecraft's death from complications of childbirth the melodramatic cast it probably had for the girl herself. That Mary Shelley was conscious, moreover, of a strangely intimate relationship between her feelings toward her dead mother, her romance with a living poet, and her own sense of vocation as a reader and writer is made perfectly clear by her habit of 'taking her books to Mary Wollstonecraft's grave in St. Pancras' Churchyard, there', as Muriel Spark puts it, 'to pursue her studies in an atmosphere of communion with a mind greater than the second Mrs Godwin's [and] to meet Shelley in secret'.

Her mother's grave: the setting seems an unusually grim, even ghoulish locale for reading, writing, or lovemaking. Yet, to a girl with Mary Shelley's background, literary activities, like sexual ones, must have been primarily extensions of the elaborate, gothic psychodrama of her family history. If her famous diary is largely a compendium of her reading lists and Shelley's that fact does not, therefore, suggest unusual reticence on her part. Rather, it emphasizes the point that for Mary, even more than for most writers, reading a book was often an emotional as well as an intellectual event of considerable magnitude. Especially because she never knew her mother, and because her father seemed so definitively to reject her after her youthful elopement, her principal mode of self-definition – certainly in the early years of her life with Shelley, when she was writing *Frankenstein* – was through reading, and to a lesser extent through writing.

Endlessly studying her mother's works and her father's, Mary Shelley may be said to have 'read' her family and to have been related to her reading, for books appear to have functioned as her surrogate parents, pages and words standing in for flesh and blood. That much of her reading was undertaken in Shelley's company, moreover, may also help explain some of his obsessiveness, for Mary's literary inheritance was obviously involved in her very literary romance and marriage. In the years just before she wrote *Frankenstein*, for instance, and those when she was engaged in composing the novel (1816–17), she studied her parents' writings, alone or together with Shelley, like a scholarly detective seeking clues to the significance of some cryptic text. To be sure, this investigation of the mysteries of literary genealogy was done in a larger context. In these same years, Mary Shelley recorded innumerable readings of contemporary gothic novels, as well as a program of study in English, French and German literature that would do credit to a modern graduate student. But especially, in 1815, 1816 and 1817, she read the words of Milton: *Paradise Lost* (twice), *Paradise Regained, Comus, Areopagetica, Lycidas.* And what makes the extent of this reading particularly impressive is the fact that in these years, her seventeenth to her twenty-first, Mary Shelley was almost continuously pregnant, 'confined', or nursing. At the same time, it is precisely the coincidence of all these disparate activities – her family studies, her initiation into adult sexuality, and her literary self-education – that makes her vision of *Paradise Lost* so significant. For her developing sense of herself as a literary creature and/or creator seems to have been inseparable from her emerging self-definition as daughter, mistress, wife, and mother. Thus she cast her birth myth – her myth of origins – in precisely those cosmogenic terms to which her parents, her husband, and indeed her whole literary culture continually alluded: the terms of *Paradise Lost*, which (as she indicates even on the title page of her novel), she saw as preceding, paralleling, and commenting upon the Greek cosmogony of the Prometheus play her husband had just translated. It is as a female fantasy of sex and reading, then, a gothic psychodrama reflecting Mary Shelley's own sense of what we might call bibliogenesis, that *Frankenstein* is a version of the misogynistic story implicit in *Paradise Lost.*

It would be a mistake to underestimate the significance of *Frankenstein*'s title page, with its allusive subtitle ('The Modern Prometheus') and carefully pointed Miltonic epigraph ('Did I request thee, Maker, from my clay/To mould me man? Did I solicit thee/From darkness to promote me?'). But our first really serious clue to the highly literary nature of this history of a creature born outside history is its author's use of an unusually *evidentiary* technique for conveying the stories of her monster and his maker. Like a literary jigsaw puzzle, a collection of apparently random documents from whose juxtaposition the scholar-detective must infer a meaning, *Frankenstein* consists of three 'concentric circles' of narration (Walton's letters, Victor Frankenstein's recital to Walton, and the monster's speech to Frankenstein), within which are embedded

pockets of digression containing other miniature narratives (Frankenstein's mother's story, Elizabeth Lavenza's and Justine's stories,
Felix's and Agatha's story, Safie's story), etc. As we have noted,
reading and assembling documentary evidence, examining it, analyzing it and researching it comprised for Shelley a crucial if voyeuristic
method of exploring origins, explaining identity, understanding
sexuality. Even more obviously it was a way of researching and
analyzing an emotionally unintelligible text, like *Paradise Lost*. In a
sense, then, even before *Paradise Lost* as a central item on the
monster's reading list becomes a literal event in *Frankenstein*, the
novel's literary structure prepares us to confront Milton's patriarchal
epic, both as a sort of research problem and as the framework for a
complex system of allusions.

The book's dramatic situations are equally resonant. Like Mary
Shelley, who was a puzzled but studious Miltonist, this novel's key
characters – Walton, Frankenstein and the monster – are obsessed
with problem-solving. 'I shall satiate my ardent curiosity with the
sight of a part of the world never before visited', exclaims the young
explorer, Walton, as he embarks like a child 'on an expedition of
discovery up his native river' [letter 1, 2]. 'While my companions
contemplated . . . the magnificent appearance of things', declares
Frankenstein, the scientist of sexual ontology, 'I delighted in
investigating their causes' [ch. 2, 22]. 'Who was I? What was I?
Whence did I come?' [ch. 15, 113–15] the monster reports wonder-
ing, describing endless speculations cast in Miltonic terms. All three,
like Shelley herself, appear to be trying to understand their presence
in a fallen world, and trying at the same time to define the nature
of the lost paradise that must have existed before the fall. But unlike
Adam, all three characters seem to have fallen not merely from
Eden but from the earth, fallen directly into hell, like Sin, Satan
and – by implication – Eve. Thus their questionings are in some
sense female, for they belong in that line of literary women's
questionings of the fall into gender which goes back at least to Anne
Finch's plaintive 'How are we fal'n?' and forward to Sylvia Plath's
horrified 'I have fallen very far!'

From the first, however, *Frankenstein* answers such neo-Miltonic
questions mainly through explicit or implicit allusions to Milton,
retelling the story of the fall not so much to protest against it as to
clarify its meaning. The parallels between those two Promethean
over-reachers Walton and Frankenstein, for instance, have always
been clear to readers. But that both characters can, therefore, be
described (the way Walton describes Frankenstein) as 'fallen angels'
is not as frequently remarked. Yet Frankenstein himself is perceptive

enough to ask Walton 'Do you share my madness?' at just the moment when the young explorer remarks Satanically that 'One man's life or death were but a small price to pay . . . for the dominion I [wish to] acquire' [letter 4, 13]. Plainly one fallen angel can recognize another. Alienated from his crew and chronically friendless, Walton tells his sister that he longs for a friend 'on the wide ocean', and what he discovers in Victor Frankenstein is the fellowship of hell.

In fact, like the many other secondary narratives Mary Shelley offers in her novel, Walton's story is itself an alternative version of the myth of origins presented in *Paradise Lost*. Writing his ambitious letters home from St Petersburgh [sic], Archangel and points north, Walton moves like Satan away from the sanctity and sanity represented by his sister, his crew and the allegorical names of the places he leaves. Like Satan, too, he seems at least in part to be exploring the frozen frontiers of hell in order to attempt a return to heaven, for the 'country of eternal light' he envisions at the Pole [letter 1, 1] has much in common with Milton's celestial 'Fountain of Light' [*PL* III 375]. Again, like Satan's (and Eve's) aspirations, his ambition has violated a patriarchal decree: his father's 'dying injunction' had forbidden him 'to embark on a seafaring life'. Moreover, even the icy hell where Walton encounters Frankenstein and the monster is Miltonic, for all three of these diabolical wanderers must learn, like the fallen angels of *Paradise Lost*, that 'Beyond this flood a frozen Continent / Lies dark and wild . . . / Thither by harpy-footed Furies hal'd, / At certain revolutions all the damn'd / Are brought . . . From Beds of raging Fire to starve in Ice' [*PL* II 587–600].

Finally, another of Walton's revelations illuminates not only the likeness of his ambitions to Satan's but also the similarity of his anxieties to those of his female author. Speaking of his childhood, he reminds his sister that, because poetry had 'lifted [my soul] to heaven', he had become a poet and 'for one year lived in a paradise of my own creation'. Then he adds ominously that 'You are well-acquainted with my failure and how heavily I bore the disappointment' [letter 1, 2–3]. But of course, as she confesses in her introduction to *Frankenstein*, Mary Shelley, too, had spent her childhood in 'waking dreams' of literature; later, both she and her poet-husband hoped she would prove herself 'worthy of [her] parentage and enroll [herself] on the page of fame' [*xii*]. In a sense, then, given the Miltonic context in which Walton's story of poetic failure is set, it seems possible that one of the anxious fantasies his narrative helps Mary Shelley covertly examine is the fearful tale of a female fall from a lost paradise of art, speech, and autonomy into a hell of sexuality, silence, and filthy materiality, 'A Universe of death, which God by curse / Created evil, for evil only good, / Where all life dies, death lives, and Nature breeds, / Perverse, all monstrous, all prodigious things' [*PL* II 622–5].

Walton and his new friend Victor Frankenstein have considerably more in common than a Byronic (or Monk Lewis-ish) Satanism. For one thing, both are orphans, as Frankenstein's monster is and as it turns out all the major and almost all the minor characters in *Frankenstein* are, from Caroline Beaufort and Elizabeth Lavenza to Justine, Felix, Agatha and Safie. Victor Frankenstein has not always been an orphan, though, and Shelley devotes much space to an account of his family history. Family histories, in fact, especially those of orphans, appear to fascinate her, and wherever she can include one in the narrative she does so with an obsessiveness suggesting that through the disastrous tale of the child who becomes 'an orphan and a beggar' she is once more recounting the story of the fall, the expulsion from paradise, and the confrontation of hell. For Milton's Adam and Eve, after all, began as motherless orphans reared (like Shelley herself) by a stern but kindly father-god, and ended as beggars rejected by God (as she was by *God*win when she eloped). Thus Caroline Beaufort's father dies leaving her 'an orphan and a beggar', and Eliabeth Lavenza also becomes 'an orphan and a beggar' – the phrase is repeated [ch. 1, 18, 20) – with the disappearance of her father into an Austrian dungeon. And though both girls are rescued by Alphonse Frankenstein, Victor's father, the early alienation from the patriarchal chain-of-being signalled by their orphanhood prefigures the hellish fate in store for them and their family. Later, motherless Safie and fatherless Justine enact similarly ominous anxiety fantasies about the fall of woman into orphanhood and beggary.

Beyond their orphanhood, however, a universal sense of guilt links such diverse figures as Justine, Felix and Elizabeth, just as it will eventually link Victor, Walton and the monster. Justine, for instance, irrationally confesses to the murder of little William, though she knows perfectly well she is innocent. Even more irrationally, Elizabeth is reported by Alphonse Frankenstein to have exclaimed 'Oh, God! I have murdered my darling child!' after her first sight of the corpse of little William [ch. 7, 57]. Victor, too, long before he knows that the monster is actually his brother's killer, decides that his 'creature' has killed William and that therefore he, the creator, is the 'true murderer': 'the mere presence of the idea', he notes, is 'an irresistible proof of the fact' [ch. 7, 60]. Complicity in the murder of the child William is, it seems, another crucial component of the Original Sin shared by prominent members of the Frankenstein family.

At the same time, the likenesses among all these characters – the common alienation, the shared guilt, the orphanhood and beggary — imply relationships of redundance between them like the solipsistic relationships among artfully placed mirrors. What reinforces our sense of this hellish solipsism is the barely disguised incest at the heart of a number of the marriages and romances the novel describes. Most notably, Victor Frankenstein is intended to marry his 'more than sister' Elizabeth Lavenza, whom he confesses to having always considered 'a possession of my own' [ch. 1, 21]. But the mysterious Mrs Saville, to whom Walton's letters are addressed, is apparently in some sense *his* more than sister, just as Caroline Beaufort was clearly a 'more than' wife, in fact a daughter, to her father's friend Alphonse Frankenstein. Even relationless Justine appears to have a metaphorically incestuous relationship with the Frankensteins, since as their servant she becomes their possession and more than sister, while the female monster Victor half-constructs in Scotland will be a more than sister as well as a mate to the monster, since both have the same parent/creator.

Certainly at least some of this incest-obsession in *Frankenstein* is, as Ellen Moers remarks, the 'standard' sensational matter of Romantic novels. Some of it, too, even without the conventions of the gothic thriller, would be a natural subject for an impressionable young woman who had just spent several months in the company of the famously incestuous author of *Manfred*. Nevertheless, the streak of incest that darkens *Frankenstein* probably owes as much to the book's Miltonic framework as it does to Mary Shelley's own life and times. In the Edenic cosiness of their childhood, for instance, Victor and Elizabeth are incestuous as Adam and Eve are, literally incestuous because they have the same creator, and figuratively so because Elizabeth is Victor's pretty plaything, the image of an angelic soul or 'epipsyche' created from his own soul just as Eve is created from Adam's rib. Similarly, the incestuous relationships of Satan and Sin, and by implication of Satan and Eve, are mirrored in the incest fantasies of *Frankenstein*, including the disguised but intensely sexual waking dream in which Victor Frankenstein in effect couples with his monster applying 'the instruments of life' to its body and inducing a shudder of response [ch. 5, 42]. For Milton, and therefore for Mary Shelley, who was trying to understand Milton, incest was an inescapable metaphor for the solipsistic fever of self-awareness that Matthew Arnold was later to call 'the dialogue of the mind with itself'.

If Victor Frankenstein can be likened to both Adam and Satan, however, who or what is he *really*? Here we are obliged to confront both the moral ambiguity and the symbolic slipperiness which are at the heart of all the characterizations in *Frankenstein*. In fact, it is probably these continual and complex reallocations of meaning, among characters whose histories echo and re-echo each other, that have been so bewildering to critics. Like figures in a dream, all the people in *Frankenstein* have different bodies and somehow, horribly, the same face, or worse – the same two faces. For this reason, as Muriel Spark notes, even the book's subtitle 'The Modern Prometheus' is ambiguous, 'for though at first Frankenstein is himself the Prometheus, the vital fire-endowing protagonist, the Monster, as soon as he is created, takes on [a different aspect of] the role'. Moreover, if we postulate that Mary Shelley is more concerned with Milton than she is with Aeschylus, the intertwining of meanings grows even more confusing, as the monster himself several times points out to Frankenstein, noting 'I ought to be thy Adam, but I am rather the fallen angel' [ch. 10, 84], then adding elsewhere that 'God, in pity, made man beautiful . . . after His own image; but my form is a filthy type of yours. . . . Satan had his companions . . . but I am solitary and abhorred' [ch. 15, 115]. In other words, not only do Frankenstein and his monster both in one way or another enact the story of Prometheus, each is at one time or another like God (Victor as creator, the monster as his creator's 'Master'), like Adam (Victor as innocent child, the monster as primordial 'creature'), and like Satan (Victor as tormented overreacher, the monster as vengeful fiend).

What is the reason for this continual duplication and reduplication of roles? Most obviously, perhaps, the dreamlike shifting of fantasy figures from part to part, costume to costume, tells us that we are in fact dealing with the psychodrama or waking dream that Shelley herself suspected she had written. Beyond his, however, we would argue that the fluidity of the narrative's symbolic scheme reinforces in another way the crucial significance of the Miltonic skeleton around which Mary Shelley's hideous progeny took shape. For it becomes increasingly clear as one reads *Frankenstein* with *Paradise Lost* in mind that because the novel's author is such an inveterate student of literature, families and sexuality, and because she is using her novel as a tool to help her make sense of her reading, *Frankenstein* is ultimately a mock *Paradise Lost* in which both Victor and his monster, together with a number of secondary characters, play all the neo-biblical parts over and over again – all except, it seems at first, the part of Eve. Not just the striking omission of any obvious Eve-figure from this 'woman's book' about Milton, but also the barely concealed sexual components of the story as well as our earlier analysis of Milton's bogey should tell us, however, that for Mary Shelley the part of Eve *is* all the parts.

On the surface, Victor seems at first more Adamic than Satanic or Eve-like. His Edenic childhood is an interlude of prelapsarian innocence in which, like Adam, he is sheltered by his benevolent father as a sensitive plant might be 'sheltered by the gardener, from every rougher wind' [ch. 1, 19–20]. When cherubic Elizabeth Lavenza joins the family, she seems as 'heaven-sent' as Milton's Eve, as much Victor's 'possession' as Adam's rib is Adam's. Moreover, though he is evidently forbidden almost nothing ('My parents [were not] tyrants . . . but the agents and creators of many delights'), Victor hints to Walton that his deific father, like Adam's and Walton's, did on one occasion arbitrarily forbid him to pursue his interest in arcane knowledge. Indeed, like Eve and Satan, Victor blames his own fall at least in part on his father's apparent arbitrariness. 'If . . . my father had taken the pains to explain to me that the principles of Agrippa had been entirely exploded. . . . It is even possible that the train of my ideas would never have received the fatal impulse that led to my ruin' [ch. 2, 24–5]. And soon after asserting this he even associates an incident in which a tree is struck by Jovian thunder bolts with his feelings about his forbidden studies.

As his researches into the 'secrets of nature' become more feverish, however, and as his ambition 'to explore unknown powers' grows more intense, Victor begins to metamorphose from Adam to Satan, becoming 'as Gods' in his capacity of 'bestowing animation upon lifeless matter', laboring like a guilty artist to complete his false creation. Finally, in his conversations with Walton he echoes Milton's fallen angel, and Marlowe's, in his frequently reiterated confession that 'I bore a hell within me which nothing could extinguish' [ch. 8, 72]. Indeed, as the 'true murderer' of innocence, here cast in the form of the child William, Victor perceives himself as a diabolical creator whose mind has involuntarily 'let loose' a monstrous and 'filthy demon' in much the same way that Milton's Satan's swelled head produced Sin, the disgusting monster he 'let loose' upon the world. Watching a 'noble war in the sky' that seems almost like an intentional reminder that we are participating in a critical rearrangement of most of the elements of *Paradise Lost*, he explains that 'I considered the being whom I had cast among mankind . . . nearly in the light of my own vampire, my own spirit let loose from the grave and forced to destroy all that was dear to me' [ch. 7, 61]. Even while it is the final sign and seal of Victor's transformation from Adam to Satan, however, it is perhaps the Sin-ful murder of the child William that is our first overt clue to the real nature of the bewilderingly disguised set of identity shifts and parallels Mary Shelley incorporated into *Frankenstein*. For as we saw earlier, not just Victor and the monster but also Elizabeth and Justine insist upon responsibility for the monster's misdeed. Feeling 'as if I had been guilty of a crime' [ch. 4, 41] even before one had been committed, Victor responds to the news of William's death with the same self-accusations that torment the two orphans. And, significantly, for all three – as well as for the monster and little William himself – one focal point of both crime and guilt is an image of that other beautiful orphan, Caroline Beaufort Frankenstein. Passing from hand to hand, pocket to pocket, the smiling miniature of Victor's 'angel mother' seems a token of some secret fellowship in sin, as does Victor's post-creation nightmare of transforming a lovely, living Elizabeth, with a single magical kiss, into 'the corpse of my dead mother' enveloped in a shroud made more horrible by 'grave-worms crawling in the folds of the flannel' [ch. 5, 42]. Though it has been disguised, buried, or miniaturized, femaleness – the gender definition of mothers and daughters, orphans and beggars, monsters and false creators – is at the heart of this apparently masculine book.

Because this is so, it eventually becomes clear that, though Victor Frankenstein enacts the roles of Adam and Satan like a child trying on costumes, his single most self-defining act transforms him definitively into Eve. For as both Ellen Moers and Marc Rubenstein have pointed out, after much study of the 'cause of generation and life', after locking himself away from ordinary society in the tradition of such agonized mothers as Wollstonecraft's Maria, Eliot's Hetty Sorel, and Hardy's Tess, Victor Frankenstein has a baby. His 'pregnancy' and childbirth are obviously manifested by the existence of the paradoxically huge being who emerges from his 'workshop of filthy creation', but even the descriptive language of his creation myth is suggestive: 'incredible labours', 'emaciated with confinement', 'a passing trance', 'oppressed by a slow fever', 'nervous to a painful degree', 'exercise and amusement would . . . drive away incipient disease', 'the instruments of life' [ch. 4, 39–41], etc. And, like Eve's fall into guilty knowledge and painful maternity, Victor's entrance into what Blake would call the realm of 'generation' is marked by a recognition of the necessary interdependence of those complementary opposites, sex and death: 'To examine the causes of life, we must first have recourse to death', he observes [ch. 14, 36] and in his isolated workshop of filthy creation – filthy because obscenely sexual – he collects and arranges materials furnished by 'the dissecting room and the slaughterhouse'.

Pursuing 'nature to her hiding places' as Eve does in eating the apple, he learns that 'the tremendous secrets of the human frame' are the interlocked secrets of sex and death, although, again like Eve, in his first mad pursuit of knowledge he knows not 'eating death'. But that his actual orgasmic animation of his monster-child takes place 'on a dreary night in November', month of All Souls, short days and the year's last slide toward death, merely reinforces the Miltonic and Blakean nature of his act of generation.

Even while Victor Frankenstein's self-defining procreation dramatically transforms him into an Eve-figure, however, our recognition of its implications reflects backward upon our sense of Victor-as-Satan and our earlier vision of Victor-as-Adam. Victor as Satan, we now realize, was never really the masculine, Byronic Satan of the first book of *Paradise Lost*, but always, instead, the curiously female outcast Satan who gave birth to Sin. In his Eve-like pride ('I was surprised . . . that I alone should be reserved to discover so astonishing a secret' [ch. 4, 37]), this Victor-Satan becomes 'dizzy' with his creative powers, so that his monstrous pregnancy, bookishly and solipsistically conceived, re-enacts as a terrible bibliogenesis the moment when, in Milton's version, Satan 'dizzy swum / In darkness, while [his] head flames thick and fast / Threw forth, till on the left side op'ning wide' and Sin, Death's mother-to-be, appeared like 'a Sign / Portentous' (*PL* ii 753–61). Because he has conceived – or, rather, misconceived – his monstrous offspring by brooding upon the *wrong* books, moreover, this Victor-Satan is paradigmatic, like the falsely creative fallen angel, of the female artist, whose anxiety about her own aesthetic activity is expressed, for instance, in Mary Shelley's deferential introductory phrase about her 'hideous progeny', with its plain implication that in her alienated attic workshop of filthy creation she has given birth to a deformed book, a literary abortion or miscarriage. 'How [did] I, then a young girl, [come] to think of and to *dilate* upon so very hideous an idea?' is a key (if disingenuous) question she records. But we should not overlook her word play upon *dilate*, just as we should not ignore the anxious pun on the word *author* that is so deeply embedded in *Frankenstein*.

If the adult, Satanic Victor is Eve-like both in his procreation and his anxious creation, even the young, prelapsarian and Adamic

Victor is – to risk a pun – *curiously* female, that is, Eve-like. Innocent and guided by silken threads like a Blakeian lamb in a Godwinian garden, he is consumed by 'a fervent longing to penetrate the secrets of nature', a longing which – expressed in his explorations of 'vaults and charnelhouses', his guilty observations of 'the unhallowed damps of the grave', and his passion to understand 'the structure of the human frame' – recalls the criminal female curiosity that led Psyche to lose love by gazing upon its secret face, Eve to insist upon consuming 'intellectual food', and Prometheus's sister-in-law Pandora to open the forbidden box of fleshly ills. But if Victor-Adam is also Victor-Eve, what is the real significance of the episode in which, away at school and cut off from his family, he locks himself into his workshop of filthy creation and gives birth by intellectual parturition to a giant monster? Isn't it precisely at this point in the novel that he discovers he is not Adam but Eve, not Satan but Sin, not male but female? If so, it seems likely that what this crucial section of *Frankenstein* really enacts is the story of Eve's discovery not that she must fall but that, having been created female, she *is* fallen, femaleness and fallenness being essentially synonymous. For what Victor Frankenstein most importantly learns, we must remember, is that he is the 'author' of the monster – for him alone is 'reserved . . . so astonishing a secret' – and thus it is he who is 'the true murderer', he who unleashes Sin and Death upon the world, he who dreams the primal kiss that incestuously kills both 'sister' and 'mother'. Doomed and filthy, is he not, then, Eve instead of Adam? In fact, may not the story of the fall be, for women, the story of the discovery that one is not innocent and Adam (as one had supposed) but Eve, and fallen? Perhaps this is what Freud's cruel but metaphorically accurate concept of penis-envy really means: the girl-child's surprised discovery that she is female, hence fallen, inadequate. Certainly the almost grotesquely anxious self-analysis implicit in Victor Frankenstein's (and Mary Shelley's) multiform relationships to Eve, Adam, God and Satan suggest as much.

SOURCE: section on 'Horror's Twin: Mary Shelley's Monstrous Eve', in *The Madwoman in the Attic: The Woman Writes and the Nineteenth-Century Literary Imagination* (New Haven, Con., and London, 1979), pp. 221–34.

References above are to the Bantam/Pathfinder (1967) edition of *Frankenstein*.

*Mary Poovey*      My Hideous Progeny: Mary
Shelley and the Feminization of
Romance   (1980)


To most of her acquaintances, the mature Mary Shelley was
simply a conundrum. 'Your writings and your manner are not in
accordance', Lord Dillion observed in 1829.

I should have thought of you – if I had only read you – that you were a
sort of my Sybil, outpouringly enthusiastic, rather indiscreet, and even
extravagant; but you are cool, quiet, and feminine to the last degree – I
mean in delicacy of manner and expression. Explain this to me.[1]

Leigh Hunt, who had known Shelley longer than most of her new
London set, found her friends' confusion amusing enough to rhyme:

> And Shelley, four-famed – for her parents, her lord,
> And the poor lone impossible monster abhorred.
> (So sleek and so smiling she came, people stared,
> To think such fair clay should so darkly have dared.)[2]

The puzzle Shelley presented to her contemporaries is well worth
our consideration, for what seems to suggest a simple discrepancy
between art and life actually points to a lifetime of self-division, the
result of one woman's attempt to conform simultaneously to two
conflicting prescriptive models of behavior. On the one hand, both
as the daughter of William Godwin and Mary Wollstonecraft and
as the lover and then wife of Percy Shelley, Mary was encouraged
from her youth to fulfill the Romantic model of the artist, to prove
herself by means of her pen and her imagination. 'In our family',
Mary's stepsister Claire Clairmont once wryly remarked, 'if you
cannot write an epic poem or novel, that by its originality knocks
all other novels on the head, you are a despicable creature, not
worth acknowledging'.[3] On the other hand, this pressure to be
'original' was contradicted by the more prevalent social expectations
that a woman conform to the conventional feminine model of
propriety, that she be self-effacing and supportive, devoted to a
family rather than to a career. Caught between these two models,
Shelley developed a pervasive personal and artistic ambivalence
toward feminine self-assertion. Each of her six novels reflects this

ambivalence to a greater or lesser degree; they are all riddled with competing tendencies because they simultaneously fulfill and punish her desire for self-expression. Because her works demonstrate the difficulties that the conflicting expectations of this transitional period posed for a woman writer, Mary Shelley emerges as an important figure, even though she never fully achieved the personal or the aesthetic self-confidence necessary to integrate her imaginative efforts.

The sources and the extent of Shelley's ambivalence are vividly set out in the two editions of her most famous novel, *Frankenstein*. The first edition, published in 1818, when Mary was just twenty and not yet married, is as bold and original a work as the novelist ever conceived. But even though the 1818 *Frankenstein* addresses an undeniably unorthodox subject, it does so with conservative reservations, which have been largely overlooked by both nineteenth and twentieth-century commentators. For in the course of her unladylike metaphysical speculations, Shelley explodes the foundations of Romantic optimism by demonstrating that the egotistical energies necessary to self-assertion – energies that appear to her to be at the heart of the Romantic model of the imagination – inevitably imperil the self-denying energies of love. To accommodate this reservation, which implicitly indicts all artistic endeavors as well as more insidious forms of egotism, Shelley essentially feminizes Romantic aesthetics, deriving from her contemporaries' theories strategies that enable her to fulfill her desire for self-expression in an indirect, self-effacing and therefore acceptable manner.[4] But in the 1831 edition of her youthful production, Shelley finds even this qualified self-assertion too audacious. Despite her claims to 'have changed no portion of the story, nor introduced any new ideas or circumstances,[5] the Introduction she added to the third edition and the revisions she made in the text suggest that by 1831 Shelley wants to apologize for her adolescent audacity, to explain that she, like Frankenstein, is terrified by the product of what she now considers a 'frightful transgression'. Even in 1831, however, Shelley does not fully accept responsibility for her earlier 'crime', nor does she wholly renounce the artistic enterprise she claims to find so blasphemous. For by dramatizing herself – just as she does the 1831 Frankenstein – as the victim of forces beyond her control, she elevates the dilemma of the female artist to the status of myth and sanctions the very self-expression she professes to regret. The reversals within each of the texts reveal the contradictions of a painfully self-divided desire; taken together, the two editions of *Frankenstein* provide a case study in the tensions inherent in the feminine adaptation of the Romantic 'egotistical sublime'. . . .

Shelley's exposition of the degeneration of incipient desire into full-fledged egotism begins when Frankenstein leaves his childhood home. At the University of Ingolstadt he is alone, left to 'form [his] own friends, and be [his] own protector' [p. 40].[6] Cut loose from domestic regulations, the youth exercises a bold confidence in his innate impulses and capacities; he believes that his desire to conquer death through science is fundamentally unselfish and that he can be his own guardian. But, as Mary Shelley ruthlessly proves, both these comforting assumptions are only tricks, by which his desire – or, as Frankenstein calls it, his 'ardent imagination' – blinds him to its own essential 'self-devotion'. The course of Frankenstein's decline suggests, in fact, that in the absence of social regulation the formation of the ego is primarily influenced by the imagination's longing to deny fundamental human limitations – in particular, the body's determinate bondage to nature and to death. Frankenstein 'penetrate[s] into the recesses of nature' in search of the secret of life, but what he discovers in the 'vaults and charnel houses' is the 'natural decay and corruption of the human body'. Death is the initial and obsessive focus of the imagination, just as it will be, through the agency of the monster, its final product. But Frankenstein's imagination, swollen with self-importance, refuses to acknowledge that his own body is a part of this chain of natural processes; Victor rationalizes his absorption in 'corruption and waste' as necessary to the intellectual mastery of death, and he plots his perpetuity even as he plans the creature that will express and eventually put an end to his egotism.

Frankenstein's fatal impulse also has profound social consequences, for the vanity that convinces the scientist of the benevolence and power of his imagination is one expression of the essential, egotistical drive to assert and extend the self – to deny not only one's own mortality but also, to use Kant's phrase, the otherness of others. Thus Frankenstein's love for his family is the first victim of his growing obsession. His filial affection is displaced by 'supernatural enthusiasm': 'I wished, as it were, to procrastinate all that related to my feelings of affection until the great object, which swallowed up every habit of my nature, should be completed' [p. 50]. He isolates himself in a 'solitary chamber', refuses to write even to his fiancée, Elizabeth, and grows 'insensible to the charms of nature'. 'I became as timid as a love-sick girl', Frankenstein realizes in retrospect, 'and alternate tremor and passionate ardour took the place of wholesome sensation and regulated ambition' [p. 51].

In criticizing the indulged imagination, Mary Shelley is more concerned with this antisocial dimension than with any metaphysical implications. In ch. v, for example, at the grotesque heart of her story, she elaborates the significance of Frankenstein's self-absorption primarily in terms of his social relationships. After animating the monster, the product and symbol of self-serving desire, the exhausted scientist is immediately confronted with a dream explication of his crime: having denied domestic relationships by indulging his selfish passions, he has, in effect, murdered domestic tranquillity:

> I thought I saw Elizabeth, in the bloom of health, walking in the streets of Ingolstadt. Delighted and surprised, I embraced her; but as I imprinted the first kiss on her lips, they became vivid with the hue of death; her features appeared to change, and I thought that I held the corpse of my dead mother in my arms; a shroud enveloped her form, and I saw the grave-worms crawling in the folds of the flannel.                                    [p. 53]

Lover and mother, the presiding female guardians of Frankenstein's 'secluded and domestic' youth, are conflated in this tableau of the enthusiast's guilt. Only now, when Frankenstein starts from his sleep to find the misshapen creature hanging over his bed (as Frankenstein will later hang over Elizabeth's), does he recognize his desire for what it really is – a monstrous urge, alien and threatening to all human intercourse.

In effect, animating the monster completes and liberates Frankenstein's egotism, for his indescribable experiment explicitly objectifies desire. Paradoxically, in this incident Shelley simultaneously literalizes the ego's destructiveness and sets in motion the more figurative, symbolic character of the monster. The significance of this event for the monster I discuss below; for Frankenstein, this monument, which cuts short his process of maturation, has the dual effect of initiating self-consciousness and, tragically, perfecting his alienation. Briefly 'restored to life' by his childhood friend Clerval, Frankenstein rejects that 'selfish pursuit [which] had cramped and narrowed' him and returns his desire to its proper objects, his 'beloved friends'. But ironically, the very gesture that disciplines his desire has already destroyed the possibility of establishing relationships with his loved ones. Although liberating the monster allows Frankenstein to see that personal fulfilment results from self-denial rather than from self-assertion, that action also condemns him to perpetual isolation and, therefore, to permanent incompleteness.

This fatal paradox, the heart of Mary Shelley's waking nightmare, gives a particularly feminine twist to one important Romantic myth of human maturation through self-consciousness. . . .

. . . The imagination, as it is depicted in Frankenstein's original transgression, is incapable of projecting an irradiating virtue, for in aiding and abetting the ego the imagination carries death-dealing, selfish desire into the domestic arena. By extension, nature is also suspect because, as the avatar of death, it lacks altogether the humane, moral aspect institutionalized in the family and society. Thus Mary Shelley does not depict numerous natural theatres into which individuals can project their growing desires and from which affirmative echoes will hasten maturation. Instead, she continues to dramatize personal fulfilment strictly in terms of the child's original domestic harmony, with the absent mother being replaced by the closest female equivalent; ideally, Elizabeth would link Frankenstein's maturity to his youth, just as Mrs Saville would anchor the mariner Walton. Ideally, in other words, the beloved object would be sought and found only within the comforting confines of pre-existent domestic relationships. In this model, Shelley therefore ties the formation of personal identity to self-denial rather than to self-assertion, to a sort of perpetual childhood, entailing relational self-definition and independence, rather than to the Wordsworthian model of adulthood, which involves self-confidence, freedom and faith in the individualistic imaginative act.

The remainder of Frankenstein's narrative proves beyond a doubt that his original transgression culminates not in maturity but in death. The monster is simply the agent that carries out Frankenstein's desire: just as Frankenstein figuratively denied his family, so the monster literally destroys Frankenstein's domestic relationships, blighting both the memory and the hope of familial harmony with the 'black mark' of its murderous hand. William Frankenstein, Justine Moritz, Henry Clerval, even Elizabeth Lavenza are, as it were, *possessed* by this creature, but, as Frankenstein knows all too well, its victims are by extension his own: Justine is *his* 'unhappy victim' [p. 80]; *he* has murdered Clerval [p. 174]; and the creature consummates *his* deadly desire on '*its* bridal bier' [p. 193].

For Mary Shelley, indulging desire leads to this massacre of social relationships because of the kinship she perceives between essential human nature and the ghastly essence of the natural world. Shelley most graphically describes nature's fateful fraternity with death in the setting for the final action of *Frankenstein*, the random upheavals of the glacial ice floes. Like Percy Shelley's version of this scene in 'Mont Blanc', Mary Shelley's image suggests an inhumane, icy nature, 'terrifically desolate', strewn with uprooted and broken trees and partially shrouded by impenetrable mists. Yet, unlike her future husband, Mary Shelley does not temper this presentation of nature by claiming for the imagination a saving supremacy − 'And what were thou, and earth, and stars, and sea, / If to the human mind's imaginings / Silence and solitude were vacancy?' ['Mont Blanc', 142–4]. In her inhospitable world, the most likely answer to a human cry is an avalanche, and all momentary social contact is severed by the breaking up of the icy ground. These fields of ice, deadly to individuals like Frankenstein, provide a fitting home only for essential, uncivilized human nature – for the monster, who can achieve no community with those whose energy culture has regulated and refined into 'sensibility'. . . .

The monster carries with it the guilt and alienation that attend Frankenstein's self-assertion; yet, by having the monster itself realistically detail the stages by which it is driven to act out its symbolic nature, Shelley compels the reader to identify with the creature's anguish and frustration. The first-person, symbolic presentation of the monster within a literalized landscape thus qualifies Shelley's condemnation of self-assertion – so effectively, in fact, that generations of critics and cinematographers have awarded the creature its maker's name and place. For Mary Shelley, displacing the emotional dimension of Frankenstein's transgression onto the essentially powerless monster is primarily a means of *indirectly* dramatizing her emotional investment in Frankenstein's creative act – and her profound ambivalence toward it. The degree of pathos in the monster's cry suggests that Shelley most unequivocally identifies with the product, and the price, of Frankenstein's transgression: the objectified ego, helpless and alone. Perhaps, as we will see when we discuss her 1831 Introduction, the monster's condition seemed to Shelley the appropriate fate for the self-assertive, 'masculine', and therefore monstrous female artist.

Shelley's depiction of the monster allows for indirection because a symbol is able to accommodate different, even contradictory meanings. Although in an important sense Frankenstein's imagination loses potential semantic richness by being literalized in the monster (e.g., its possibilities of transcendent power or beneficence), this narrative strategy does allow Shelley to express her sympathy for the creative enterprise without explicitly retracing her earlier judgment of it. In other words, using symbolism at this point in the narrative enables Shelley to express two opinions, to record precisely her own divided attitude toward Frankenstein's imaginative act.

We can best understand the function symbolism plays for Mary Shelley by contrasting her use of it with Percy Shelley's significantly different description of the symbolic in his Preface to the 1818 *Frankenstein*. In his well-known justification for the central scene, Percy stresses not the ambivalence of the symbol but its comprehensiveness and its power: 'However impossible as a physical fact, [this incident] affords a point to view to the imagination for the delineating of human passions more comprehensive and commanding than any which the ordinary relations of existing events can yield' [p. 6]. Although we know from the Shelleys' letters and from the surviving manuscript of *Frankenstein* that Percy was instrumental in promoting, and even in revising, the text,[7] Mary did not uncritically or wholeheartedly embrace the aesthetic rationale by which Percy justified this self-confident use of symbolism or the artistic enterprise of which it is only a part. In fact, Mary Shelley feminizes Percy's version of the Romantic aesthetic, using her lover's theories to justify the very strategies that enabled her to find an acceptable, non-assertive voice.

Percy Shelley defended this aesthetic doctrines, like his political and religious beliefs, with a conviction Mary later called a 'resolution firm to martyrdom'.[8] Scornful of public opinion, he maintains in his *Defence of Poetry* (1821) that a true poet may be judged only by legitimate peers, a jury 'impanelled by Time from the selectest of the wise of many generations'. Society's mistaken accusation of artistic immorality, Percy explains, rests on 'a misconception of the manner in which poetry acts to produce the moral improvement of man'. According to Percy, the audience's relationship to poetry is based not on reason but on the imagination; true poetry encourages not imitation or judgment but participation. It strengthens the moral sense because it exercises and enlarges the capacity for sympathetic identification, that is, for relationship. Following Plato, Percy declares that the primary reflex of the moral imagination is the outward gesture of love:

The great secret of morals is Love; or a going out of our own nature, and an identification of ourselves with the beautiful which exists in thought, action, or person, not our own. A man, to be greatly good, must imagine intensely and comprehensively; he must put himself in the place of another and of many others; the pains and pleasures of his species must become his own. The great instrument of moral good is the imagination; and poetry administers to the effect by acting upon the cause.[9]

Each of Percy Shelley's aesthetic doctrines comes to rest on this model of the imagination as an innately moral, capacious faculty. Because the imagination, if unrestrained, naturally supersedes relative morals (and in so doing compensates for the inhumaneness of the natural world), poets should not discipline their efforts according to a particular society's conceptions of right and wrong. Because the imagination tends to extend itself, through sympathy, to truth, poets should simply depict examples of truth, thus drawing their readers into a relationship that simultaneously feeds and stimulates the human appetite for 'thoughts of ever new delight'.

This model of the artwork as an arena for relationships is the only aspect of Percy's aesthetics that Mary Shelley adopts without reservation. The notion that the artist establishes and nurtures relationships with an audience is compatible not only with the valorization of relationship we have already seen in *Frankenstein* but with society's insistence that a woman achieve her identity through and within relationships. For, unlike her defiant lover, Mary was not immune to public opinion or oblivious to conventional propriety. Percy's defiance of society was based on his confidence in the innate morality of the imagination, an assumption Mary did not share, and it resulted in a bold self-confidence that would appear, in a woman, to border on unconscionable self-assertion. In *Frankenstein*, therefore, Mary Shelley harnesses Percy's aesthetic theories to her own more conservative assumptions and thus fundamentally alters the implications of his ideas. By adopting a narrative strategy that insists on the reader's sympathetic engagement with even the monstrous part of her self, she simultaneously satisfies Percy's standards for true art and her own conflicting needs for self-assertion and social acceptance. The three-part narrative structure enables her to establish her role as an artist through a series of relationships rather than through an act of self-assertion; and because she does not limit herself to a single perspective she also avoids taking responsibility for any definitive position on what is undeniably an unladylike subject. In other words, the narrative strategy, like the symbolic presentation of the monster, permits Mary to express and efface herself at the same time. . . .

. . . The revisions Mary Shelley prepared for the third edition of *Frankenstein*, published as part of Colburn and Bentley's Standard Novels series in 1831, reveal that her interest had changed in two significant ways during the thirteen-year interval. The most extensive revisions, some of which were outlined soon after Percy's death in 1822,[10] occur in chs I, II and V of Victor Frankenstein's narrative; their primary effects are to idealize the domestic harmony of Victor's childhood and to change the origin – and thus the implications – of his passionate ambition. The first alteration makes Frankenstein's imaginative aggression seem a more atrocious 'crime', and the second transforms Frankenstein from a realistic character to a symbol of the Romantic over-reacher. The revisions thus extend the critique of imaginative indulgence already present in the 1818 text and direct it much more pointedly at the blasphemy Shelley now associates with her own adolescent audacity. Yet, paradoxically, even as she heightens the domestic destruction the egotist causes, Mary Shelley qualifies his responsibility. For her new conception depicts Frankenstein as the helpless pawn of a predetermined 'destiny', of a fate that is given, not made. The 1831 *Frankenstein* seems quintessentially a victim, like the monster, who now symbolizes more precisely what this kind of man is than what he allows himself to become. In both the text and her Author's Introduction, Shelley suggests that such a man has virtually no control over his destiny and that he is therefore to be pitied rather than condemned.

The revision almost all critics have noted is the transformation of Victor's fiancée, Elizabeth, from cousin to foundling. Shelley redefines her in this way partly, no doubt, to avoid insinuations of incest but also to emphasize the active benevolence of Frankenstein's mother, who, in adopting the poor orphan, becomes a 'guardian angel'. This alteration, however, is only one of a series of changes that idealize the harmony of Victor's childhood home. In this edition, for example, Shelley gives more space to the protectiveness of Victor's parents [pp. 233–4] and to the happiness of his childhood ('My mother's tender caresses, and my father's smile of benevolent pleasure while regarding me, are my first recollections' [p. 234]. Not surprisingly, Elizabeth, as the potential link between Victor's childhood and his mature domesticity, receives the most attention. In 1831 Shelley presents her as a celestial creature, 'a being heaven-sent', 'a child fairer than pictured cherub' [p. 235]. Elizabeth is both Victor's guardian and his charge; explicitly she embodies the regulating reciprocity of domestic love. 'She was the living spirit of love to soften and attract: I might have become sullen in my study, rough through the ardour of my nature, but that she was there to subdue me to a semblance of her own gentleness' [p. 237]. By emphasizing Elizabeth's pivotal role in what is now an ideal of domestic harmony, Shelley prepares to heighten the devastating social consequences of Frankenstein's imaginative transgression and to underscore further the loss *he* suffers through his willful act.

Despite this idealization of the family, in the 1831 *Frankenstein* the seeds of Victor's egotism germinate more rapidly within the home, for Shelley now attributes Frankenstein's fall not primarily to formative accidents or to his departure but to his innate 'temperature' or character. 'Deeply smitten with the thirst for knowledge', Frankenstein is now from his birth set apart from his childhood companions. Unlike the 'saintly' Elizabeth or the 'noble' spirit[ed]' Clerval, Frankenstein has a violent temper and vehement passions. His accidental discovery of Agrippa is now preceded by a description

of a more decisive factor, the determining 'law in [his] temperature';
it is this inborn predilection that turns his desire 'not towards
childish pursuits, but to an eager desire to learn . . . the secrets of
heaven and earth' [p. 237]. The 1831 edition retains Frankenstein's
suggestion that his father's negligence contributed to his 'fatal
impulse', but almost every alteration contradicts the implication
that circumstances can substantially modify inherent character. The
1831 Frankenstein resists modern science not because 'some accident'
prevents him from attending lectures but because 'one of those
caprices of the mind' distracts him from scientific speculations. By
abandoning the mechanistic model of psychology and adopting
instead the notion of desire as organically affixed to innate character,
Shelley radically reduces the importance of external circumstances
and emphasizes the inevitability of the over-reacher's fall; at the
same time, she pushes what had been a realistic narrative, framing
the symbolic story of monstrous egotism, in the direction of allegory. . . .

. . . Walton too is a pawn of internal forces that syntactically,
seem not his own ('there is a love . . . which hurries me'). Thus,
although in the 1831 text Walton's ambition is more pronounced,
more like the young Frankenstein's, he is not wholly responsible for
his actions. Just as Mr Waldman is the external catalyst that
precipitates Frankenstein's 'destiny', so Frankenstein serves as the
critical agent for Walton. Frankenstein's narrative resolves Walton's
internal conflict and restores to him that domestic affection which
has been all along the innate 'ground-work of [his] character'.
Walton does not really assert himself or actively choose; rather, true
to his character, to his original self-denying nature, he allows himself
to be acted on by others, to respond to the needs of Frankenstein,
then to those of the sailors in his charge.

Of the three narrations that compose *Frankenstein*, the monster's
history receives the least attention in the 1831 revisions – no doubt
because by this time Shelley sympathized even more strongly with
the guilt and alienation that attend the egotist's crime. Moreover,
by implication, the monster has become the appropriate extension
of the curse of the artist, not the product of the self-indulgent ego.
The monster's grotesqueness, its singularity are still signs of an
essential transgression, but its pathetic powerlessness is now a more
appropriate equivalent of the helplessness of Frankenstein himself.
. . .

The terror Shelley associates with artistic creation, however,
comes not just from the guilt of superseding one's proper role or
from a fear of the literal but also from the fear of failure that

accompanies such presumption. The creation Shelley imagines is 'odious', 'horrid', 'hideous', imperfectly animated – a failure for all to see. The suggestion that the burden of the artistic creation consists in large part in its profoundly public nature also appears in the 1831 Introduction. There Shelley distinguishes between her youthful, private fantasies of pure imagination ('waking dreams . . . which had for their subject the formation of a succession of imaginary incidents' [p. 222]) and the stories she actually wrote down, the 'close imitations' she shared with her childhood friend Isabel Baxter. 'My dreams were at once more fantastic and agreeable than my writings', she explains. 'The airy flights of . . . imagination', in fact, she considers her only 'true composition', for what she wrote was in 'a most common-place style'. To write, for Shelley, is necessarily to imitate, and her models, almost all masculine, are both intimidating and potentially judgmental of her audacious foray into their domain and of what seems the monstrous inadequacy of her objectified self. The fear of public scrutiny and judgment lies behind most of Shelley's disclaimers of the artistic enterprise: 'What I wrote was intended at least for one other eye – my childhood's companion and friend; but my dreams were all my own; I accounted for them to nobody; they were my refuge when annoyed – my dearest pleasures when free' [p. 223]. Thus when Mary Shelley places her imagination in the service of a text, a discomforting transformation occurs: what was a harmless pastime becomes tantamount to a transgression, and fuelling the attendant guilt, the fear surfaces that if she does compete she will be found inadequate. Only the unbound and therefore non-binding imagination can escape censure and thus protect the ego against exposure and pain.

Shelley's distinction between imagination and imaginative creation would have surprised many of her male contemporaries. In his *Defence*, for example, Percy Shelley does not even consider the possibility of keeping imaginative insights private, for, in his theory, poets have a profoundly public responsibility – they are the 'unacknowledged legislators of the World'. Percy's description centres on the self-expressive function of art; his authority derives from a masculine tradition of poet-prophets and his self-confidence from the social approbation accorded masculine self-assertion. Mary Shelley, however, lacking the support of both tradition and public opinion, separates the permissible, even liberating expression of the imagination from the more egotistical, less defensible act of public self-assertion.[11] For Mary Shelley, the imagination is properly a vehicle for escaping the self, not a medium of personal power or even of self-expression. She therefore associates the imagination with images of flight, escape, freedom; writing she associates with monstrosity transgression, literalization and failure. . . .

The 1831 *Frankenstein* is neither Mary Shelley's first nor her last embrace of powerlessness. *The Last Man* (1826), for example, is a protracted study of the 'indissoluble chain of events' that sweeps mankind inexorably toward universal destruction, and even the more conventional *Falkner* (1837) presents 'each link of the chain' of the past as having 'been formed and riveted by a superior power for peculiar purposes.' In the course of her career, Shelley's explanation of that power changes, as does her evaluation of it, but consistently after 1818 she invokes some version of Necessity to link the turnings of plots and, more important, to explain her own behavior. Paradoxically, this wholehearted acceptance of an essentially subordinate position – like the symbolic presentation of the monster – affords Shelley precisely the grounds she needs to sanction her artistic endeavors. For the claim to powerlessness not only exonerates her from personal responsibility but also provides a socially acceptable rationale for self-aggrandizement – and thus a means of satisfying simultaneously her need for social approval and her desire to 'prove [herself] worthy' of her parents and Percy Shelley. In her depiction of the monster and the 1831 Frankenstein, Mary Shelley essentially raises feminine powerlessness to the status of myth,[12] and thus, as we see in a diary entry from her journal of 1831, she is able to distinguish herself in the very gesture with which she seems to efface herself. As commentary on her life as a self-divided artist, her 'apology' is worth quoting at length:

To hang back, as I do, brings a penalty. I was nursed and fed with a love of glory. To be something great was the precept given me by my Father. Shelley reiterated it. Alone and poor, I could only be something by joining a party; and there was much in me – the woman's love of looking up, and being guided, and being willing to do anything any one supported and brought me forward – which would have made me a good partisan. But Shelley died, and I was alone. My Father, from age and domestic circumstances, could not '*me faire valoir*'. My total friendlessness, my horror of pushing, an inability to put myself forward unless led, cherished and supported, – all this has sunk me in a state of loneliness no other human being has ever before, I believe, endured – except Robinson Crusoe.

In her subordinate position Shelley finds something genuinely remarkable – a singular state worthy of dramatic presentation, like the competent victim-vanquisher Robinson Crusoe himself.

SOURCE: extracts from 'My Hideous Progeny: Mary Shelley and the Feminization of Romanticism', *MPLA*, 95 (1980), pp. 332–3, 334–5, 335–6, 338–9, 340–1, 342–3, 344, 345

NOTES

[Reorganised and renumbered from the original – Ed.]
1. In Julian Marshall, *The Life and Letters of Mary Wollstonecraft Shelley* (London, 1889), II, p. 197.
2. From Hunt's 'Blue Stocking Revels' (1837); quoted by R. Glynn Grylls, *Mary Shelley: A Biography* (London, 1938), p. 211, n.2.
3. Marshall, p. 248.
4. Shelley's reading of her contemporaries' egotism, while certainly colored by the inhibitions she, as a woman, had internalized, is an understandable interpretation. For example, Coleridge's depiction of the artistic act as a repetition of 'the eternal act of creation in the infinite I AM' appropriates godlike power for the poet, whatever Coleridge's own doubts might have been in practice. The Bryon of *Childe Harold*, parading his bleeding heart for all Europe, also conveys a sense of self-importance, and Percy Shelley's image of the artist as priest-lawgiver-prophet assumes that the poet is all-powerful, or ought to be. In *The Madwoman in the Attic: The Woman Writer and the Nineteenth-Century Literary Imagination* (1979), Sandra M. Gilbert and Susan Gubar discuss both this masculine image of the poet and the 'anxiety of authorship' it causes for women. Although I think that the dilemma was intensified by the Romantic image of the artist as creator, I essentially agree with their perceptive analysis of the self-doubts this image causes women, who read into the claims of male writers more confidence than the poets' works sometimes reveal (see esp. pp. 45–63 and the discussion of *Frankenstein*, pp. 213–17) – [the latter reproduced above in our selection – Ed.]
5. Mary Shelley, Introduction to the 3rd edn (1831), as cited in *Frankenstein or the Modern Prometheus (the 1818 Text)*, edited by James Rieger (Indianapolis, 1974), p. 227.
6. This and all other citations, for both editions, refer to the above-mentioned text, in which Appendix B consists of a collation of the two editions.
7. For a discussion of Percy Shelley's participation in the revision of *Frankenstein*, see Rieger's Introduction, op. cit. Rieger goes so far as to assert that Percy's 'assistance at every point in the book's manufacture was so extensive that one hardly knows whether to regard him as editor or minor collaborator' (p. *xviii*). The microfilms of the Frankenstein manuscript that I have examined in Duke University's Perkin Library (Abinger Collection, Reel 11) suggest that, while Percy made many marginal suggestions and probably helped recopy the manuscript, his contributions were largely stylistic and grammatical.

8. Mary Shelley, Preface to the 2nd edn of Percy Shelley's *Collected Poetry* (1839), cited in Thomas Hutchinson (ed.), *Shelley: Poetical Works*, new edn, corrected by G. M. Matthews (London, 1970), p. *xxi*.

9. P. B. Shelley, 'A Defence of Poetry, or Remarks Suggested by an Essay Entitled "The Four Ages of Poetry"' (1821), reproduced in Donald H. Reiman and Sharon B. Powers (eds), *Shelley's Poetry and Prose* (New York, 1977), pp. 486, 487–8.

10. Rieger, Intro., op. cit., pp. *xxii-xxiii*.

11. Mary Shelley's endorsement of the non-textualized imagination is clear both from her portrait of Clerval, 'a boy of singular talent and fancy', who gives up his childish composition of stories to become simply a connoisseur of natural beauty [p. 159], and from this journal entry of 1834: 'My imagination, my Kubla Khan, my 'pleasure dome', occasionally pushed aside by misery but at the first opportunity her beaming face peeped in and the weight of deadly woe was lightened' – see Frederick L. Jones (ed.), *Mary Shelley's Journal* (Norman, Okla., 1947) p. 203.

12. In *Literary Women: The Great Writers* (New York, 1977), Ellen Moers proposes that *Frankenstein* is specifically 'a birth myth', that the novel is 'most feminine . . . in the motif of revulsion against newborn life, and the drama of guilt, dread and flight surrounding birth and its consequences' (p. 142). While Moers's insights seem to me suggestive, I think her equation of the monster and the newborn too limiting. Childbearing is only one kind of expression or projection of the self, and Shelley conflates several meanings in this central incident.

# SELECT BIBLIOGRAPHY

P. Arnaud, *Ann Radcliffe et le fantastique* (Paris, 1976).

E. A. Barber, *The History of the English Novel*, 10 vols, (London, 1929–39), Vol. 5, 'The Gothic Romance'.

E. Birkhead, *The Tale of Terror: A Study of the Gothic Romance* (London, 1921).

D. Blakey, *The Minerva Press 1790–1820* (London, 1939).

R. Jackson, *Fantasy: the Literature of Subversion* (London, 1982).

M. Lévy, *Le Roman 'Gotique' Anglais: 1764–1824* (Toulouse, 1960).

D. J. McNutt (ed.), *The XVIIIth Century Gothic Novel, an annotated bibliography of criticism*, Introduction by D. P. Varma and M. Lévy (London, 1975).

E. Moers, *Literary Women* (London, 1975).

D. Punta, *The Literature of Terror* (London, 1980).

E. Railo, *The Haunted Castle* (New York, 1964).

V. Sage, *Horror Fiction in the Protestant Tradition* (London, 1988).

# NOTES ON CONTRIBUTORS

JANE AUSTEN (1775–1817): her satire of the genre in *Northanger Abbey* reveals her as both a devoted reader and an acute critic of the mystery and horror tales of her day.

ANDRÉ BRETON: founder and leader of the surrealist movement in 1917, poet, artist, critic, writer, publicist, whose works include 'What is Surrealism?', the Manifesto of Surrealism, and (with Trotsky, in 1930) 'Towards an Independent Revolutionary Art'. He organised the international Exhibition of Surrealism.

EDMUND BURKE (1729–97): statesman and political theorist, he also exerted strong influence on aesthetics through his *Philosophical Enquiry into . . . the Sublime and the Beautiful* (1757).

S. T. COLERIDGE (1771–1834): poet and critic, co-doyen with Wordsworth of the Romantic movement in English poetry.

WILKIE COLLINS (1824–89): novelist, most celebrated for his mystery novels *The Woman in White* (1860) and *The Moonstone* (1868).

DE SADE, MARQUIS (1740–1814): author of works excoriated by his contemporaries for their philosopical justification of cruelty and sexual licence; the term 'sadism' derives from his writings and his conduct.

LESLIE FIEDLER: American critic, until retirement Professor of English in the State University of New York, at Buffalo. His works, often controversial, have made him regarded by some as the *enfant terrible* of American literary studies; in addition to *Love and Death in the American Novel*, they include *The Stranger in Shakespeare*, *Waiting for the End* and *An End to Innocence*.

SIGMUND FREUD (1856–1939): the founding father of 'modern psychology', his interpretations of human behaviour and psychic states have had enormous influence on creative writing and literary criticism in the twentieth century. In addition to his major studies, such as *The Interpretation of Dreams* and *The Psychopathology of Everyday Life*, he also wrote a number of interesting essays in literary criticism.

SANDRA M. GILBERT: American critic, is Asst Professor in the English dept, at Indiana University at Bloomington and a member of the Modern Language Association. Her publications include *The poetry of WB Yeats*

(1966), *Acts of Attention: the poems of D.H. Lawrence* (1972) and *All the dead voices*, a study of Samuel Beckett's *Krapp's Last Tape*, Drama Survey, Spring 1968.

SUSAN GUBAR: critic, teacher and member of faculty at Indiana University, Bloomington.

CORAL ANN HOWELLS: graduate of Birkbeck College, London. Works include: *Private and Fictional Words: Canadian Women Novelists of the 1970s and 1980s*

JAMES HOGG (1770–1835): Scottish poet, novelist and essayist, known as 'the Ettrick Shepherd'. In our day his reputation resides mainly in his powerful exploration of demonic possession in *The Memoirs and Confessions of a Justified Sinner*.

RICHARD HURD (1720–1808): bishop successively of Litchfield and Worcester, and an influential critic; his works include *The Polite Arts* (1749) and *Letters on Romance and Chivalry* (1762).

SAMUEL JOHNSON (1709–84): poet, essayist, novelist, dramatist, biographer and lexicographer, perhaps his most enduring influence has been as literary critic, refining and exemplifying the humane sensibility of his age.

ROBERT KIELY: critic and Harvard academic, Associate Dean of Faculty of Arts and Sciences at Harvard in 1972 and Master of Adams House, Harvard, in 1973. Publications include *Robert Louis Stevenson and the Fiction of Adventure* (1964) and *The Romantic Novel in England* (1972).

SAMUEL KLIGER: scholar, critic, academic Harvard graduate who worked under A. O. Lovejoy, the famous historian of ideas. When this piece was written, Kliger was at Northwestern University. Subsequent works include: *The Goths In England* (New York, 1952).

THOMAS BABINGTON MACAULAY – Lord Macaulay (1800–59): historian, Liberal politician, poet and essayist; in political and literary interests he was closely associated with the critic of the *Edinburgh Review* and Lady Holland's coterie in London.

THOMAS LOVE PEACOCK (1785–1866): novelist and poet, and a close friend of Shelley. As well as his satirical 'conversational' novels, like *Nightmare Abbey*, he also wrote more overtly romantic works, *Maid Marian* and *The Misfortunes of Elphin*.

MARY POOVEY: member of faculty in the English dept, Swarthmore College, Swarthmore, Pennsylvania. Works include *The proper Lady and the Woman*

*Writer: ideology as style in works of Mary Wollstoncraft, Mary Shelley, and Jane Austen* (1984).

MARIO PRAZ (1896–1982): Italian critic and literary historian; his publications include *The Romantic Agony, The Hero in Eclipse in Victorian Fiction* and *Studies in Seventeenth–Century Imagery.*

HENRY CRABB ROBINSON (1775–1867): diarist and traveller, and special correspondent of *The Times* during the Napoleonic wars. He was acquainted with almost everyone of consequence in literary circles and Europe, and was a notable go-between for the literatures of England and Germany.

GEORGE SAINTSBURY (1845–1933): literary critic and historian, Professor of Rhetoric and English Literature in the University of Edinburgh (1895–1915). His many works include *A Short History of English Literature* (1887), *A History of Criticism* (1900–1), *A History of English Prosody* (1906–10), and writings on wine which are still highly regarded.

SIR WALTER SCOTT (1771–1832): poet and novelist, he was also a discerning and well regarded critic. As a Romantic novelist, his influence on the arts generally, not only in literature, has been immense.

ELEANOR M. SICKELS: scholar critic, graduate of Columbia. Worked under Professor H. F. Fairchild, the famous historian of religion, at Columbia University, New York.

JOYCE M. S. TOMPKINS: formerly teaching at Royal Holloway College, University of London; her publications include – in addition to *The Popular Novel in England, 1770–1800 – The Art of Rudyard Kipling* (1959, 2nd edn 1965) and an edition of Mrs Inchbald's *A Simple Story* (1967).

# ACKNOWLEDGEMENTS

The editor and publishers wish to thank the following for permission to use copyright material: André Breton, extract from 'Limites Non Frontières du Surrealisme', translated by Herbert Read in *Surrealism*, by permission of Faber and Faber Ltd.; Leslie A. Fielder, extracts from *Love and Death in the American Novel*, Stein and Day, Inc., by permission of Scarborough House Publishers. Copyright © 1975 by Leslie A. Fielder; Sigmund Freud, extracts from *The Standard Edition of the Complete Psychological Works of Sigmund Freud*, translated and edited by James Strachey (1957), by permission of Sigmund Freud Copyrights Ltd., The Institute of Psychoanalysis and The Hogarth Press; Sandra Gilbert and Marion Gubar, extracts from *The Madwoman in the Attic* (1979), by permission of Yale University Press; Coral Ann Howells, extract from *Love, Mystery and Misery: Feeling in Gothic Fiction* (1978), by permission of The Athlone Press. Copyright © 1978 Coral Ann Howells; Robert Kiely, extract from *The Romantic Novel in England*, by permission of Harvard University Press. Copyright © 1972 by the President and Fellows of Harvard College; Samuel Kliger, article, 'The Goths in England', *Modern Philology* (1945), by permission of The University of Chicago Press; Mary Poovey, extracts from article, 'My Hideous Progeny; Mary Shelley and the Feminization of Romanticism', *PMLA*, 95 (1980) by permission of the Modern Language Association of America; Mario Praz, extract from *The Romantic Agony*, translated by Angus Davidson, 2nd edition (1970), by permission of Oxford University Press; Eleanor M. Sickels, extracts from *The Gloomy Egoist: Moods and Themes of Melancholy from Gray to Keats* (1932), by permission of Columbia University Press.

Every effort has been made to trace all the copyright holders but if any have been inadvertently overlooked the publishers will be pleased to make the necessary arrangement at the first opportunity.

# INDEX

Page numbers in **bold type** denote essays or extracts in this Casebook.